THE

RECORDER

BOOK

Kenneth Wollitz

THE
RECORDER
BOOK

ALFRED A. KNOPF   NEW YORK   1982

THIS IS A BORZOI BOOK
PUBLISHED BY ALFRED A. KNOPF, INC.

Portions of Chapters 2 and 3 have appeared previously in
somewhat different form in *The American Recorder.*

LIBRARY OF CONGRESS CATALOGING IN PUBLICATION DATA
Wollitz, Kenneth.
The recorder book.

Bibliography: p.
Includes index.
1. Recorder (Musical instrument)—Instruction and
study. I. Title.
MT350.W64   788'.53   81-47518
ISBN 0-394-47973-4   AACR2

Manufactured in the United States of America
First Edition

For Judith and Kathy

CONTENTS

ACKNOWLEDGMENTS

There are a number of people whom I wish to thank for their help in writing this book. Martha Bixler made many valuable suggestions for the chapter on ensemble. She and Joan Munkacsi are largely responsible for the meticulous task of preparing the music list. Steve Silverstein gave unstintingly of his expert knowledge for the chapter on selecting and caring for one's recorder. I am grateful to Colin Sterne, Professor of Music at the University of Pittsburgh, for providing a clear, concise chapter on the history of musical forms as they relate to the recorder. I would also like to thank the many people whom I have taught over the years, for it is through them that I have learned the things that I have set down in this book.

Most of all, I wish to thank my editors, Judith Jones and Kathy Hourigan, whose patience and encouragement have been indispensable.

K.W.

INTRODUCTION

The recorder is a charming instrument. It is beguiling in its sweetness of sound and appealing in its simplicity and directness of construction. All instruments are fascinating to the music lover, and every musician has a particular love for his chosen instrument, but certain instruments have an almost magical aura about them that touches every listener and makes him, in turn, want to touch them. The harp is such an instrument, and so is the guitar. When you see them and hear them played you want to play them yourself, and even though both have a formidable technique it is possible to pluck out a tune on one or strum a few simple chords on the other with great satisfaction. The recorder is similarly inviting.

I first encountered a recorder when I was about twenty. It was a simple wooden soprano, lying rather forlorn and dusty in a friend's bookcase, abandoned because it didn't seem to give the right notes. At the time I played clarinet, oboe, and bassoon, so I was quickly able to figure out the fingerings that did give the right notes. I was enchanted, and the very next day went to a music store and bought myself an alto recorder in pearwood which set me back exactly nine dollars! It was not, truth to tell, a very good instrument, but it sufficed for many happy hours, both alone and playing with friends; and although it was several years before I became involved as a professional teacher and performer, my recorder was my constant companion and it always led me to find others with whom to play. It also led me to a musical literature not usually encountered in high school bands and orchestras.

Many people have told me similar stories about their first encounter with the recorder: love at first sight. The recorder, in its simplicity, seems to evoke Arcadian scenes of shepherds piping to their flocks, and, indeed, they may have been playing something very similar, since whistles with finger holes are common throughout much of the world and apparently have a very ancient lineage. What characterizes a whistle is that you blow air through a slot which directs it against a sharp edge to produce a sound. A whistle can be made from a tube of wood, cane, bone, clay, or whatever, by inserting a plug in the upper end, which almost completely closes it, leaving only a narrow passage on one side for the air to pass through. At the bottom of this passage a window is cut into the tube with its lower side sharpened into a blade. Holes cut into the side of the tube further down are opened and closed by the fingers to get different notes. The principle is the same for a simple pipe of willow bark as it is for the recorder. However, what distinguishes the recorder from other whistle flutes with finger holes is the number and disposition of these holes. A recorder has holes for seven fingers above, and a hole for the upper thumb on the back. The tapering bore, which becomes gradually narrower from the top to the bottom of the instrument, is another characteristic of the true recorder.

Precisely when recorders first came into use is hard to say, since the earliest instruments do not survive. The oldest recorder known at present is called the "Dordrecht" recorder since it was found beneath a fifteenth-century stone house in that Dutch town. It is eleven and three-quarters inches long, just a little longer than a modern soprano, made in one piece, of elmwood. The date of its construction, whether there were others like it, or in different sizes, are all questions with no sure answers. Pictorial and sculptural evidence for earlier recorders is too ambiguous for certain identification—it may be a recorder or it may be a shawm. The artist doesn't show the instrument's bore or whether there is a hole in back for the thumb.

By the early 1500's, however, we are on firmer ground. Various practical treatises on the art of making music begin to appear, and the recorder is treated in some detail in several of them. Sebastian Virdung's *Musica getutscht und Ausgezogen,* Strasbourg and Basel, 1511, describes a quartet in three sizes: a bass in F, two tenors in C, and a discant (alto) in G. Woodcuts (out of scale) indicate the presence of the thumbhole by a circle to one side of those for the finger holes; the thumbhole is confirmed in the fingering charts which Virdung provides for each size. He also shows a prevalent—but for us, curious—feature: a *ninth* finger hole. This is placed alongside hole number 7 on the top of the instrument and is for the convenience of players who wish to place their right hand uppermost on the instrument. The choice was up to the player, and whichever hole was redundant for the seventh finger, right or left, was stopped up with wax. For the same reason, the key on the bass for the seventh finger has a double touch piece (variously called a "butterfly," "fishtail," or "swallowtail" key) so that the key would be within reach of whichever pinky happened to be down there. The keywork is protected by a perforated barrel called a "fontanelle." Keywork, given the state of metallurgy in the Renaissance, was fragile, and either fontanelles or little perforated brass boxes were standard protection during that period. The duplicated hole on number 7 was also standard, indeed, well into the eighteenth century, thus giving the recorder the seemingly anachronistic name, among many others, of *flûte à neuf trous,* or flute with nine holes, even though we use only eight to play it!

Virdung's work heralds the sixteenth-century preoccupation with families of instruments, many different sizes of the same kind, to be played in "whole consorts," as opposed to the mixed sonorities favored in earlier times. There were families of flutes, viols, krummhorns, shawms, racketts, etc., but few reached the eventual size of the recorder family. Nowadays recorder ensembles tend to reflect sixteenth-century practice by playing in consorts of soprano, alto, tenor, and bass, which fits the music nicely. But in the later sixteenth and early seventeenth centuries they did the same thing an octave lower: Tenors for sopranos, basses for altos, great basses (in C) for tenors, and contras (in F) as the true bass instruments of this profound quartet. There were even lower basses, down to Great C, below the bass clef, appropriately operated by pedals. Such instruments were very rare. To give an idea of where our modern-day consort stands next to this late-sixteenth-century "grand jeu" the lowest notes of the respective consorts are given below:

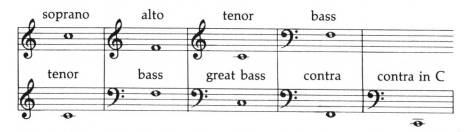

Michael Praetorius was a stupendous example of the Renaissance musician, providing and performing music for every liturgical occasion,

composing in, and describing, all contemporary secular forms, and writing a great *Syntagmum Musicum* ("Musical Treatise") in three volumes (a fourth was projected but didn't appear) in which he attempted and, to an astonishing extent, achieved an explanation of all music up to his time. Volume II of this work, published in Wolfenbüttel in 1618, describes musical instruments in exhaustive and explicit detail. It was followed two years later with a set of woodcut plates, carefully showing the instruments in proper scale. The plate on recorders, reproduced at right, shows nine sizes, from a contra in F to a sopranino in G.

I had occasion to hear such a grand jeu of recorders when I was teaching at the Northern Recorder Course, in England in the spring of 1979. We Americans tend to employ mixed ensembles at our workshops for performing large pieces such as masses and ceremonial motets, with a chorus of voices as the central force, enriched at various places by recorders, krummhorns, viols, shawms, dulcians, cornets, sackbuts, harps, and whatever other instruments are available, the sackbuts, bass viols, and dulcians providing the underpinning. The English, by contrast, favor the sound of the recorder orchestra unadulterated by reeds, strings, or brass, with half-a-dozen great basses and two or three contras to provide the bass. These all-recorder ensembles perform music especially written for them as well as arrangements of nineteenth- and twentieth-century orchestral pieces. To the American purist, the idea of playing anything but early music on a consort of recorders, however extended, is a bit shocking, but in fact the results are highly successful. I was delighted and impressed by the sound that emerges from an English recorder orchestra. The playing is very precise and musical, with a great variety of tone color. I would have loved to hear how the music of Michael Praetorius would sound when performed by such a magnificent consort of recorders, but the compositions I did hear were most effective and beautiful.

The great size of the recorder family in the sixteenth century is one evidence of the instrument's popularity. Another, more striking proof is found in the inventories of instruments from large musical establishments. Henry VIII, for example, owned seventy-six recorders of various sizes, according to a list made in 1547, shortly after his death. Out of 507 wind instruments listed as belonging to the Stuttgart Town Band in 1589, 299 were recorders. Similar inventories of the period usually show a preponderance of recorders among the instruments listed.

These vast numbers of recorders were not all played at once. The

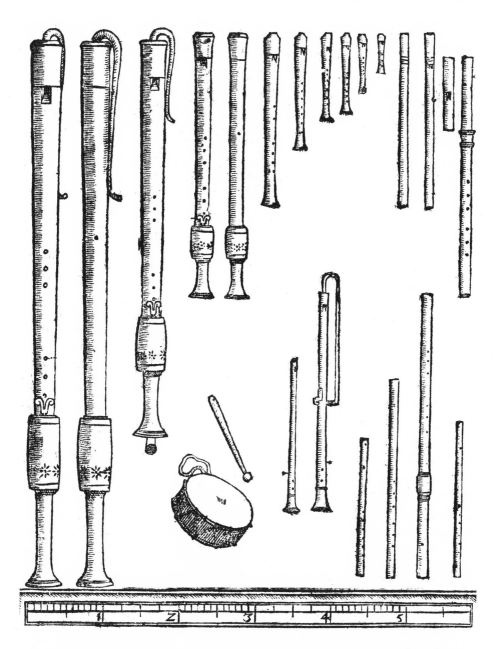

Recorders, from Michael Praetorius, Syntagmum Musicum, *1620: from contra (sounding F an octave a fifth below Middle C) through great bass, bass, tenor, alto, soprano, to sopranino in G. Also shown are various sizes of flutes and tabor pipes, and a drum.*

Renaissance professional musician was a doubler, playing on all kinds of instruments, specializing on one or two, and singing as well. Praetorius, writing toward the end of the Renaissance, describes a Great Consort of recorders as one contra, two great basses, four each of basses, tenors, altos, and sopranos, topped off with two sopraninos—a total of twenty-one instruments. This was probably as big as things ever got until the second half of the twentieth century!

In the sixteenth century, Venice was the center of woodwind instrument manufacture. It was customary to order recorders in sets—perhaps two sopranos, two altos, two tenors, and a bass—presumably so as to ensure that they would be in tune with each other, because standard pitch, A–440, is a quite recent phenomenon. These instruments were simple in outline and, except in the largest sizes, made in one piece. Surviving examples evince superior craftsmanship and, when in playing condition, they play very well indeed. Modern makers have copied them with excellent results.

In the second half of the seventeenth century, innovation in woodwind instrument-making shifted to France, where a family of instrument maker-musician-composers, the Hotteterres, were then revolutionizing woodwind design by transforming the Renaissance one-piece construction of recorders, flutes, shawms, and dulcians into instruments made in several joints—the Baroque recorder, flute, oboe, and bassoon. The bores of these instruments were altered to improve range, tone quality, and intonation; and the simple outline of the Renaissance instruments was replaced by the richly turned bulges characteristically found at the sockets of Baroque instruments, intended both to provide strength and to enhance their decorative quality. It is, of course, upon this Baroque design that most modern recorders are modeled.

The Hotteterre design quickly became the standard for recorder makers throughout Europe, and although recorders continued to be made in many sizes they began to be used less in consorts than as solo instruments, the favored size being the alto. The alto recorder became a popular instrument for the amateur player. In France, the silken shepherds and shepherdesses of Le Petit Trianon warbled mock-rustic dances on pairs of recorders or exquisitely turned little bagpipes called musettes. In London, the gentleman-about-town carried a recorder in his pocket to pull out at an odd moment and pipe some popular tune from *The Beggar's Opera* or play with a friend the latest duets by Valentine or Paisaible.

Baroque composers continued a long-standing tradition of associating certain instruments with particular dramatic situations: drums and
trumpets for kings, horns for the hunt, bagpipes for rustics, etc. The
recorder announced pastoral scenes, as in Bach's familiar "Sheep May
Safely Graze." Recorders were associated with birds, as in Handel's
"Hush, ye pretty warbling quire," from *Acis and Galatea,* where a sopranino provides the irrepressible birdsong. Neither of these associations
surprises us, nor does the idea of the recorder's sweet sound to set the
mood for a love scene. For heavenly apparitions we might have expected
harps, but the chaste, otherworldly sound of the recorder consort was
deemed correct for the descent of gods, angels, and other such supernatu-
ral beings. It was apparently this use of recorders, exerting their unique
charm, that prompted Samuel Pepys to record the following in his Diary
for February 27, 1668:

> With my wife to the King's house, to see "The Virgen Martyr,"
> the first time it hath been acted in a great while: and it is mightly
> pleasant; not that the play is worth much, but it is finely acted
> by Berk Marshall. But that which did please me beyond any-
> thing in the whole world was the wind-musique when the angel
> comes down, which is so sweet that it ravished me, and indeed,
> in a word, did wrap my soul so that it made me really sick, just
> as I have formerly been when in love with my wife; but neither
> then, nor all evening going home, and at home, I was able to
> think of any thing, but remained all night transported, so as I
> could not believe that ever any music hath that real command
> over the soul of man as did this upon me: and makes me resolve
> to practice wind-musique, and to make my wife do the like.

Pepys returned for a second performance and found the music for
the coming down of the angel still moved him "as nothing ever did, and
the other musique is nothing to it." He then betook himself to Drum-
blely's to buy a recorder and resolved to learn to play it, "the sound of
it being, of all sounds in the world, most pleasing to me." I feel a great
sense of kinship with Samuel Pepys.

Henry Purcell (c. 1659–1695) was the greatest English composer of
the Baroque period, the "British Orpheus," as he was dubbed by his
musical contemporaries. He was admired both for his compositions and

for his countertenor voice. He was fond of coupling songs for counter-tenor with two "flutes," as recorders were then termed in England. Upon his early death, John Blow, who was both his mentor and his successor as organist at Westminster Abbey, wrote an "Ode on the Death of Henry Purcell" for two countertenors, two alto recorders, and continuo.

Clearly, Purcell and recorders had a close affinity. In his ode for Queen Mary's birthday, "Come, ye sons of art" (1694), there is an aria which is quintessentially Purcellian, "Strike the Viol." The voice is coun-tertenor, Purcell's own; over a ground bass (a short pattern repeated throughout the composition), a favorite device of Purcell's; with an ob-bligato of two recorders. The first quatrain, twelve words in thirteen syllables, is my favorite verse about music:

> *Strike the viol*
> *Touch the lute*
> *Wake the harp*
> *Inspire the flute.*

The bow does indeed strike the viol; the fingers do touch the lute; the harp sleeps until we wake it; and we inspire our flutes. Purcell not only agreed with the words by singing them with his own voice, but by putting a striking viol on the ground bass, and two inspiring flutes as accompaniment. A harp and a lute may well have taken up the rest.

The early eighteenth century was the recorder's heyday. Bach and Handel wrote for it, although it is interesting to note that Bach wrote no solo sonatas for recorder, choosing instead the flute, a sign of things to come. Among the Baroque composers, Telemann has provided us with more beautiful music for the recorder than any other: sonatas, trio sona-tas, and music for larger ensembles, including the ravishing Suite in A Minor for Recorder and Strings. Telemann's musical gifts were not en-couraged by his family. Nonetheless, as a boy of ten he managed to teach himself to play the violin, cittern, and recorder. Perhaps because it was one of his first instruments, he seems to have had an unusual fondness for the recorder, although instruments of all kinds were well served in his prodigious output of music.

The recorder's turn as a Baroque solo instrument, though brilliant, was brief, for it soon began to be eclipsed by the Baroque flute, with its greater dynamic possibilities. Later Baroque music became increasingly preoccupied with nuances of loud and soft, sudden crescendos and decrescendos, none of which were possible on the recorder. Its cool, even sound did not suit the subjective emotionality of the emerging *stile galant.* Still less could it compete with other instruments in the developing ensemble of strings, woodwinds in pairs, and brass that became the classical orchestra. Gentlemen-about-town began carrying flutes in their pockets instead of recorders. The recorder became an antiquarian curiosity, and so it remained for a hundred and fifty years.

Before we consign the instrument to this long sleep, let us consider some of the names by which it was known during its extended first incarnation. Some of these describe its appearance, as the archaic German *Schnabelflöte* and the name by which it is still called in France, *flûte à bec,* both referring to the beak through which we blow. The old Italian term *flauto diritto* describes how the instrument is held, straight as opposed to the sideways position of the *flauto traverso.* Features of the instrument's construction are reflected in the archaic *flûte à neuf trous;* the German name *Blockflöte* and the old English *fipple flute* refer to the plug in the recorder's head. Its sweet tone is referred to in the Italian *flauto dolce* and French *flûte douce.* Its popularity in England gave it the names *flûte d'Angleterre, English flute, common flute,* and, as we have noted, simply *flute.* Perhaps the hardest name to account for is the word *recorder* itself. Edgar Hunt, in his excellent book *The Recorder and Its Music,* examines the question in some detail. While it has proven impossible to determine exactly how the name got attached to the instrument, Mr. Hunt leads us to the Latin *recordari: to remember* or *recollect.* Among many tenuous but intriguing possibilities, Mr. Hunt lays one definitively to rest—the verb *to record* in the obsolete meaning of "to sing like a bird"—since the recorder had its name a century-and-a-half before the bird got its verb. Perhaps we should think of the recorder as a "memory flute," although it resembles a nightingale more than a tape machine.

The twentieth-century revival of the recorder began, as most reawakenings do, quite slowly. In the late nineteenth century some scholars and musicians began to interest themselves in the largely neglected literature of music written before Bach and Handel. This, in turn, led them to wonder how the music was performed. The first experiments with early instruments were not always revelatory, but nonetheless served to get things started. The chief galvanizing force in reviving the ancient sounds was Arnold Dolmetsch (1858–1940), whose genius was perfectly suited to the task. He was trained as an instrument maker (piano and organ), and was an excellent violinist. His interest in early music led him to make reconstructions of viols, clavichords, harpsichords, and, eventually, recorders. He also compiled a book on the performance of early music, *The Interpretation of the Music of the XVII & XVIII Centuries* (1916), quoting extensively from the original sources, which over sixty years later remains a reliable guide.

Arnold Dolmetsch, and his son Carl, not only provided us with recorders (since we cannot all own museum specimens), but demonstrated their viability as musical instruments. Other makers soon took up the pattern, but not always correctly. German makers of the late twenties and early thirties changed the position of the holes in order to simplify the fingering of the recorder's basic scale, to the so-called "German fingering," which upset the delicate balance needed for successful cross-fingering. This step backwards was made on the false assumption that the instrument would then be easier for schoolchildren, for in Germany the recorder was widely used in school music instruction. German fingering does indeed make it easier to play F on a soprano recorder, but what about F-sharp? There are still many German-fingered recorders about,

but anyone who makes them or uses them is declaring his conviction that the recorder is an inferior instrument by promoting an inferior version of it.

Fortunately, most makers have chosen to follow the perfected design of the historical instruments, and in recent years ever more exactly. Several makers produce Baroque instruments at Baroque pitch, approximately one half-step lower than modern standard pitch. Recorders of Renaissance design are also being made. It is usually the smaller workshops, and individual craftsmen, who adhere most closely to the originals, producing the best, and most expensive, instruments. Such instruments are for the specialist, the professional player, or the wealthy amateur. For the public at large, instruments of neo-Baroque design are manufactured, in both wood and plastic, in quantities that would stagger the members of the late-sixteenth-century Stuttgart Town Band. Many of these instruments are excellent for their purpose, avocational music making, but if you are buying a recorder in wood you must find the instrument that suits you (for further advice, see the chapter "Selecting and Caring for Your Recorder").

It is astonishing to think that in the past twenty years more recorders have been made (by how many times over, I couldn't imagine) and more lips laid to fipple, than ever before in the recorder's long history. This reflects, I suppose, our modern, mass-produced approach to something good. I take a kind attitude because there is no doubt in my mind that the recorder is good. Since there are more of us in this egalitarian society than there were in eighteenth-century London or Paris, or Europe in general in preceding centuries, and certainly more than perched on the knolls of Arcady, we need more recorders. The virtues of this endearing instrument far exceed its shortcomings.

Its role in reviving the sound of early music has been that of leader. With the recorder came lutes, and viols, and krummhorns; then cornets, and shawms, and sackbuts; Baroque oboes, and flutes, and bassoons; citterns and theorbos; racketts and rommelpots. You may think I am making this up, but I assure you that at workshops over the past twenty years I have witnessed a revival of early sounds that never fails to amaze me. Some are produced very well, and others very badly; but both get better, and delight and amusement prevail. The recorder, like a guileless page, opens the door to this musical garden of flowers, fruits, and vegetables. It is the seminal instrument that has led the way.

I first began teaching the recorder in 1958, when a few people who had heard me play asked me for lessons. I agreed to try and by the end of 1959 I was teaching adult classes several nights a week, teaching a children's class one afternoon a week, and teaching a group of teenage girls on Saturday afternoons, as well as giving many private lessons. I found myself dealing with people of all ages and all levels of musical sophistication from the absolute novice to the trained musician. Some people learned quite readily but others suffered from learning blocks and inhibitions—and often I found these people the most fun to teach because they tested my ingenuity. I soon found that there were a great many people who wanted to learn the recorder and I was in the fortunate position of being, at that time and in that place—the San Francisco Bay Area—the best recorder player around, so I was very busy.

For me every new student was a fresh challenge. I worked out my own ways of explaining a technical musical point to a particular person in a particular situation and developed techniques for allaying tensions, nervousness, and self-deprecation, for finding a nonthreatening way of solving a problem, for leading people to the musical results they so much desire. I have great respect for anyone who chooses to learn a musical instrument, for it is a process which makes him vulnerable to himself and to the rest of the world. This is something that should be understood by any good teacher. A student gives a teacher his trust and the teacher must respond with all the tact, sensitivity, and patience at his command. It is a very rewarding relationship.

Over the years that I have taught, I naturally learned a great deal and I developed routines for solving various problems and refining definitions of just what the problems are. Again and again students have suggested that I put this accumulated experience down in a book, so that is what I have finally done.

First, I offer the why and wherefore, in "Technique." This is what you should know in order to play the instrument well. I aim to set novices on the right track, and to provide some insights for the more experienced player or teacher. At the end of this section we consider for the first time, but not the last, how it all works in the act of making music. Next comes "How to Practice." Having done a good bit of practice myself, I tell you what tricks of mind and action I have found useful in getting the parts of myself to work together to get the results I want. The chapter on ornamentation is an introduction and a bridge to get you across the fearsome abyss between ignorance and the standard scholarly explanations. Alternate fingerings are required for fast movements, usually ornaments. It is good to know the fingerings and the ornaments, but it is better to know fast movement, so finger action is the basis of my presentation of alternate fingerings.

Compound articulation is a concern of players whose tongues can't keep up with their fingers. They have to learn to double-tongue and triple-tongue. Compound articulation also has an historical aspect which is quite different, so read the chapter in question and find out.

Unless you want to play by yourself for the rest of your life, the courtesies and techniques of ensemble playing are what you should look at next. There's more to it than you might think. When we know how to get along together in the musical ensemble, we must look for music to play. Colin Sterne, Professor of Music at the University of Pittsburgh, and a pioneer, with his wife, Roberta, in the performance of early music, has provided us with a chapter on the repertoire of music available to the recorder. This general survey is supplemented by an explicit list of editions for recorders, compiled with the help of two knowledgeable colleagues, Martha Bixler and Joan Munkacsi.

Finally, we come to the care and feeding of your recorder, upon which I had excellent advice from Steve Silverstein. Probably the reason that Steve is one of the world's best makers of recorders is that he is also one of the best players. For those of you who have never played the recorder before, there is a special section in the Appendix, "The Beginner's First Lesson," to help you get started.

The book does not contain lists of specific instrument makers, or of shops that specialize in recorders and music for them, or where you can buy a krummhorn or a psaltery, and so forth. For current information on what is available, you should join the American Recorder Society and receive quarterly issues of its journal, *The American Recorder.* For more about the American Recorder Society, see the Appendix, p. 243.

Many topics in this book invite examination in greater detail than I have given. As you develop, you will look in many directions for guidance. Signposts along the way are listed in "For Further Reading." The purpose of this book is to till the soil and plant the seeds so that your musical experience will grow and flourish with our sweet flute, the recorder.

THE

RECORDER

BOOK

Chapter 1

TECHNIQUE

THE IMPORTANCE OF TECHNIQUE

Playing a musical instrument is rather like ice-skating. At the beginning, one's interest is most often engaged by observing an expert performer. Who has not been thrilled seeing a lithe figure flashing across the ice on silver blades, suddenly reversing direction, making startling leaps and dazzling spins, or gliding in graceful arcs? The polished blades beneath his feet allow an almost magical freedom, so the variety of his movements seems to be determined only by his fancy. The wistful, earthbound observer, wishing to experience this liberated and expressive movement, may decide on the spot to get a pair of these skates which put wings on one's feet. But one's first time on ice is usually a cruel disappointment. Obviously, the magic does not lie in the skates but in the skill of the skater, and as the beginner progresses he learns that he must control his movements precisely as the skates dictate. Only when these movements are automatic does he begin to enjoy the expressive freedom which the skates allow.

We are usually drawn to the recorder by hearing it played by an expert. We are charmed by its apparently effortless sweetness and simplicity, and we hurry out to buy one of these sweet flutes so that we too can make such charming sounds. But when we begin to blow on our own recorder the sound is not the same, and the surprise is no less disconcerting than are those first slippery moments on skates. The truth is that the expressive lyricism which we seek lies not in the instrument but in the skill with which we play it.

Technique is the process of mastering the movements we make when we play. We must analyze these movements, know them in intimate detail, and repeat them over and over until they are automatic.

Then they become the servants of our expression. We learn to play *ourselves* in the mode dictated by our instrument.

We use three distinct systems of muscles in playing the recorder, the breath, the tongue, and the fingers. Breath is primary, providing energy to create and sustain tone. The tongue is a valve which starts and stops the tone by releasing or cutting off the airstream. Fingers, by stopping or unstopping their respective holes, produce different pitches. None of these movements requires much effort. Strength is not needed to play the recorder. No special muscles need to be developed for extraordinary exertions. A cellist must have a steely grip in his fingering hand to press the strings against the fingerboard. A pianist belaboring a grand piano in concert with a full symphony orchestra is truly heroic, and he has spent years of practice to develop the necessary strength of finger, hand, wrist, and arm. Trained singers drive their voices with breathing muscles of astonishing strength and development. Slip an arm around a singer's waist and ask for a high note delivered mezzo-forte—you will receive an experience worth remembering the next time you hear Violetta or Mimi dying of consumption in the last act.

The recorder is the most lightly blown of all the instruments which are sounded by the player's breath. The variations in breath pressure required in playing other wind instruments reflect corresponding variations of resistance created by the player's lips, his *embouchure.* The recorder does not have an embouchure. The embouchure is built in, so to speak. A recorder's windway is relatively large, and therefore offers but slight resistance to the player's breath, compared to the constricted apertures against which players of embouchure instruments must blow; and since it is unchangeable, it offers the same resistance to high and low notes alike, which accounts for the prevailing low breath pressure employed in blowing the recorder.

So, as you can see, we recorder players are not subject to the athletic demands of the cello, piano, trained voice, or modern wind instruments. Our muscles already have more than enough strength for the recorder's modest requirements. However, the gestures of our breath, tongue, and fingers must be precise and sensitive. The breath must be relaxed and free, with a quick and delicate flexibility in meeting particular requirements of each note with good intonation and clear sonority. *Articulation,* the spacing between notes and the quality of attack and release, is controlled by the tongue and the breath, which by their combined action can produce a great variety of effects. Fingers move lightly and quickly, with precise coordination among themselves and with the tongue. Fingers and tongue are in charge of executing the rhythmic aspect of the music. Therefore their movements must be rhythmically exact and expressive.

Our concern is to coordinate all these actions while maintaining the necessary lightness. Thus we must be particularly alert for signs of tension, cramped fingers, heavy tongue, or harsh, overblown tone. These are indications that we are trying too hard, moving our muscles with excessive and misplaced force. Such tensions are most likely to creep into our playing when there are technical problems. Fast notes, wide leaps, very high notes, complicated rhythms, or extended phrases lead to overexertion in our efforts to maintain control. Tension replaces lightness, to the immediate detriment of our playing. To play any instrument well one must use just the amount of effort the instrument demands, neither more nor less.

Practice routines, to be useful, must allow us to be aware of our muscles and our sound. We use fragmentation, simplifying complex situations into their component actions, and we practice them over and over. Muscles learn by repetition. The aim of good practice is to use repetition efficiently by isolating and solving problems one at a time mechanically so we don't have to think of everything at once. We can focus our attention on our movements to be sure that they are light and free of strain. Most important, we can *listen* to the sounds we are making. How can we ever know we are playing pleasingly unless we hear ourselves adequately?

Neat execution must be sought from the very beginning as a foundation for rapid and reliable progress untrammeled by irksome remedial work. The meticulous fragmentation of a technical problem works best when one is in the right frame of mind—calm, patient, and objective. Sometimes we are in the mood to pay attention to tiny details, and sometimes we are not. It is only realistic to acknowledge our state of mind as we begin a session of practice. Good technique is making all the right movements effortlessly, knowing the instrument so well that every muscle responds automatically to just the right degree from one note to the next. By dint of practice, the muscles are programmed to the instrument's requirements. Technical mastery is a state of self-knowledge, immediate and corporeal. It is exhilarating to achieve, but not an end in itself. Beautifully and expressively played music is the goal; technical mastery is one of the essential means.

Basic technique has the same meaning for the beginner and the

experienced player. It is something you must renew each time you begin
to play. Pablo Casals used to say that the first thing he did each morning
when he picked up his cello was to relearn where to put his fingers. We
all must learn basic technique, and each time we begin to play, we learn
it anew.

Note: In the discussions that follow, whenever I refer to notes, these
are for the alto recorder, which we are taking as our standard size for this
purpose. In order to give each note a specific designation, I have adopted
the following system: The seven bottom notes are identified by capital
letters, F through E; the next seven notes are shown by capital letters
followed by a prime, F′ through E′; the six highest notes are shown by
capital letters followed by a double prime, F″ through C″. Showing the
actual notes that the alto recorder sounds, it works out like this:

F G A B C D E F′ G′ A′ B′ C′ D′ E′ F″ G″ A″ B″ C″

BREATH

What emerges again and again about blowing the recorder is that one's
breath must be relaxed. But there is a real contradiction inherent in this
simple statement of fact, a fact absolutely determined by the physical
structure of the instrument. The difficulty is in trying not to try. How
does one direct one's efforts towards effortlessness? We invest a lot of
ourselves in the endeavor of playing a musical instrument. This self-
expression is most meaningful and our desire is to do it supremely well,
so we try hard to do that which must be done effortlessly. And the force
and intensity of this effort throttles our breath; tone becomes tight when
looseness is what is needed.

How can we *try* to be more relaxed? By a ruse, by a deception, by
doing something else, with the recorder to our lips, than the avowed
purpose of making beautiful sounds. In short, by heaving sighs through
the recorder. A sigh is a gesture of the breath characterized by a totally
relaxed exhalation. There is no effort in emitting a sigh. That is its virtue,
as a sigh, and as an expressive gesture of the breath that will inform our
efforts in relaxed breathing.

Here are the steps in using the sigh:

Step 1: Heave a sigh. It must be a genuine sigh, not some artificially forced push of air obediently produced on command. And as you sigh, observe the sensation. We sigh daily, hourly, indeed from moment to moment, but usually we don't notice it. Now is the time to observe this habitual, profound, personal, and useful gesture of the breathing apparatus. Know what it feels like, in relaxation, to heave a deep and honest sigh.

Step 2: The next step is to heave a sigh through your recorder. Place the recorder loosely in your mouth, with your lips and cheeks relaxed, and emit a sigh through the recorder. This is a delicate moment. No beautiful tone is going to emerge, but a rush of overblown sound which collapses into a pathetic dying fall, a noise precisely the opposite of what one wishes. At this moment you must remember what a true sigh feels like and be sure you are making that gesture of the breath through the recorder. You will be appalled by the sound, but never mind. At this stage we are not concerned with the sound, but rather with the sensation of blowing a completely relaxed and uncontrolled breath through the recorder. From here we can move to blowing with the minimal control required by the minimal resistance offered by the instrument.

It is more difficult than you might think to blow a sincere sigh through the recorder. Our monitoring ears will try to persuade us to mitigate the first overblown gust and to sustain the tone that follows rather than letting it passively die. But a sigh is passive; we fill our lungs deeply with air and then let it all rush out, neither holding it back nor pushing it to sustain the flow. We should think about the sigh and be sure it is genuine and let the sound come out as it will. We can observe the sound but we musn't try to control it. At the outset there will be too much air, and the sound will be overblown. The deeper the sigh, the greater the overblowing. Let it be over-blown. Contemplate this sudden, free rush of air. Know what it represents and be unafraid of the sound it produces. After the initial gust of escaping breath comes the dying fall, a smooth, sliding *morendo* of pitch and volume, ending in nothingness. If there are wobbles in this descent they indicate attempts at control or tightness in the throat, both unwanted. At this step we seek a totally free and uncontrolled exhalation from which we will move to the light and virtually effortless breath control appropriate to the instrument.

Step 3: Once we have (and only if we have) succeeded in making the completely relaxed gesture of a sigh through our recorder, we begin to alter the size of our sighs. We take in less air so when we sigh it out through the recorder the sound is not overblown at all, although it still ends in a smooth, dying fall. At this point we are truly delivering a relaxed breath stream into the recorder at the level appropriate to the instrument.

Step 4: Here minimal control enters. We simply make the same gesture of the breath as a small sigh, light and relaxed, and sustain it. No dying fall, but just a continued blowing through of the original, easy puff of air. If the tone does not sustain easily and smoothly, without wobbles from extraneous muscular events, one would do well to go back to the beginning of this sequence, and heave a deep sigh.

When you understand it, the sequence is much shorter in the doing than in the telling: Heave a deep sigh; heave a deep sigh through the recorder; heave a smaller sigh through the recorder; make the same breath gesture as the smaller sigh through the recorder and sustain the tone. That's about how long it takes, and it does remind you of how it feels to blow a relaxed breath through the recorder. My students begin every lesson (and, I hope, every practice session) with this routine. It works. We go up and down a scale; I do it, and they answer, and we are all reminded of what relaxed breathing feels like. Then we proceed to the vibrato exercise for further relaxed breath control (see p. 45).

TONGUE

The precise posture and action of the tongue are nicely demonstrated by the phrase "Who edited it?" If you say this phrase quickly the distinction between various consonants and vowels gets blurry, and the phrase comes out "Who edududut?" Now drop the "who" and just say "dudududut" in the same rhythm as a quickly spoken "Who edited it?" In musical notation it looks like this:

dudududut

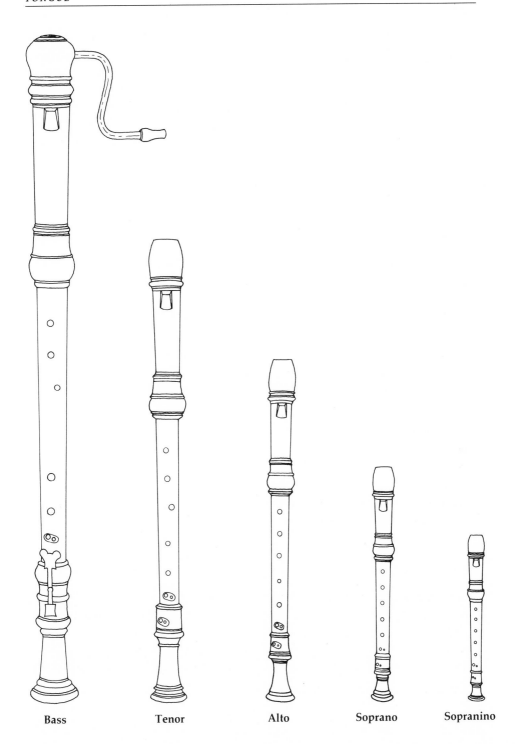

Bass   Tenor   Alto   Soprano   Sopranino

"Dudududut" provides a perfect verbal analogy for the basic action of tonguing on the recorder. Say it over several times and observe exactly what is happening. The tongue is in a state of light tension, so that it keeps a stationary posture. It is not so loose that it lolls around in the mouth, nor so stiff as to inhibit the quick repercussions of the tip. It is gently anchored at either side against the molars and is cupped at the tip so that the very edge of the tip strikes against the palatal ridge, just in back of the front teeth. It would be a good idea to say "Who edited it?" again, to get the right rhythm, and then "dudududut," to observe that the action is indeed as described.

What may surprise you is that your tongue can move so fast and so crisply; and it can move just as fast and crisply while blowing the recorder as when speaking. Put this to the test by going up and down the C scale, "dudududut-ing" on each note (no vocalizing, of course, just the tongue action). You may forget, when confronted with a menacingly black group of fast notes, just how fast your tongue already knows how to move. Thinking of "Who edited it" and "dudududut" at such moments helps to untie the tongue.

Starting the lowest notes, F, G, and A, and notes in the upper register, from high C'-sharp upwards, requires a different relationship between tongue and breath than that described by "Who edited it?" For the lowest notes the breath must be started very gently and the tongue must come away from the palate at the same instant that the breath begins. Any buildup of pressure behind the tongue that gives even a slight explosive quality to the release of air into the recorder will cause the note to pop into its second mode of vibration. Instead of a low F, for example, you will get a note a bit more than an octave higher, roughly an F'-sharp. The low notes are fragile and you must ease into them gently. An analogy that a student of mine found useful for getting the low C on her tenor is to start the air as if you were blowing on a spoonful of hot soup. A gusty blow spills the soup, or overblows the note.

In articulating notes in the highest register, from C'-sharp on up, the tongue action is virtually the same as I have just described, but the gesture of the breath behind it is almost exactly the opposite of what is required in the lowest register. The breath must move considerably faster and it must commence instantly and precisely at the appropriate speed for the given note. And at the same instant the breath delivers this exactly gauged and initiated puff of air, the tongue moves away from the palatal ridge, so that there is no buildup of pressure behind it, and no explosiveness.

A little experiment with the note D in the lower and upper registers will clarify the details of the description:

- First play a D in the lower register, but with no articulation. Use neither the tip nor the back of the tongue, and certainly do not start it with a grunt from the throat. Rather, begin it simply with a huff of air, and try to make that huff so cleanly and instantaneously that the note sounds as if it had been tongued in the normal way. It may take a few tries before you acquire the necessary instant gesture of the breath, but be patient and listen very critically. You are on the verge of an important discovery!

- When you have succeeded in producing an absolutely clean attack using the breath alone, open the thumbhole just a tiny bit, and make that same instant gesture of the breath but with a bit more air (i.e., a faster breath stream) as is required in the upper register; and now start the note with a very quick and light tongue stroke which comes away from the palatal ridge at the same moment that the breath stream starts, and a clean D' should result.

After a few tries you should find yourself producing clean and perfectly articulated high D's; and you will be in possession of the great secret of how to articulate the high notes. For indeed the method is the same for all of them. What varies from note to note, and certainly from instrument to instrument, is the precise amount and speed of air to be delivered by this instantaneous gesture of the breath. On certain notes, for instance, on high C'-sharps, high D's, and high F's, there is very little margin for error. One must proceed with calm and patience in mastering these, and one must master them anew each time one picks up the recorder. There are very few activities that require quite the minute precision of movement involved in drawing beautiful music from an instrument, and the recorder is no exception in this regard.

Besides having the correct attack for the high notes there is, of course, the crucial element of just how much to crack the thumbhole. (The whole topic of cracking the thumbhole will be discussed in detail later in this chapter [pp. 16–20].) When one has gotten both the attack and the thumbing right, the high notes come out with surprising ease.

The action of the left thumb in cracking the thumbhole forms a part of our consideration of how we should move our fingers. As you will see, to get the proper relaxed action in our fingers requires relaxation and looseness in the entire arm, and indeed, in the entire body.

FINGERS

Sitting comfortably upright in a chair that has no arms, lean over to the right and let your arm dangle from your shoulder. Your entire arm must be relaxed for this to happen. The whole arm and hand should hang loose, like a clapper in a bell. This is precisely the way both arms should always hang from the shoulders when you are playing the recorder. Tension, when it occurs, usually starts with stiff, grasping fingers, but it soon is transferred to the forearms, the biceps, the shoulders, and even the muscles of the back. I have heard people complain that after a session of practicing they have gotten a backache. That is the result of stiff fingers trying too hard, and it is not an unnatural result. When we are trying to do something with our fingers it is very easy to try too hard, to use too much muscular force in the effort to make the fingers move the way we want them to. Unwanted tension will creep in again and again. If our fingers start getting stiff, they won't behave the way we want them to, so the best way to allay stiffness when it starts to creep in is to lean over sideways and let the arm dangle. It won't hang loose from the shoulder if there is any tension below, so a dangling arm is a good reminder of the relaxation we should feel in these parts.

Now, with arms hanging loose, reach up and touch your shoulder. This demonstrates the hinge action at the elbow. Next, with your elbows at your side, hold your hands out in front of you and swivel your forearms so that you see first the backs of your hands and then the palms. This demonstrates the swivel action at the elbow. While performing this maneuver, be aware of your elbows, which should be hanging loosely at your sides. If you find your elbows sticking up and out, there is tension in your upper arms that holds them in that position. Drop them. The tension is unwanted and unneeded. Being aware of the swivel action of the forearm from the elbow is useful in positioning the hands on the recorder.

Now lift your forearms more or less vertically in front of you and let the hands dangle from the wrists. They will hang at right angles from the forearms. With the fingers of one hand pointing at the fingers of the other, lift your index fingers only. Try to move just these first fingers, with no sympathetic movement from the other fingers. You will find that to succeed you must move the index fingers very lightly. Be sure that your hands are indeed hanging loosely from the wrists. Next try moving middle fingers only. Here the action must be even lighter in order to confine the movement to just these fingers. It is virtually impossible to move the ring fingers without some movement of the fingers on either side. The pinkies, however, turn out to be more independent. The point of this little exercise is to direct your attention to the correct action of the fingers in playing the recorder, which is to move the entire finger from the third knuckle where the finger attaches to the hand. This action is achieved by long, slender muscles on the forearm extending from the wrist to the elbow. If you look at your bared forearm and move each finger in turn, you will see a slightly different movement of the anatomy beneath the skin for each finger. These are made by the muscles that move our fingers in playing the recorder correctly.

There are also powerful gripping muscles in the palm of the hand that are used for grasping things and making fists. These are the muscles that we do not want to use. They make our fingers stiff and heavy; they are for tasks of strength, not agility, and when they come into play they make the proper muscles work harder. So stiffness sets in, and if unchecked, it could give you a backache. Therefore every time your fingers become stiff, let your arm dangle. Facile fingers move with very little force. Each finger moves as a whole, like a lever, from the third knuckle hinging it to the hand.

Position

We seek a position of the hands on the recorder that allows each finger to fall neatly and accurately on the hole which it governs, securing a complete seal with the center of the fleshy pad opposite the nail, more or less at the center of the whorl of the fingerprint, which is also the most tactilely sensitive part of the finger. This ideal spot cannot always be used because of the size of the instrument, the positioning of its holes, the size and shape of individual hands and fingers, and, in certain cases, the sequence of notes to be played. When not covering the holes, the fingers should hover about a half-inch above them. The fingers' movements are always quick, neat, and crisp, whether one is playing slow notes or fast.

There is usually only one position of the hands on the instrument which allows each finger to meet its hole exactly and accurately with the desired light action, and this position must be found by each individual according to the shape of his hand and the placement of the holes on his recorder. Some instruments are made with the holes slightly offset to make the reach for each finger easier. Others have a perfectly vertical alignment of holes, which is less convenient. The position of the hands that most people find comfortable is as follows, beginning with the left, uppermost hand:

The line of the knuckles is at an angle to the shaft of the instrument, nearer above and further away below, so that the third finger is straight and extending obliquely downward to cover the third hole with its fleshy pad. Fingers 1 and 2 are slightly arched, and they also cover with their fleshy pads. The lefthand pinky, of course, is not used. This angling away of the line of the knuckles is achieved by a slight swiveling of the forearm toward the body, accompanied by a slight bending back of the hand at the wrist. The left thumb is placed on the back of the instrument, angled slightly upwards from horizontal, and covers its hole with the top of the digit, close to the nail, just before the point where the nail enters the cuticle. This spot provides the best reference point for accuracy in cracking the thumbhole for the upper registers (see pages 16–20 for a more thorough discussion of this action).

The position of the lower hand, the right, is very similar to that of the left: the line of the knuckles angling away from the instrument, the third finger straight, and the first and second fingers slightly arched. However, when the hand is in this position the pinky cannot reach the seventh hole which it is supposed to stop, and it may not even reach the instrument. Therefore there is more than one position for the right hand, depending on whether or not the pinky is involved. When it must perform, the entire hand moves further onto the instrument. The pinky now becomes the finger which is extended straight and obliquely downward to cover its double holes. The first finger will still be covering with its fleshy pad but the second and third fingers will now be covering further along, even so far as the first knuckle. Thus, the right hand is inclined to move about a bit on the instrument, and it is perfectly normal that it should do so. The right hand is furthest across the shaft of the instrument when the pinky is covering both its double holes for the low F. It moves off slightly for the F-sharp, and off further still for G, so the fingers for holes 5 and 6 can cover with their best parts, the fleshy pads. For G-sharp/A-flat the hand draws away even slightly more. Unlike the upper hand, the left, the right hand's position is not stationary on the recorder.

The right thumb, which has nothing to do otherwise, can help support the weight of the instrument by means of a thumbrest.

The Thumbrest

I recommend that every recorder of alto size or larger be furnished with a thumbrest, a device that one fastens to the back of the instrument just above the right thumb, which allows the weight of the instrument to be sustained by that otherwise inactive digit. Thus the fingers can move freely in their patterns without having to hold up the instrument at the same time. The thumbrest provides a more secure hold on the instrument and promotes lightness of finger action. Thumbrests are made of metal, plastic, or wood. Rubber erasers and wine bottle corks are popular objects for makeshift thumbrests. The usual position for the thumbrest is rather low, about midway between holes 4 and 5, so that the right thumb, placed on the recorder at a right angle to the shaft, carries the weight on its upper side. Most thumbs have a depression between the first joint and the thumb nail, a saddle in which the thumbrest fits quite nicely. If the thumbrest sits too close to the nail, it will tend to irritate the cuticle. Smaller thumbs, lacking a "saddle," may have difficulty in finding a comfortable resting place for the thumbrest, which seems irritating in every position. One solution is to cushion the bottom of the thumbrest with sponge or some other soft and springy substance. This will usually eliminate the discomfort. Some people find the hand is more comfortable if they hold the right thumb vertically, in which case the thumbrest sits on the end of the thumb. Some like the thumbrest higher or lower than midway between holes 4 and 5. You will want to do some experimental moving around until you find the most comfortable spot, and for this reason it is best to begin with a temporary attachment with some kind of adhesive tape. Attaching a thumbrest permanently with tiny screws that actually penetrate the wood of the recorder is a tricky business, and should be done by a repairman who specializes in recorders. There is no single correct position for the thumbrest. If it allows you to hold the instrument securely, without strain or irritation, it is in the right place.

There is no evidence that thumbrests were used on old instruments. Indeed, fingering charts from the seventeenth century onward provide evidence to the contrary by inclusion of the so-called "buttress finger," the sixth finger (righthand ring finger), to help steady the recorder for the notes from C to G', which involve only the fingers and thumb of the upper hand. Since the buttress finger is only a mechanical expedient, and since the thumbrest does the same thing better, I see no reason not to accept this untraditional but mechanically superior device.

Cracking the Thumbhole

If the right thumb beneath its thumbrest has a mere supporting role, certainly the left thumb is the star in our cast of digits. It has a more difficult and delicate task than any of the other fingers. By slightly opening, "cracking," its hole, it helps us to get into the upper registers of the recorder. In doing this we are blowing various notes of the lowest register in their second, third, and fourth modes of vibration. For example, when we finger a low A and open the thumbhole slightly, the A sounds in its second mode of vibration, that is, A', an octave higher. Lifting the third finger causes the note to vibrate in its third mode, giving a high E', a fifth above the second mode and an octave and a fifth above the basic mode of the low A. Blowing harder with this same fingering produces the fourth mode of vibration. Theoretically this should be an A" two octaves above the basic mode but in fact the note produced is one tone higher, a B".

How far to open the thumbhole varies from recorder to recorder, and quite often from note to note on the same recorder. Also the thumb has to be extremely agile in moving from cracked to closed to open position as the recorder skips back and forth between the upper and bottom registers. All of this leads us to one conclusion: we want the simplest and most economical movement from closed to cracked thumb that we can find.

There are two methods, *pinching* and *rolling. Pinching* involves pressing the thumbnail against the thumbhole. *Rolling* involves swiveling the thumb slightly to uncover the hole. Pinching is the recognized method.

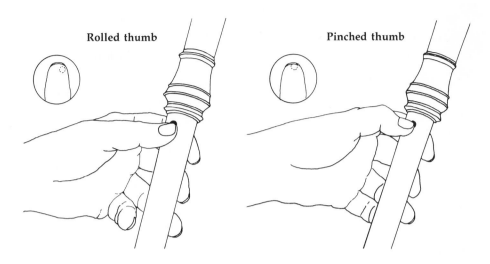

Rolled thumb   Pinched thumb

It is used by most people, taught by most teachers, described in most method books, and historically correct. Most amateurs do it incorrectly. Rolling is practiced by a renegade minority, many of whom are former (or present) clarinetists who are familiar with thumb-rolling from that instrument. Pinching is defended as being easier to control exactly, and some feel that the hard edge of the nail has a better acoustical effect than the softer flesh of the rolled thumb. We thumb-rollers are not aware of the difficulties imputed to our method, and we prefer it because the movement is simpler. However, the pinched thumb, when done properly, is a very simple movement too; so I think it's all in what you are used to. Either method is satisfactory. I actually use both, switching to a pinched thumb in treacherous registers on the soprano and tenor, specifically, from the second octave G on up.

The rolled thumb: This method takes advantage of a slight swiveling action of the thumb at the joint with the hand. Hold your left thumb between right thumb and index finger and try swiveling it; you will see that it moves readily. The action is performed on the recorder as though you were going to make a downward stroking motion on the barrel of the recorder. In fact you might try actually making this stroking motion just to get a feel of the action. What actually happens, though, is that the thumb does not slide down because its flesh catches against the bottom edge of the hole, so it swivels away from the hole slightly instead. In order to have control of this action you must close the hole at a particular spot on the thumb, on the upper side, very near the nail and close to where the nail enters the flesh. The thumbnail provides a point of reference which allows you to gauge how much you have opened the hole. The movement is certainly very quick and simple; a slight push downwards rolls the thumb away, and a push upwards rolls it back.

The pinched thumb: Here, too, the closed position of the thumb determines the success of the movement. It is very nearly the same spot as with the rolled thumb, just a bit more towards the center of the nail. The action is to bend the first joint of the thumb, which draws the tip down past the upper edge of the hole and points the nail into the space that is revealed, so that it forms the lower edge of the aperture. A closed position very near the nail minimizes the amount of movement required. The thumbnail must be very precisely manicured—not too long, not too short. The lighter the thumb presses against the recorder, the easier it is to move between closed and pinched positions. A great many people forget this fact, which is why one sees so many gouged-out thumbholes. Often so much wood will be worn away by these brutal thumbs that the hole has to be rebushed with ivory or some other hard substance that can resist the wearing action of the thumbnail. Worn thumbholes are a sure sign of improper and overly forceful movement of the thumb. Wearing a slight groove in the edges of the thumbhole does provide a point of reference for the thumbnail. It should settle in the same place every time, namely, where the groove is. But if the groove begins to become an excavation, reference points will be ground away.

One problem which neither rolling nor pinching quite solves is moving from an open to a cracked thumbhole. One has to depend on spatial memory, since there are no tactile clues. Therefore one must train the thumb to restrict its movements and to stay close to home. If one learns to always take the thumb off and put it on the recorder with exactly the same movements one develops a spatial sense of where to drop the thumb in going from open to cracked position. Thumbs are very mobile and like to wander. This is very bad discipline for recorder playing, and these wandering thumbs must be carefully trained.

After we have studied the techniques of pinching or rolling to open the thumbhole, the most important question remains to be answered: How much to open the thumbhole? This is a difficult and elusive topic because the answer varies so from one instrument to the next, or even from note to note. A few general remarks and some generalizations will help you find the answer for your particular instrument. First of all, one opens less rather than more, opening perhaps from one-twentieth to one-tenth of the hole. Don't misunderstand the graphic device, encountered in fingering charts, of a half-blackened circle to indicate the cracked thumbhole. This does not mean that you uncover the hole halfway! Usually the higher you go, the less aperture required. High notes are more often persnickety about the precise size of the opening; but one must remember that these are the notes for which the breath and the tongue must modify their gestures, so the solution to obtaining these notes is not in the size of the thumb aperture alone. Nonetheless there are some instruments on which certain notes will only respond to the tiniest amount of cracking, and others that require a disconcertingly large opening. Usually the former have to be attacked very lightly, and the latter with a good deal of force. It is bothersome to have an instrument with one or two notes that require radically different thumbing from the rest. Sometimes the condition can be solved by revoicing, but this should only be undertaken by an expert. If the instrument is of high quality (and therefore expensive), particularly if it is the product of an individual craftsman rather than a factory, you can send it back to the maker with precise descriptions of what you find unsatisfactory and how you would like the instrument changed. Free-lance experts at revoicing are very hard to find. They live in either large but distant cities or obscure and inaccessible hamlets.

It should be remembered that the larger the aperture of the cracked thumbhole the sharper the note will be. This provides a useful means of controlling intonation in the upper registers, either in compensating for a faulty note or for blowing softer or harder for dynamic effects.

Producing the high notes successfully is a matter of delicate control and precise coordination of breath speed, attack, and the amount the thumbhole is uncovered. There is little margin for error, so when these notes elude one, the tendency is to tense up in one's efforts to find them, squeezing and pressing very hard with the thumb and trying to force the notes out with an explosive tongue and too much air. Needless to say, this does not help at all. To the contrary, it makes the thumb action stiffer, slower, and less sensitive; and in the case of the pinching action, you may even be damaging the instrument. Leaping to the high notes is rather like a cat leaping to a high, narrow shelf. The cat usually makes it, and, with a little practice, so should we.

Some Further Hints About Covering the Holes

One must be sure to have one's fingers far enough on the recorder so that they offer a flat surface to their holes for instant sealing. Pay particular attention to holes 3 and 6. If you close too near the tip of the finger where it begins to curve away toward the nail, there is the danger either of leaking or of not achieving an instantaneous seal. Leaking gives a false note, which is recognized at once. The non-instantaneous seal is signaled by a *portamento* effect, a sort of sliding down to the note. This unwanted effect is cured by getting the finger further on the recorder. A useful trick for seeing if your fingers are really covering the holes is, without blowing into the instrument, to slap each finger down on it with quite a bit of force, much more than one would normally use, so that it makes a percussive pop as it strikes the hole. If the finger hits squarely, and all other fingers that are down are sealing properly, this pop will sound at the pitch of the note just fingered. Thus, if you have your thumbhole covered, and you drop your first finger sharply and accurately on its hole, then the second finger, and finally the third, you will produce three pitches: *mi, re, do,* in the key of C major, the first phrase of "Hot Cross Buns." One can play entire tunes this way. But remember, this is just a device to check that your fingers are falling accurately and completely on their holes. It is not to be taken as an exercise showing the amount of force with which one drops the fingers. Obviously, one uses much less force.

Some very fine players, possessing great facility, like to hold their fingers rather high above the holes, and to slap them down with almost the force of the popping exercise. These are highly energized fingers, expressing a strong rhythmic drive. For most players, however, a lower position and lighter movement are preferable, especially at the beginning, when the fingers have not yet learned to move automatically.

Having examined the proper action in moving the fingers on the recorder, let us proceed to discuss each note of the recorder's range, establish the correct fingerings, and note any particular problems.

FINGERING THE NOTES

To show the fingerings for the notes, I'll use two systems: (1) A vertical series of circles representing the holes on the recorder—black circles to indicate closed holes and white circles to indicate open holes. (The thumbhole is indicated by a circle to the left of the figure, and if the thumbhole is to be cracked, the lower half of the circle is black.) (2) A digital display. This is a vertical column of seven numbers to indicate the seven finger holes on top of the recorder, 1 for the top hole, through 7 for the bottom hole. The thumbhole is indicated by a 0 to the left of the column between numbers 1 and 2. If a hole is to be uncovered, there is a space where the corresponding number would appear. The thumb in cracked position is indicated by a horizontal line through the zero: θ. When only one of the double holes on 6 and 7 is to be covered, this is shown by a slash through the corresponding digit: 6 or 7. The details of this system will be clear as you examine the individual fingerings and compare the figure of the recorder with the digital display. This digital system of showing the fingerings appears elsewhere in this book in a horizontal format—e.g., B-flat = 0 123/4 67.

Each note is identified by its most familiar name only, since I assume readers are aware that F-sharp is also G-flat, G-sharp is A-flat, etc. Anyone who is a little hazy about scales should consult the Appendix, page 239.

Remember that in order to get the pinky on hole 7 without cramping the rest of your hand you must allow fingers five and six to extend beyond the shaft of the instrument. Blowing the low F, you start the airstream rather slowly, an easy gesture of the breath with almost no tongue action. The tongue comes

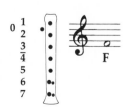

away at the same instant that one starts the breath. If you start the low F with too much air the note will overblow, producing something near an F'-sharp, an octave and a semitone higher. If you do tend to get this cracking effect on the low F and some of the other low notes, check first to see that you are not starting the breath stream too fast, or putting too strong an articulation at the beginning of the note. If neither of these is the problem, then check to see if one finger or another is not quite sealing its hole.

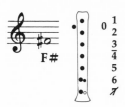

The low F-sharp has the same fingering as the F, except that the pinky is not quite so far onto the instrument, and therefore covers only the righthand hole, speaking from the player's point of view, and looms over the lefthand hole somewhat. The action of going from one to the other (i.e., F to F-sharp) is one of pulling the little finger back away from the instrument just a little bit. The low F-sharp is even more fragile than the low F, and has to be started very delicately. On most instruments it is a weak note, one of relatively slight conviction.

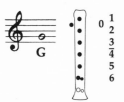

For the low G, unless it is preceded or followed by fingerings requiring the pinky (F and B-flat), the position of the right hand is as the left hand, finger number six of the right hand being extended and straight, as is finger number three of the left hand. Low G is an ambiguous note. It's richer in overtones, usually, than the low F, and the overtones usually are not quite in tune with the basic harmonic of the sound. Therefore if one blows too strongly on the note, thereby bringing in more of the upper harmonics, these will begin to beat in an unpleasant way with the basic vibration. A low G will have its best sonority if you don't blow it too hard but rather try to focus in on the tone. The note is more telling if blown softly but in tune.

A-flat involves pulling finger six away from the in- strument just a little bit, in a fashion analogous to what one does with the pinky for the low F-sharp. Moving quickly from the low G to the A-flat is re- quired in some music, including, of course, Bach's (he never spared the performer); there are two ways

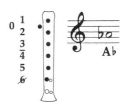

of making the action. One is to quickly pull the sixth finger away the little bit necessary to uncover one of the double holes. The other is to push the knuckles of the sixth finger down a little bit so that the end of the finger rises up and away from the instrument just enough to uncover the left hole, while still covering the right. Either way is awk- ward and takes some practice, and that practice will be done when the musical situation requiring it arises. A-flat is another rather weak note and may tend to be sharp. If it is slightly sharp, you can correct it by blowing softer. If it is more than slightly sharp, try adding half of hole 7.

Low A is a good, solid note, and can be delivered with a fairly strong stream of air. But caution: This note is sharp on some recorders.

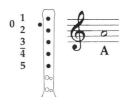

B-flat is usually a very secure note, solid in intona- tion, and doesn't require a special accommodation of the breath. Some people fall into the bad habit of not putting the seventh finger down. On any properly made recorder the B-flat will be too high in pitch unless that seventh finger is down. Thus, the finger-

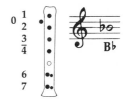

ing for the B-flat, like the fingering for the low F, requires the right hand to be more on the instrument.

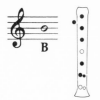

B is one of the weakest of the cross-fingered notes. It tends to be too sharp, and therefore should be blown more gently than the notes surrounding it. For example, in a sequence A, B, C, the A and the C can take more breath than the B. One should be aware of this particularly if the B occurs as a sustained note.

C is a very solid, clear, easy-to-blow note.

C-sharp will always require half of 6, and on some instruments all of 6 will be necessary to bring the note really into tune. But the simplistic fingering of

$$0 \quad \begin{matrix} 1 \\ 2 \end{matrix}$$

$$\begin{matrix} \overline{4} \\ 5 \end{matrix}$$

is not adequate on most instruments, usually being too sharp. Therefore one uses this fingering only in very fast passages where the normal fingering would be inconvenient; for example, a fast run of notes, A, B, C-sharp, D. It is awkward to go from B, with all of the sixth finger down, then swiftly to half-fingering for the C-sharp. However, over time you will find that you become more and more adept at inserting the requisite half-finger on 6 for the C-sharp in faster and faster passages.

D is a solid note; no problems.

On some instruments the sixth finger may also be required, although usually not. Fingerings on the recorder are complicated enough to start with, so one always looks for the simplest true fingering for each note.

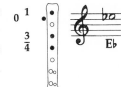

No problems.

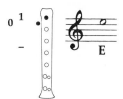

No problems.

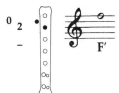

No problems.

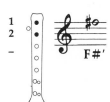

No problems.

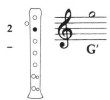

A'-flat is the first note in the second register. This is the standard fingering with the thumbhole uncovered, unlike the cracked thumb used for all other notes in the upper registers.

The same as the lower A, but with a faster airstream. Use this fingering. I know that 2

$$\frac{3}{4}$$
5

gives almost the same result, but only to an uncritical ear, since this secondary fingering is often harsher in sound.

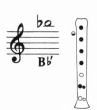

B'-flat presents no peculiar problems.

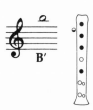

B' again is a slightly sharp note on many instruments, and you have to be sensitive.

No problems. Obviously, a faster airstream than for the C an octave lower.

C'-sharp is a delicate note. It is the first note in the second register that requires special articulation. This is one of the notes described earlier in the section "Tongue," wherein you start the note as much by a gesture of the breath as by a gesture of the tongue. You can tongue rather strongly from C to C', but 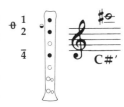 from C'-sharp on upward, the tongue action must be quicker and lighter, and the breath action takes over as the major source of articulation. The degree to which this is true varies from recorder to recorder, but C'-sharp is definitely a delicate note.

D' is also a delicate note, requiring the previously described articulation and breath modifications.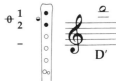

E'-flat is the first note of the third register. You may be interested to know that it is really low G in its third mode of vibration. If you want to check this out, you can try playing a low G; and then, blowing with a little stronger huff of air, using the same fingering, you will overblow at somewhat more than 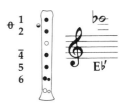 an octave, somewhere between a G' and an A'-flat. And then, if you can get it, with the appropriate huff of air, you will strike the next mode of vibration, which will be approximately the E'-flat. This E'-flat, from the third mode of vibration, of course comes much more easily with the appropriate venting of fingers, that is, the fingering given above. This note is easy to produce.

High E' is easy to produce.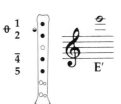

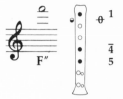

1 F″ is a fragile and delicate note, as we will all attest. Again, it is a note that requires a very precise gesture of the breath, and a very slight but quick presence of the tongue. We're really on the high wire with this note. If breath and tongue are just right we can produce the F″ cleanly, but the parameters are narrow!

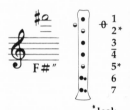

F″-sharp is the most problematical note on the alto recorder. It is problematical because there is no really satisfactory fingering for it, and yet it is a required note in some compositions, most notably in Bach's Fourth Brandenburg Concerto, and it often appears as well in compositions for other instruments into whose bailiwick recorder players choose to venture. Perhaps, but only perhaps, the fingering given here is the best solution. This fingering introduces a new concept, that of *leaking.* Leaking is doing the opposite of what one normally tries to do—that is, to close the hole fully and securely. To "leak," one closes the hole in question but not quite, and the amount of not-quiteness varies from leakage to leakage; which is to say, from esoteric fingering to esoteric fingering. There are two ways of leaking: either by arching the finger, or by drawing the finger back a little. Arching leaks from the underside of the finger, furthest from the tip. Drawing back leaks from the tip of the finger. Usually the arching technique works better in terms of the fingering requirements which surround a note requiring this technique. Thus you arch your finger slightly so that it will leak on the *underside.* For the F″-sharp, a leaking 5 is more helpful than a leaking 2.

Another, and radically different, way of getting the high F″-sharp is to finger the high G″ just above it, and stop the bell hole of the recorder against your knee; the result will be a perfect F″-sharp. But the technique is hazardous to the front teeth, especially if the note has to be gotten out quickly.

The high G″ speaks much more easily than the notes just below it. A clear, strong stream of air is all that is needed. Often the G″ is too sharp unless one adds either a half of 7, or all of 7. Thus, you must check the fingering of this highest G″ against the G′ an octave lower to be sure that it is not too sharp.

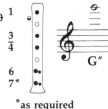

θ 1
3
4
6
7*

*as required

G″

There are notes above a high G″, very seldom required in most recorder music, but these notes are useful in another context, to be explored in terms of coming to ease with the highest registers (see "High Notes," p. 68).

At this point we are in the stratosphere, and fingerings vary. Another possibility, somewhat flatter, is θ 2
3
4
5   A sharper alternative is θ 2
3
6

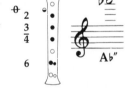

θ 2
3
4
6

Ab″

One has to experiment with one's recorder to find the best fingerings.

High A″ is a note which requires quite a blast of air. But it can come out quite clearly if one hits the note with a breath stream of the appropriately fast speed.

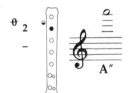

θ 2
–

A″

This hypothetical note works on some instruments, but not all.

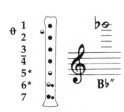

θ 1
2
3
4
5*
6*
7

*leak

Bb″

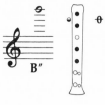

The high B″ is fingered exactly like a high E′, but one addresses the note with a much stronger, faster stream of air. This is a very strong, brisk note, and one which, like many of these extremely high notes, is not required in most musical contexts, although it has excellent value as an extender of one's technique in playing high notes.

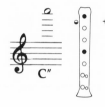

This note(?) requires a veritable blast of air. And usually the C″ produced will be quite sharp. It is very raw—but required, nonetheless, by at least one composition of Telemann's. I have yet to hear this note sound *pretty.*

PUTTING IT ALL TOGETHER

Now that we have carefully examined the actions of our breath, tongue, and fingers and have learned some routines for getting them under relaxed control, there are a few other basic matters to consider. Even experienced recorder players sometimes neglect them as important factors in the quality of our overall playing: how we sit when we play, how we employ our diaphragms to take in large quantities of air, and how the shape of our oral cavities affects tone.

Then, at last, we'll be ready to consider how we put it all together for the act of making music. It is at this point that we'll consider when and how to use vibrato, how dynamics work on the recorder, the role of articulation, and how to develop expressive playing.

Putting it all together does have to do with the way we sit, and breathe, and shape our mouths; when, and how, we use vibrato, dynamics, and articulation. Everything, of course, does rest upon proper basic technique. But at a certain point we need to put all technical considerations aside and seek to commune with the spirit of the music. The eighteenth-century writers had an excellent term for it: they spoke of finding the "affect" of the music, that ineluctable quality which resides only in the notes, which words can't describe. If words could do it, why would we need music? I remember being reduced to tears, at the age of seven, by a sudden poignant nostalgia, hearing "Take Me Out to the Ball Game." I don't know what ball game I had in mind, but the tune sure went straight to my heart. The rapture communicated by music is what draws us to play it. Every bit of music has its message, nearer than words. It may be simple, but there is no other means of saying it. When we play the music, we want to express how it affects us. That is the main point of the enterprise.

Posture

Relaxation is the keynote. A stiff, rigid posture tends to infect your playing with rigidity. A loose, easy posture, which allows you to take in deep breaths and exhale them gently, is all that is required. Don't carry this too far, however—you should not sit back in your chair in a stolid, unmoving slouch which betokens passivity and lack of involvement in the music. Looking at the violin section of a symphony orchestra is very instructive as regards the meaning of playing posture. The concertmaster is usually perched on the very edge of his chair and moves his torso as he bows his violin; you seldom see a back touching a chair among the first violins. Among the second violins we may see players leaning back against their chairs, but with their torsos erect and their instruments held high. But among the third violins we often see passive slouchers sawing away with a discouraged air.

Sit forward on your chair, letting the back muscles hold your torso erect in a free and flexible stance, your arms hanging loosely from the shoulders and your head held lightly and freely by the neck muscles. With your head bent slightly forward your throat becomes more open and relaxed. Your head feels loose on your neck and the recorder seems to hang loosely from your lips. The angle of the recorder to the head is about 45 degrees, but since your head is bent a little forward, the angle of the instrument to your body is less. If you purse your lips lightly and blow out a stream of air against your open hand, you will get an approximate idea of the angle at which to hold your recorder. The sound is best when you blow air directly into the recorder, so it should be held more or less at the same angle as the breath stream issuing from your mouth.

A certain amount of expressive body movement while playing is desirable, indicating looseness which promotes deeper breathing, and involvement with the music. Excessive body movement, however, is unsightly and distracting. You should beware of putting your expression into your movement rather than your playing. If you are guilty of this, you must train yourself to move less and to focus more on your instrument. If, on the other hand, you are inclined to sit immobile as you play, you would do well to consciously unbend and try to get a little body movement into your playing.

Our playing posture, like our posture in general, is a reflection of our selves, so naturally we are not all going to sit alike as we play. A recorder consort is not a military band. But we should avoid either slouching forward with the ribcage collapsed on the viscera, inhibiting the intake of air, or slumping back in our chairs. A correct playing posture will not be tiring. If you arise from a playing session feeling stiff and weary, you should give some attention to your playing posture. Remember that a loose, easy posture makes it easier for us to take in the really deep breaths of air that our recorders require from us.

How to Take Breaths

When we are out of breath, we don't need to know how to take a deep breath. The body needs it and the body takes it in the most efficient and energetic fashion without our conscious volition. When we take a deep breath by decision rather than need, we are usually not so efficient because we tend to move the wrong parts. Think, for example, of what we did as little children in school when the teacher told us to stand up next to our desks and take a deep breath. We all stuck out our chests and sucked in our tummies and tried to look like little Tarzans. We were moving the wrong parts, lifting our shoulders and chests when the real expansion should have been down below, from our diaphragms, which should have been pushing our tummies out instead of our sucking them in.

A voice teacher gave me the following routine for becoming aware of the diaphragm's action in taking a deep breath: Stand before a mirror that allows you to observe your chest and shoulders, and fill yourself up with as much air as you can *without* lifting your chest or shoulders. Then hiss the air out while counting slowly to yourself and see how far you can get before running out of air. Do this a couple of times each day, and try to increase the count each time. Now of course this hissing and counting are a pretty rough measurement of how much air you are taking in, but that doesn't matter. What does matter is that you watch your shoulders and chest to be sure you are not lifting them as you take in air. Your chest will of course rise as the lungs fill up but the real action will be below the rib cage. For a really deep breath your abdomen should swell out, and you will look more like a toad than like Tarzan. By the time you have done this exercise for a week, you will begin to be aware of how to use your diaphragm to take a breath while playing the re-corder. Why do you want to use your diaphragm? Because you can get more air in that way, and the recorder does take a lot of air.

Many people are confused about just what the diaphragm is, where it is located, and how it works. It is not that part of our facade just below the ribs that swells out when we take a deep breath. *That* is the abdomi-nal wall, and it swells out because the diaphragm is pushing down from inside. The diaphragm is a dome-shaped muscular structure that divides our innards into two cavities, the thoracic (above), which contains the heart and lungs, and the abdominal (below), which is full of various other slippery things. The diaphragm is the primary muscle of respira-tion. It is our bellows, so to speak. The action of this bellows is to flatten downwards, about an inch for a shallow breath, and about three inches for a deep breath. The diaphragm is on automatic control from the respiratory center, located in the lower brain, which directs its movement according to the body's need for oxygen. As the diaphragm moves down-ward it creates a vacuum in the lungs which is filled by inrushing air. As it relaxes and resumes its dome shape, air is pushed out of the lungs, and so respiration proceeds. As the diaphragm moves downward it pushes on the contents of the visceral cavity which push in turn against the muscu-lar wall of the abdomen. This wall reflects each intake of breath by moving outward; the deeper the breath, the greater this movement.

From all of this you can see that when we sucked our tummies in as little Tarzans we were working at cross-purposes to the real action of our diaphragms in taking a deep breath. We have all been taught, espe-cially the ladies, that it is good and proper posture to hold our stomachs in. That is why I recommend wearing something loose and blousy when you play the recorder. We feel freer when we draw a curtain over the action.

It is not always possible to take in a deep, diaphragmatic breath. Sometimes we are confronted with an extended string of notes too long to play on one breath and with no resting place to allow a refill. In such situations we must learn to catch tiny, quick breaths in the fraction of a second between one note and the next. The trick in successfully catching a quick breath is in not trying to make it a deep breath, which tends to throttle and disrupt the outward flow of air. Rather, just take in that little bit of air that the brief moment allows. A series of these quick little breaths will get you through the passage, and when you get to the end you can really fill up again.

Sometimes an extended passage that we could negotiate if we started with our lungs full to capacity is preceded by a rest too brief to allow this. In such cases we must plan ahead, starting to fill up well in advance by taking in air at every opportunity so that our last breath before the long passage will be simply topping off a full tank.

When playing the soprano or sopranino, which consume less air, you can encounter the problem of having too much air, so that you are obliged to expel stale air at the end of a phrase before taking in a fresh breath. In such situations, rather than worrying about getting enough air, you must plan ahead in order not to take in too much. On the larger-size recorders, however, this will not be a problem. In general, recorder playing requires more air than most other wind instruments, and our concern is to learn to use our diaphragms to take in the large quantities of air that we pour out through our recorders.

Inside the Mouth

Changing the size and shape of the oral cavity has an effect on the tone of the recorder. Specifically, blowing with a very open, enlarged oral cavity, with the jaw dropped so that there is a space between the upper and lower teeth, produces a brighter, clearer, more silvery tone. This effect is particularly noticeable in the upper registers. Blowing with the teeth closed and the oral cavity relatively small gives a duller, softer, fuzzier sound. Both timbres are pleasing, and it is useful to be able to produce either one, or to move from one to the other on the same note.

The brighter, open sound requires some explanation. The openness is achieved in two ways: by dropping the jaw so that there is a space between upper and lower teeth, and by cupping the tongue at the bottom of the mouth, one creates space in the front of the mouth. The back of the mouth is made more open by stretching the throat with the same action as in yawning, and by lifting and closing the velum. The velum is a flap of flesh at the back of the soft palate which closes to stop off the nasal passages where they connect with the throat. The velum closes automatically every time we swallow to keep whatever we are swallowing from getting up into the nasal passages. You can get a sense of the action of consciously closing your velum by talking as though you have a cold in your nose and the nasal passages are all stopped up. Try saying "I've got a cold in my nose," and make it sound as though you really did have a cold in your nose. It will sound something like "I've got a colt in by dose." To imitate the sound of a stuffed-up nose, you will lift your velum to stop off the nasal passages, and by stretching the throat as though yawning, you will enlarge the back of the oral cavity. When you blow with both the front and back of the mouth thus enlarged, you will have the sensation that you are delivering air into the recorder from the back of the mouth rather than from the lips, and a brighter sound will result. Blowing with an enlarged oral cavity and parted teeth feels very light and easy. You may have to experiment a bit until you get the hang of it, but once you do you will notice a marked change in timbre. I don't know just why this more silvery sound occurs. Perhaps it is because the air is going into the recorder with fewer eddies than if you were blowing with your teeth closed. In any case it is a technique well worth acquiring, particularly for the ease it brings in blowing high notes, which sound sweeter and more focused.

As I have said, you may not necessarily want to blow with your mouth in this enlarged shape all the time. For one thing, certain articulations such as the "deedle" (see Chapter 5, p. 115) require the tongue to be close to the roof of the mouth. For another, it is preferable to have as much variety of sound as possible, since the recorder's fixed windway structure makes it a relatively rigid instrument as compared, say, to the flexibility of timbre that is available on the flute. The point is to be aware of what you are doing with the inside of your mouth and your sound will become more flexible.

The Role of Vibrato in Expressive Playing

Vibrato in musical tone is a regular pulsing of pitch and intensity. Its function is to enliven the tone and make it more telling. Vibrato is a wonderful device for imparting expression to your playing, and thus it is particularly useful for recorder players, but the danger for us is to overuse it. Vibrato is lavishly employed by modern instrumentalists and singers. Use of an almost constant vibrato is common on most modern instruments and in most contemporary voices. The clarinet is the only modern instrument that customarily is not played with vibrato. Its expression derives instead from its enormous dynamic range. Other modern instruments have great dynamic flexibility as well, so vibrato for them does not have quite the unique expressive importance that it does for our rigid whistles. But we must save our vibrato for special expressive effects. If it is constantly present in the tone, its expressive force is diminished. We must think carefully about how we use vibrato in order to get the maximum expressive benefits it can provide.

Different instruments produce vibrato in various ways, some of which are well known while others are somewhat mysterious. String players rock their fingers (actually the entire hand and forearm) on the fingerboard as they stop the strings. This technique is clear because it is visible. Wind players use the diaphragm, the throat, or, in the case of reed instruments, even the jaw. What goes on inside a singer's throat is to a certain degree a mystery. What we recorder players do will be explained under "Vibrato as an Exercise for Relaxed Blowing," page 45.

There has been much discussion of whether vibrato is a variation from the true pitch of the note to above, equally above and below, or just below. In point of fact, it can be any of the three, depending on the expressive context, although it is my opinion that the general movement is from the pitch to below and back.

Finger vibrato—described by Hotteterre under the name *flattement* and by Quantz in connection with the *messa di voce* (a swelling and then diminishing of volume on a single note)—clearly goes below the pitch. This technique, commonly employed by French Baroque woodwind players, involves striking, but only partially covering, an open hole one or two steps below the bottom stopped hole of the regular fingering with a trilling action of the finger. A *flattement* on C, for example, can be produced by beating finger five against part of its hole (0 123/ 5⤳). The action of finger five obviously is lowering the pitch of the C.

In teaching, I am reluctant to impose my musical expression to such a degree as to dictate where and how to use vibrato on a specific piece of music. Vibrato is so tied up with personal expression that it is difficult to give hard and fast rules. Usually it appears where the expression calls for it, just as the Oriental painter with ink on paper varies the width of his brush stroke in a spontaneous expressive gesture. In either case, however, perfect control is required to arrive at this spontaneous expressivity.

I remember the first time I became conscious of using a vibrato for expressive purposes. I was playing music with an amateur pianist friend. The piece (I think it was by Handel) opened with a long, sustained note for the recorder, and my friend said, "Can't you make the note grow as it goes along? Why not put a crescendo into it?" I replied that on the recorder that would be impossible without going sharp. "Well, do *something!*" he replied. And as we started to play again I found myself gradually introducing vibrato into the note, which satisfied my friend, and me as well. I like to say that I received vibrato the way St. Francis received the stigmata. It wasn't until some years later, after I had started teaching, that I began to analyze what was actually involved in producing vibrato and how to teach others to do it, and I discovered that the exercises involved in learning it have a very salutary effect in developing relaxed breath control.

Although exactly when and how to introduce vibrato into your playing is a matter of personal expression and therefore sounds most convincing when it comes from within rather than from someone else's direction, there is much that can be said in a general way. Vibrato can be used much more freely when the recorder is functioning as a solo instrument, in sonatas, trio sonatas, and the like. In consort music it must be used very discreetly, if at all, and only at those moments when your line has genuine melodic importance. Even then it must be delicate and not too wide, and if you don't have such delicate control it is better to play without. If all lines of a consort piece are played with vibrato, the texture gets muddy and perfection of intonation becomes an impossibility. (I wish more of my colleagues shared my conviction in this matter!)

The speed of the vibrato depends in part on the speed of the piece. Allegros generally sound best with a faster vibrato, which is often rhythmically in time with the meter, thus imparting pace and drive to the tempo. An example of where this metered, equal vibrato is effective is in the opening measures of the second movement, Allegro, of Handel's C major recorder sonata. The time signature is 3/8 and the first three measures each contain a dotted quarter, leading from G' up to C', a strong melodic movement from dominant to tonic, whereupon the recorder bursts into a rapid movement of eighths and sixteenths. The drive of the three opening dotted quarters is enhanced by giving each six equal pulses of vibrato.

Short notes do not take vibrato well. Usually any fewer than four pulses on a note sounds silly, so if the note is too short for four pulses, don't use vibrato.

Vibrato is usually slower in adagios, largos, and similar slow movements, and the pulses of the vibrato are less likely to be tied to the tempo of the music. The speed of the vibrato, when it is used, will be more likely to vary. A quick vibrato will give accent to a note. A slower vibrato gives it warmth.

The width of the vibrato varies with its speed, faster vibrato tending to be narrower. Thus, in fast movements the vibrato is usually more narrow. In slow movements a wider vibrato can be used, both to give emphasis to a note and to mask sharpness resulting from blowing it stronger. For this effect the vibrato should move equally above and below the pitch. When blowing a note softly, you can use vibrato to mask flatness. In this case the pulse of the vibrato is to the pitch of the note, and the valleys between dip below. You must listen closely to your sound in employing either of these effects to be sure you are not carrying them too far, and indeed sounding sharp or flat.

The gradual introduction of vibrato to a long note makes it grow and creates the effect of a crescendo, as I have already described. Coupling this with the change in timbre produced by gradually enlarging the oral cavity enhances the effect. Removing vibrato from a long note and then reintroducing it to reflect the harmonic changes occurring beneath it can be very effective. In Diego Ortiz's second *recercada* on the chanson "Doulce Memoire," the highly embellished version of the top voice which he presents concludes with just such a long note, while the voices below do a repeated modulation leading to the final cadence. When the top voice reaches the final long note, the player can make it sing out above the movement below by gently bringing in vibrato, then remove it on the penultimate chord, and lightly bring it back upon the final resolution. The effect is breathtaking, and, I might add, takes a lot of breath!

A slight, imperceptible vibrato, very quick but *very* light, after a breath accent helps to focus the proper pitch, and gives further energy to the note. This is a very delicate effect, and if overdone, becomes an obtrusive mannerism. The key word here is "imperceptible." The vibrato should be so quick and light that it is inaudible except as a subtle energy in the note.

The more flexible your breath stream becomes, the greater the variety of effects you can obtain with the use of vibrato. But remember that we do not rely on vibrato alone for our expression. Much can be done with articulation. It is possible to play expressively using articulation alone, and it is a good discipline to try doing exactly that. Then when you add vibrato it will be much more telling, and your sense of when to use it will be much clearer.

Articulation for Phrasing and Expression

Articulation, in the sense we discuss it here, refers to the amount of space we put between one note and the next. The *slur* represents the least space, which is actually no space. There is no interruption, either by tongue or breath, of the flow of air into the recorder as we move fingers to go from one note to the next. *Staccatissimo* is when the notes are shortest and the spaces of silence between them most extended. Articulation encompasses these extremes and all gradients that lie between them. It's a matter of placing and spacing. Articulation is at the center of expressive playing on the recorder. Since we don't have loud and soft as flutes and oboes do—any more than the harpsichord and organ have, compared to the piano—recorders, harpsichords, and organs *articulate* to create their expressive effects, molding phrases and infusing emotion by ever-changing spacing, attack, and release. As this description suggests, is *meant* to suggest, the breath has a role in articulation equal to the tongue. Articulation is important to all musical instruments, but for recorder players it is the principal expressive device.

WHEN DO WE ARTICULATE? Here are some general principles. They are by no means hard and fast rules but they should be helpful in showing how to begin:

- Notes that proceed by step should be more smoothly connected; when they proceed by leap, a little space usually makes them sound better.

- Fast pieces like separation: allegros, gigues, dance music in general. Even stepwise figures may want separation in allegros. Even wide leaps may want to be connected in slow movements.

- The thicker the texture (number of voices, number of doubled parts), the more you must articulate. Otherwise it becomes difficult to hear individual lines.

- Articulate more in acoustically live spaces than in dead ones. Otherwise room resonance and echo will muddy the sound.

- If you are playing vocal music with the words printed below the notes, it helps to read both and try to express the phrasing, accent, and spacing of the words. Parisian chansons and Italian *frottole* of the mid-sixteenth century are examples of music closely allied to text, and reading the words helps you to play the music with variety in your articulation.

In general, use a lot of spacing. We are accustomed to playing the notes as written and only adding articulation where indicated, but we must keep in mind that it was only in the Baroque period that composers even began to supply articulation signs; previously, the matter had simply been left to the performer. Early music, with its lively rhythmic textures, sounds better when generously articulated. It's hard to say just how much space, how connected or separated the notes. I offer this advice: Do it enough to produce the effect but not enough to show how it was done. It's a matter of developing taste.

SOME SPECIFIC SUGGESTIONS Rules about articulation are like egg timers; you can stand them on their head and they still tell you the truth. Any thoughtful scheme of articulation will enhance the music, so you're welcome to try these ideas in reverse to see what comes of it.

- If you have two notes repeated on the same pitch, separate the first from the second.

- When a piece or a phrase begins with a pick-up note, make it short and leave space between it and the ensuing downbeat, thereby giving more force and accent to the downbeat.

- Put space between a dotted note and the short note that follows. The shorter the note values and the faster the tempo, the more this applies.

play as

- In music where the beat divides into triplets (3/8, 6/8, 9/8, 12/8) the third note of each triplet is shortened to enhance the next downbeat.

- Syncopated figures. The short note on the downbeat should be curtailed to some degree. The space between it and the ensuing long note gives the latter more force.

Expressive delivery of lively music on the recorder is more akin to the speaking voice than to the singing voice. When the line is slow and broad, we sing; when it is quick and lively, we speak, by varying degrees of spacing—i.e., by articulation. Thus, less spacing for slower tempos and longer notes, more for shorter notes and faster tempos.

In early music, almost every note is articulated to some degree. In even the smoothest phrases a flick of the tongue can put a dent in the ongoing breath stream. Notes might be slurred in pairs, but even here a slight articulation between the downbeat note and the upbeat note is more common than not. Only very fast ornamental figures, runs, trills, etc., will be slurred. Otherwise, some degree of articulation is always desirable.

Very short, crisp articulation is done with the tongue: "dit . . . dit . . . dit." Articulative spacings at slower speeds involve the breath as well: "dah . . . dah . . . dah." In the first instance, the tongue sharply cuts off the breath stream, its tip stopping at the hard palate. In the second, the breath stops with the tongue and the effect is less abrupt;

it is important that the tongue catch it before the pitch drops. Cutting off the breath stream with the tongue alone sounds silly at slow speeds; at fast speeds the crispness of the tongue stop sounds great. The point here is that at slower tempos the breath participates in the release of the note.

Every attack, every note, should involve breath accent to some degree. As we know, the recorder is so sensitive that even the slightest huff of air is audible. The airstream that sounds our recorder doesn't come from just a wind-chest. We use our pulmonary apparatus all the time, with varying starts and stops, to express ourselves in words. The huffs and puffs of verbal expression serve us very well for expression on the recorder.

A strong attack will perforce be overblown and must fall away immediately to the true pitch, or some vibratoed approximation of it. Soft attacks might start below and quickly slide up to pitch. Either effect must be done within the wink of an eye, lest it be discovered. The parameters are narrow, but the space in between is very expressive. How you start a note, how you stop it, and the spacing between notes comprise articulation.

Dynamics

Dynamics in music, as we know, refers to playing with various degrees of loudness and softness, and crescendoing or decrescendoing. Short of dicey finger slides, dynamics of this sort are not available on the recorder. Loud into soft, or soft into loud, rests on simpler grounds for the average recorder player. It is a generality that musical phrases as they rise want to get louder and as they descend want to get softer. The recorder, fixed whistle that it is, is louder with each ascending note and quieter as it goes down. So unless a phrase is unnaturally charged with a descending crescendo or an ascending diminuendo, the recorder and the phrase generally agree about loud and soft. If, as you play them, you think of rising phrases as getting louder and descending ones as getting softer you will adhere to the natural dynamics of your instrument and the generality of dynamics for the music that you play. Don't be gross; be delicate. But think crescendo as you go up and decrescendo as you go down. The expressive results are surprising. It is easy, however, to forget, so remind yourself again and again: Rising phrases get louder, falling ones softer. Play the instrument, and the phrase, as they are.

The Sense and Sensibility of Expressive Playing

One can teach or learn the sense, playing the right notes, in time and in tune. But the sensibility, the expression, can only be demonstrated. No words can describe the actual experience of musical playing, any more than a recipe can provide the taste of a feast. The best way to develop your own expression is to listen to and then imitate performances that you love and that move you.

Let me give you an example from my own experience. I have a performance of Schubert's beautiful song cycle, *Die Schöne Müllerin,* recorded about forty years ago by Aksel Schiøtz and Gerald Moore, which is, to my mind, perfect. I love this performance because it is so completely musical and absolutely unaffected and true in its expression. When I want to reawaken my expressivity I get out the music and play every verse of each of the twenty songs, reading all the words. Then I try to give my recorder the same expression as Aksel Schiøtz's voice. Doing this always teaches me more about expression. Choose your own favorite performance and imitate it. It is the best way of putting all the details of technique to their intended use, which is to play music beautifully and expressively.

Chapter 2

HOW TO PRACTICE

The point of practicing is to acquire physical, muscular skills. Muscles learn by repetition, by doing things over and over again as we carefully observe and correct the results of their action. Practice is not creative activity like painting a picture, composing a tune, or writing a book. It's more like hitting tennis balls against a wall, or swimming laps, or jogging. It's not even playing pretty tunes for one's own pleasure, not usually. Practice is not self-expression, it is the exercise that precedes and prepares for self-expression. In order to get the most out of practice we must be aware of what we are about and not confuse one thing with another. We must be in the right frame of mind, contemplative but self-aware, always listening, our ears on the qui vive. We must be wary of the dangers of wishful imagination, rapt in a dream of what we wish to sound like rather than awake to the reality of what we do sound like. It is only through hearing the reality that we can transform it gradually into our dream.

Practice has a certain hypnotic quality. We focus our attention on limited areas of small detail. Not all of our mind or imagination is engaged. The lady who knits and converses at the same time is like the piano student who practices his scales while reading the morning newspaper. Some practice takes more attention, some less. We must learn to give it what it requires, enough for all the requisite details. We must know thoroughly what it is we are trying to do with a particular bit of practice so that if something goes wrong we can identify the detail and correct it. Even the most mechanical, repetitive practice isn't quite like knitting, at least not for most of us, but I can do justice to the short trill exercise while gazing out the window at the passing scene. Give it as much attention as it needs, not one whit less, and let the rest of your mind roam free. In this way the repetition of practicing becomes restful and soothing. You lay aside the big concerns of the real world to contemplate little details of fingers, tongue, and breath. Start slowly, listen carefully, be analytical. Be objective. In effect, be your own teacher. Eventually we all must, so it's just as well to start early.

PRACTICING WITHOUT NOTES

Practicing without staring at a printed page has the advantage that you don't have to read and decipher notation simultaneously with all the other things you must do to make the instrument work. You remove some of the complications and your attention is freed to concentrate on the sounds you are making, and the movements that produce them. By the same token it is possible, and useful, to practice the music without an instrument, simply reading through the notes and, if possible, imagining their sound in your head. This can be done in the noise and bustle of a bus or train, or in the silence of a library reading room, and many reading problems can be solved without the distraction of working the instrument. You can practice the notes without the instrument and you can practice the instrument without the notes. In fact, if you expect to ever control it, you *must* practice the instrument without the notes.

Tone

The first thing to practice, for any player, at any level, is tone—breath control. A good beginning is the sighing routine (see pp. 6–8). This takes only a minute or two and at once reminds you of the gentle level at which the breath operates in blowing the recorder. This exercise leads naturally into vibrato routines.

VIBRATO AS AN EXERCISE FOR RELAXED BLOWING The vibrato exercise starts very much like blowing the easy sigh through the recorder. We start on pitch, then let the tone begin to die away; but here comes the great difference, for we then bring it back. We can let it die away to nothingness, as a gesture of resignation. But if we know that we are going to bring it back, we are reluctant to let it go in the first place. We are afraid that if we let it go we will lose it altogether. That is what we learned in blowing sighs through the recorder, to let it go altogether. But there is still some air left, and with a gentle push we can bring it back up again. To use the analogy of skating, it's like learning to lean from the perpendicular, trusting that your momentum will bring you upright again, perhaps to lean in the other direction. Learning skating is much easier if someone who knows how has an arm around your waist. You feel the movement, and dare to lean with it. By the same token, hearing someone who knows how to drop his breath and bring it back again gives you courage to try it yourself.

Since my sound cannot emerge from the pages of this book, I offer you this encouragement to try. The worst thing that can happen is that you will make a funny sound, and that, by the way, is also the best thing that can happen. A slow dip, from pitch down and back up again, is not a pretty, musical sound, but it is precisely the sound I would be making if you were listening to me. If you heard it, then you would believe it and find it much easier to do the same. "Is *that* what he wants me to do? Well, I guess I'd better try to do it," you well might think.

I should also tell you that, although vibrato as an exercise for relaxed blowing is basic to breath control on the recorder and forms a part of every lesson I teach to players at every level (except children), perfect control is not easy to achieve. Perfectly controlled vibrato is a paradox in what I teach, because it is both the most basic and the most advanced exercise for breath control. People who arrive innocent of vibrato are usually those best served, because I don't have to try to replace an *idée fixe* with an *idée flexible.* Nonetheless, I serve all with the vibrato exercise, and I hope you will find it palatable.

The following exercises are not concerned with the musical uses of vibrato, but rather with its function in relaxing the breath. The fact that the exercises will also teach you how to produce a vibrato is an extra dividend. For the use of vibrato for musical purposes, see page 35. Everything that follows refers to fingerings on the alto recorder, which is really the best size for beginning these exercises in breath control.

EXERCISES FOR THE VIBRATO

Step 1: Blow a note (E is a good one to start with) and slowly dip it down as far as you can and then bring it back up to pitch. This will feel very much like blowing a sigh through the recorder except that instead of letting it die away to nothing you increase the air again to bring it back to the pitch you started with. This note-droop-return sequence should be completely smooth. No little wiggles on the way. The dip should be as deep as possible because this helps you get control of the mechanism. As with the sigh, you will not be making a musical sound, but you must listen to it carefully nonetheless to be sure that you are starting on pitch, making a deep dip, and then bringing the note back up to pitch smoothly and without wobbles. When you can do this on E, proceed to do it on each note of the C scale, up and down. (See Appendix, p. 239, if you need a refresher on the scales.) You will notice that some notes dip more readily than others. Your task is to adjust your dips with even less breath on the reluctant notes so that you get the same degree of dip on every note. Notes in the upper register should not be dipped so far that the tone breaks into the lower register, but as far as possible short of that.

When you can dip equally and smoothly on the notes of the C scale, you can extend the exercise further by going on to other closely related scales, such as F, G, and B-flat, until you can do controlled dipping on every note of the recorder's compass. You will find that cross-fingered notes such as B and C-sharp are more reluctant. Low notes require very delicate control, since you are blowing them softly to start with and must blow softer still to make them dip. Notes in the highest register are difficult to dip without the note's breaking, but strive to get as much as possible from every note. When you have done this, you are ready for Step 2.

Step 2: Slow, single dips are perhaps the hardest and most nerve-racking, but when you can do them with some control you can go on to four dips per note, about 120 per minute by the metronome (MM 120). This, by the way, is standard march tempo, so you could think of yourself as dipping to "The Stars and Stripes Forever." You should still dip deep. We're not up to musical vibrato yet. We're still working on breath control. You should start on pitch, and the dips should be smooth and equal, and should get back to pitch between each dip. It might help to think of yourself as a slow siren (the firehouse variety). The first pulse comes when you start your note, on pitch. Then you dip. Each return to the true pitch creates another pulse in the sound. Don't start below pitch, and certainly don't start at pitch and *then* push for pulse. That, obviously, leads to overblowing, which is the opposite of the relaxation we are seeking. This, however, is very easy to fall into if you haven't yet got the trick of falling away from the sound and then coming back with a fresh pulse. The first pulse is at the beginning of the note, the second comes after the first dip, and so forth. Remember that this is a breath-*relaxing* exercise.

Step 3: Make six pulses per note. Think of them as two groups of three, but don't mark the second group with an extralarge pulse. The pulses will be coming a bit faster, six in the time of the previous four, or about 180 per minute (MM 180), and will almost approach the speed of a musical vibrato. As a matter of fact, you will find that when the pulses reach a certain speed the effect becomes automatic instead of deliberate. Pulsing at this speed, the dips become shallower, again more like a musical vibrato. Listen carefully to be sure you are not getting any little double pulses. These indicate that you are moving from deliberate to automatic action without perfect control, and you should move back to slower pulses.

In doing these exercises you should be warned against making any extraneous body movements, marking each pulse with a gesture of the arms or the torso. Such movement contributes nothing to producing the pulses and indicates unwanted effort and tension when relaxation is our goal. The action is going on unseen and unfelt inside. You will observe that I make no attempt to describe just what muscles are involved in making the vibrato. The movements are so slight that trying to direct the muscles involved, whatever they are, would result in exaggerated action. The ear is the guide to whether you are doing it right, which is why I have described so carefully the sounds you are trying to get.

The actual movement of the pitch in making the vibrato, if shown graphically, would not be like a sine wave curve, moving equally up hill and down dale,

but more like the stylized depiction of ocean waves, a sudden rise to the crest on the left, and a slow decline on the right before the next crest,

The moment of crest, the pulse, comes rather suddenly, and the following dip is more gradual. The shape of a vibrato will vary according to its speed and width and how it is applied in varying musical contexts, but for the purpose of our breath-relaxing exercises, the ocean-wave shape described above is useful.

Step 4: Play up and down scales, making the first note straight, the second with vibrato of four or six pulses, the third straight, the fourth with vibrato, and so on. The feeling here is that the straight notes lead into the following vibratoed notes. This exercise gives the feeling of how vibrato occurs in actual musical contexts.

Step 5: Start notes straight and introduce vibrato on the second half of them. The moment of introducing the vibrato must, of course, be preceded by a slight dip. The dip should be so brief that it is imperceptible. Don't anticipate it during the straight part of the note by a gradual decline. Keep the pitch steady until just before the first pulse of the vibrato.

All of these breath-relaxation vibrato exercises can be done in ensemble by using the following trick which I picked up from LaNoue Davenport. Let me first describe how I heard LaNoue employ this simple device. We were teaching at a week-long summer workshop in Southern California. It was a large workshop, some ninety people, and LaNoue's chief task was to rehearse the entire workshop each evening for a performance at the end of the week of Josquin's *Missa Pange Lingua.* It was LaNoue's ambition to have only a quartet of recorders, a quartet of viols, and a quartet of mixed instruments, and have the rest of the workshop members sing. This was back in the mid-sixties, when amateur recorder players were unaccustomed to the idea of using their voices to make music, so when LaNoue announced his idea at the first faculty meeting the rest of us assured him from our own experience that he would never succeed in persuading recorder players to sing. LaNoue insisted on at least trying the first evening. If he couldn't get us to sing, then the mass would, perforce, be performed instrumentally.

LaNoue did get us all to sing, and he did so through an approach that was simple, unthreatening, elegant, and musical. First he had us sing a D, an easy note in anyone's range. Then we were asked to sing it again and move a whole step upwards to E, and then again, moving a whole step downwards to C. Next he had us sing up and down the C scale. Nothing threatening in that. Next came his master stroke: He quickly divided us into three groups and had us sing up and down the scale as a three-part canon. The first group began and as it got to the third note the second group entered, and as it got to the third note the last group entered. The result was a lovely succession of rising and falling triads. We found ourselves making beautiful sounds with our voices. When we finished, LaNoue said, "Okay, let's sing the mass." We did so gladly. All fear of singing had vanished.

I have used this device of scales in canon ever since. It is particularly effective for the vibrato exercises described in Steps 2, 3, 4, and 5 because the pleasing concords encourage a relaxed and musical production. I generally start every class by playing up and down one scale or another in canon, with vibrato, bringing relaxation and flexibility in the breath, which makes it easier to play in tune.

Step 6: This is the ultimate exercise in controlled vibrato. It was my first assignment when I studied with Kees Otten in Amsterdam. It involves playing up and down the chromatic scale. One plays an F six beats long. The first beat is straight, the second has three pulses of vibrato, the third has four, the fourth six, the fifth four again, and the sixth back to three; then up a half-step to the next note. When you can do this accurately on each note of the chromatic scale over the entire range of the recorder, you will be in command of vibrato.

As soon as you get the vibrato going fast enough, aim for a musical and pleasing sound. The dips should be slight and the pulses not pushed. What you want is an easy, singing vibrato that you can produce at will at any speed within the bounds of musical usefulness. Then you can think about applying it discreetly in solo music. But that is not why you have learned it. You have learned it as a means of making your breath more relaxed and flexible.

Schemes for Practicing Vibrato

You can move up and down scales alternating straight tones and measured vibrato; you can start a tone straight for the first half then fall into vibrato, go up and down the chromatic scale using measured vibrato or alternating vibrato with straight tone; you can play through the circle of fifths in arpeggios with measured vibrato, etc. The possible schemes are endless. They can be very simple for the novice or very sophisticated for the experienced player—for example, a C scale on the one hand, and a succession of a rising fifth followed by a descending fifth one-half step higher and another rising fifth one-half step higher still, etc., on the other. It is very useful practice to alternate straight tones and tones with measured vibrato. The straight tone seems to stretch across and lead into the vibrato. The feeling is natural and leads to excellent breath control. There is no reason to exclude the minor scales from these breath-control routines; the more variety, the better. The melodic minor makes most sense to a melody instrument, but if you are interested in getting the forms of the three minor scales clear in your head, you can use all three, the natural, melodic, and harmonic. (For details of minor scales, see p. 239.) You can make further intellectual connections by playing a major scale and following with its relative minor (C Major and A Minor; G Major and E Minor, etc.) or tonic minor—again, see page 239 if you are not familiar with these scales (C Major and C Minor; G Major and G Minor, etc.). You may begin to perceive that practicing tone, playing long notes either straight or with vibrato, provides the opportunity for learning other things as well, associating the name of a note with its fingering, learning various scales and arpeggios, major and minor, and other details of practical musicianship. Since, for the purposes of breath control, you are staying on each single note for a relatively long while, there is time to think of what note is coming next in whatever scheme you are using. The point is to avoid any scheme so complicated as to engender confusion and tension. On the other hand, you don't want to do something so simple that it becomes boring. Some modicum of musical content gives breath-control exercises more meaning, and it is fun to exercise a little imagination in devising the practice routines.

If you play more than one size of recorder you should practice breath control on each. The gestures of breath that produce even, straight tones and vibrato on the bass are much broader than the requirements of an alto. For the soprano they are more delicate, so you should get to know the requirements of each instrument you play.

Sometimes it is good to play in acoustically live, resonant spaces which reflect and enhance your sound in an encouraging way, such as a tiled bathroom or small kitchen. At other times the utter objectivity of an acoustically dead practice space, like a living room or bedroom with heavy drapes and carpets, is instructive. For practicing tone, both types of environment have their uses, so don't confine yourself exclusively to one or the other.

Sometimes you may want to spend a good deal of time practicing tone, getting acquainted with a new instrument for instance. At other times you may just run through some simple routine to be sure that you are beginning your practice session with a properly relaxed breath stream. But every session should begin with some work on tone; it is the basic stuff of everything you play and nothing else rises above the level of the tone you produce. There is no virtue in building elaborate structures out of shoddy material.

Scales and Patterns

Scales provide a matrix for all kinds of pattern making that can teach us many things. For the beginner, and for many who are not beginners, simply saying the name of each note of a given scale and then playing it, up and down, helps establish notes by name with their fingerings. All too many amateurs have only an eye connection between notes and fingerings. If they see a G on the staff they can produce it, but if asked for it out of the blue they must pause and think, a process often prolonged by the confusion of embarrassment. This deficiency can be easily eliminated by devoting a little time specifically to the problem. If you are alone and out of anyone else's hearing, there is nothing embarrassing about saying "C" out loud and then playing it. I often begin warm-up sessions with a class in just this way, going up and down the scale at a very moderate pace. The act of saying the note out loud is very helpful in fixing it to its fingering. And it is no surprise that there are more hesitations descending than ascending; we learned the alphabet forwards, after all.

Once we have learned a scale, it is time to apply patterns, starting with the simplest, e.g., in C Major: C, note one step above, back to C; D, note one step above, back to D; and thus on up the C scale and back down again.

At the level of these baby steps it is helpful to say the ground note before playing the pattern to keep one's orientation. The precocious, with mental energy to spare, may want to think of the name of the note one step above as they play it, but this is not necessary. It is enough simply to remember the name of the ground note. Even this simplest of patterns can be transformed into a dexterity exercise by repeating the back-and-forth action several times.

Another simple pattern is: note, step below, note.

Then the two patterns combined to form a turn around the note:

Once the pattern is established, we can ring rhythmic changes on it:

With success comes courage; we can step away to the third above or below the ground note, with variations:

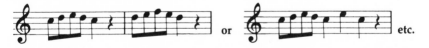

Eventually we can go on to fourths, fifths, and triads in various exciting combinations:

Up and down a fourth:

Up and down a fourth with leap:

 etc.

Down and up a fourth with leap:

 etc.

Up a fifth with arpeggio:

 etc.

Down a fifth with arpeggio:

 etc.

Arpeggios up and down:

 etc.

It is great fun to devise these sequential scale practice patterns, and the musical results are often surprising and delightful, rather like folding a piece of paper and snipping at it to produce snowflake patterns.

Needless to say, you should not confine your pattern-making to C Major, although it is the logical key to start on. When you have gotten a few patterns under your fingers in C, try them in F, B-flat, G, and D. Take them as far as you wish. Certainly any player who can do patterns with equal facility in all twelve keys can count himself expert.

Another form of sequential scale pattern practice without the notes is the alternate fingering exercises described in the chapter "Alternate Fingerings, Trills, and Fast Fingers," page 99. The procedure is described in detail there and does not need repetition. I will repeat that I and my students have found these exercises very effective and beneficial, and they are *very* hypnotic and mechanical. I can almost, but not quite, listen to the news while doing them. Maybe I need more practice.

Playing by Ear

One further form of practicing without notes is playing tunes by ear. It's fun and beneficial—fun because it realizes the dream engendered by those ads that begin, "They laughed when I sat down at the piano"; beneficial because it teaches us to be aware of what notes of the scale are used in a tune's construction.

Playing by ear is more than inspired guesswork. To do it successfully, you must know what key you are playing in, on what note of the scale the tune begins, and what notes of the scale it proceeds to. Understanding a tune in such terms involves the discipline called solfeggio, the *do-re-mi* singing many of us were taught in grammar school. Solfeggio encompasses many systems and practices for giving names to the various degrees of the scale. I propose a very simple approach, which is to identify the notes of the scale by numbers: *do* is 1, *re* is 2, *mi* is 3, and so forth; 8, the octave (if 1, or *do,* is C, the eighth note above it is again C), is synonymous with 1. If D is 2 the D an octave higher will also be 2. All of this becomes clear by parsing a few tunes by the numbers. Let's begin with "Twinkle, Twinkle, Little Star." The numbers go as follows:

1 1 5 5 6 6 5, 4 4 3 3 2 2 1. 5 5 4 4 3 3 2, 5 5 4 4 3 3 2,

1 1 5 5 6 6 5, 4 4 3 3 2 2 1.

Notated in C Major, the tune appears as follows:

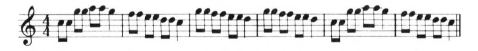

The numbers, of course, are the same in whatever key you play; in C, 1 is C; in C-sharp, 1 is C-sharp. If you know a tune by the numbers, you can play it in as many keys as you are familiar with. Here are the opening phrases of "Joy to the World" by the numbers:

8 7 6 5 4 3 2 1, 5 6 6 7 7 8

Notated in C Major:

The numbers do not show rhythm, but only pitch.

"My Country, 'Tis of Thee" shows what happens when the tune goes below 1:

1 1 2 7 1 2,   3 3 4 3 2 1,   2 1 7 1.

Not all tunes begin on 1, but they almost always end on 1, so if you are not sure where 1 is, hum the tune through to the end and discover what note it ends on. I cannot offhand think of a single melody that does not end on 1, *do,* the keynote, which is after all the note of finality. Many tunes have accidentals, a sharp or a flat momentarily introduced. Call such a note by its number plus the appropriate modifying word, "sharp" or "flat." It is not necessary to identify every note of a tune by its number in order to play by ear, but significant movements of the melody, especially if by leap, should be identified. In "Twinkle, Twinkle," for instance, the move from 1 to 5 is important. What is essential is to recognize what note of the tune is 1, and what is the number of the opening note if it is not 1.

Improvising

A final way of playing without notes that is soothing and satisfying is simply to improvise. This does not, strictly speaking, fall under the heading of practice; it is more like play. But it is a very useful and instructive kind of play, developing one's phrasing, expression, and sense of form. Free improvisation usually consists of playing around with fragments from music you have already heard. But since all tunes are inescapably composed of such preexisting bits of melody and rhythm, you needn't worry about being original. The primary purpose of improvising is to please your own ear, and prodigies of invention are not necessary for fulfillment. One good way to begin is to start on low A and gradually wander upwards. You will find yourself in A minor, and the elegaic melancholy of minor keys usually succeeds in invoking the Muse. An encouraging thought to keep in mind is that in free improvisation anything goes. Just have fun.

PRACTICING THE NOTES

There are many kinds of things to practice from the printed page; exercises, etudes, and tunes from method books; your parts from the music you are playing with your ensemble; or various kinds of solo music, such as the sonatas of Handel, Bach, and Telemann. Each of these categories requires a slightly different approach, so I will discuss them in turn.

Exercises

Exercise material from method books is very much a part of the beginner's learning experience. These exercises build into your fingers the patterns that you will be encountering again and again in the music you will be playing. They also teach you to read music, to quickly recognize a stepwise run of notes, and to distinguish a leap of a third from a leap of a fourth, a fourth from a fifth, and so on. Such practice material is usually presented in notes of equal value, all eighth notes or sixteenths. Exercises found in the Rooda book or at the back of Giesbert (see Chapter 9, page 201) are typical.

These are often termed dexterity exercises. The implication is that you should learn to play them fast, but beware: Playing fast is the goal, and you do not start at the goal, you start at the beginning. Start by playing them slowly so you are sure you are reading them correctly and playing them right. Then, by various means, you learn to read and play them faster. One means of practice that I recommend is to play exercises in various rhythms. I suggest the following rhythmic changes for exercise material that is presented on the page as a series of equal eighths or sixteenths—two patterns with dotted notes and two involving triplets:

$$\text{♫♫} = \text{♩.♫♫♩} \text{ or } \text{♫.♫.♩} \text{ or } \text{♩.♫♫} \text{ or } \text{♫♫♩}$$

The benefits of these rhythmic changes are several. First, these exercises are basic for making connections from one note to the next as quickly and smoothly as possible. By imposing a dotted rhythm on the notes, in a pattern of long, short, ♩.♫♫♩ we are making every other connection quickly, but after each quick connection comes a moment of respite on a long note. When the pattern is reversed ♫. ♩♩. the connections that were long before now become the quick ones. In effect, we are practicing half of the connections quickly with the first dotted pattern and the other half quickly when we reverse the pattern, yet we are avoiding the strain and tension of trying to practice all of the connections quickly at once. It is not necessary to adopt a fast tempo when practicing with these dotted patterns, but, at whatever tempo, the short note should move as quickly as possible to the ensuing long note. A slow tempo makes the long notes longer, giving you more time to prepare for the next quick connection. The patterns involving triplets provide three quick connections and then a restful long note.

Aside from easing the strain of an unabated series of quick connections, these patterns help train our eyes to read every note. Playing the notes as written, over and over again, we soon come to a point of semi-memorization. Our eye becomes torpid and suddenly we falter because we don't know quite where we are. By mentally imposing a rhythmic pattern on the notes, we oblige our eye to read everything. A further virtue of this system is that it makes exercises more fun to play. It is fascinating to hear how the character of an exercise changes with each of these rhythmic changes. You can go through the exercise first as written, then with each of the four rhythmic changes, and finally once again as written. You will have practiced it six times and will not have been bored. A final advantage of using the rhythmic changes is that you will get a lot of drill in the rhythms themselves. Dotted rhythms and triplets will become second nature to you.

Exercises provide good material for practicing double-tonguing (see page 116). The rule here is to go slow, play as legato as possible, and strive to make all the notes sound alike whether articulated with the tip or the back of the tongue. For perfect control, you should make your double-tonguing indistinguishable from single-tonguing. When you can do this at a slow to moderate tempo, then, and only then, it is time to speed up. The rhythmic variations with triplets described above can be used for developing triple-tonguing, with the same caveats regarding smoothness and speed as for double-tonguing.

Tunes

Many exercise books have tunes by Bach, Handel, Telemann, or even Mozart and Haydn, along with folk or English country dance tunes, interspersed with the technical material. These melodies should be played with various articulations and accents to find the most pleasing expression and to develop your musical flexibility. They are little rewards along the way. Experiment with them and enjoy them.

Ensemble Music

In practicing your parts to the music that you play with your consort, the most important thing is to achieve rhythmic precision. Consort music is usually drawn from the Renaissance or even the late Middle Ages. Although generally not as technically demanding in terms of sheer digitation as the solo literature of the Baroque, this music is often quite complex and subtle rhythmically, and each part goes its own way in a dense polyphonic texture. For it all to fit together, each part must be very accurately played. Every note must be exactly the right length. A dotted quarter must be precisely as long as three eighths, a dotted eighth as long as three sixteenths, and a dotted whole note must be just as long as twelve eighths or twenty-four sixteenths. There can be no guesswork. If any rhythm is unclear or unsteady, you should subdivide it into the equivalent number of the smallest note values that appear in the piece; this way you will be sure that the values are absolutely correct. What is true of the notes is equally true of the rests; they must be counted with the same minute precision as the notes. A place where one must exercise particular vigilance is in playing a long note at the end of a phrase which is followed by a rest. Unless you count this final note exactly, you will be unsure of when and how to start counting the rest. It is in this very situation that players often go astray. When you have parsed all the rhythms of the part and can play them exactly, you may want to try playing with a metronome to be sure your tempo is steady, but don't turn on the metronome until you are absolutely sure of what you are doing. Even then it is best to start it at a slow tempo so you know that everything is fitting in right. Once you have got it right, you can gradually build up to the desired tempo.

If your part is tacet, or resting, for a section, coming in only on the repeat, it is wise even when practicing to count out your measures of rest. This habit will serve you well when you are confronted with the distraction of hearing the other parts. You should of course observe the phrasings, breath marks, and articulations that have been agreed upon in rehearsal. It is also a sound idea to know the other parts of a piece as well as your own and, if playing from score, to keep an eye on at least one of the other parts near your own. If everyone in the group observes these rules, the ensemble will be secure indeed.

Solo Music

Solo music usually involves many fast notes. They provide brilliant display and they should be delivered with a faultless ease that belies the many hours of careful practice that went into mastering them. There is a wrong way and a right way to approach such technical passages. The wrong way is simply to go over and over a passage as fast as one can play it. This is almost invariably counterproductive. If there is a spot that tends to break down, repeating it over and over at a fast tempo does not cure the problem. To the contrary, you usually end up having practiced a mistake to the point where it becomes securely embedded in the passage. Practicing simply for speed usually results in a succession of notes devoid of shape or meaning. The correct approach to technical passages is to start slow, to break the notes up into meaningful fragments, and to practice these separately before putting them together again, and to ring various rhythmic changes on the notes so as to discover their meaning and function in the passage. We shall now examine a few characteristic passages from the Baroque literature to see how these practicing techniques apply.

In Baroque music we often encounter quasi-duet writing consisting, for example, of a four-note statement followed by a four-note answer, the patterns being repeated in a progressively rising or falling sequence. An example of this device is found in the second movement, Allegro, of the Recorder Sonata in F Major from Handel's Opus 1, in measures 20 to 24, below. The statements and answers are indicated by brackets above and below the notes. It is interesting to note how Handel demonstrates his superior musical imagination by changing the pattern at bar 23.

One way of practicing this sort of passage is to play the statements only, and rest during the answers:

Then go back and play the answers, resting during the statements:

The passage should be played each way several times before putting the parts together again. The result will be a much better understanding of the passage, both musically and technically. Similar passages abound and can be treated in a similar manner.

Another favorite device is that in which one note remains the same but is followed by three notes in changing configurations, as in the following passage from the third variation from Corelli's "Variations on *La Follía*," Opus 5, No. 12:

As the variation progresses the ground note also changes, but the method of practicing the passages remains the same. This is to play all of the ground notes but only one of the remaining three sixteenth note patterns;

all of the first pattern, then of the second, then of the third, then various combinations of two out of the three, and finally the entire passage as written.

or

or

or

and so forth.

The technique of substituting rests for some of the notes in a passage that is built on repeated patterns can be varied to suit any situation. Here are some further examples from *"La Follia"*:

Variation V from "La Follía"

practice as:

Allegro   **Variation IX from "La Follía"**

practice as:

Allegro   **Variation XI from "La Follía"**

practice as:

Subjecting a difficult passage to rhythmic variations, as described above for exercise practice, can be very helpful in mastering it.

Variation V from "La Follía"

practice as:

Variation XVI from "La Follía"

practice as:

Breaking a passage into two-note segments and repeating each of these four times, three times, twice, and finally playing the notes as written is a very thorough method of getting the notes under your fingers.

Variation XVI from "La Follía"

practice as:

then:

then:

then as is.

Any passage can be dissected and put back together in a number of ways. The more ways you try, the better you will know the passage. The technique is to break down a piece into little fragments and practice them one by one. Then you put them back together again as a sort of mosaic of tiny pieces, each one of which is done perfectly, building from phrase to phrase, and section to section, until finally a whole movement becomes a polished musical expression. The approach might be summed up as Divide and Conquer.

Practicing with the Metronome

The metronome is regarded by many with a combination of fear and distrust. It is seen (or should I say heard?) as an irksome taskmaster, impossible to keep up with, and sometimes even seeming, perversely, to change tempo. This bad reputation, however, is the result of bad use; when it is properly employed, the metronome becomes benign and helpful.

The metronome should never be set to go faster than you can—that is where the misunderstanding arises. It should be used to help you put things in their place, not to drive you to ever-faster speeds. When you use the metronome, start at a moderate tempo well within your abilities. Then you can get in step with it and it will be a steady friend. If you want it to help you move faster, move it up only a little at a time. The difference between an easy tempo and a tempo one notch faster is almost imperceptible, and such is the appropriate way to increase its, and your, speed.

When I am preparing a challenging allegro for performance, I try the music first at more or less the tempo I will want, then I turn the metronome to forty points slower than that and begin practicing. I play the movement in slow motion, with plenty of time to pay attention to every detail. I play it perfectly, in slow motion. The only thing that suffers is breathing, since the phrases are so extended, and even this can be a benefit because I am obliged to breath as deeply as possible. When I have played the movement perfectly once, or twice if I am being very rigorous, at this very slow tempo, I move the metronome up one notch and play it again perfectly at an almost imperceptibly faster speed. Then up another notch, and again perfect; and so it goes. A half-hour or so of this routine brings me up to the tempo I want, and each time I have practiced the piece perfectly. If I begin to encounter difficulties at a certain speed, I use some form of the fragmentation techniques already described. The whole process may sound boring, but it is in fact very satisfying and liberating. It gives the session structure and palpable tokens of progress. Most important, it ensures that I am playing the notes *right* each time I go through them. It does not make my playing mechanical because when the notes are secure I can do anything with them that I want. I let the metronome lead me, but it never drives me.

The metronome may be used in all kinds of practice, if you wish. Measured vibrato, for instance, or all kinds of exercise material can be performed with the discipline of the metronome's beat. If you find it helpful, use it. If you find it annoying, save it for those situations where it is particularly useful. I don't recommend the metronome for beginners: until one has acquired some modicum of control over the instrument and the notes, the metronome is more likely to be a distraction than a help. I do, however, advise a beginner to keep time by tapping his foot. I am not in favor of foot-tapping as a continuing, unconscious habit. As soon as one has acquired a sense of how to keep a steady beat, that beat should be internalized. For the beginner, keeping a steady beat at all is an unfamiliar skill, and tapping the foot is a good way to begin to develop it. If it helps, tap; and tap the toe, not the heel! Almost everyone moves his toes while playing, but what goes on inside your shoes is your own affair. Moving a toe down on the downbeat and up on the upbeat, thereby evenly subdividing the beat, is often helpful in moments of tricky counting.

This brings us to one final and very important point about using the metronome. Never try to keep time with foot or toe when the metronome is going. Tell your feet to keep still. The metronome is doing the work, and you must give your attention to it. If you tap your foot you will be trying to follow two masters, and the foot, being closer to home though more fallible, will win out and lead you astray. It is just this point that causes many people frustration when trying to play with the metronome. Unconsciously they are trying to keep the beat themselves while trying to follow the metronome's objective tick. If you are going to use the metronome, sit passively for a few moments and listen to it before you begin to play. This will give you a chance to hear and internalize the beat you are going to adhere to. Remember, when playing with the metronome, we do not keep the beat, it does. The trick is to give ourselves to it, to listen.

OTHER THINGS TO PRACTICE

Aside from practicing tone, scales, patterns, exercises, and pieces there are other skills we can develop. The person who knows only C fingering (soprano and tenor) can begin to learn F fingering (alto, bass, or sopranino), and one who knows only F fingering can begin to learn C fingering. The fingering patterns are the same on all sizes and with the two fingerings all are covered. The best way to learn a new fingering is to take a beginners' method book and start in on page one. It will go very quickly, since you already know how to play and will just be concerned with associating fingerings and notes in a new sequence. At first your gears will slip from time to time, and you will find yourself using soprano fingerings on the alto or vice versa. Don't be distressed; things will soon straighten out, and besides, everyone has an occasional slip. Some people undertake the new fingering more readily than others. Some even learn both from the very beginning. There is no need to be fearful; it is really quite easy, and the gain in musical versatility is well worth any minor initial confusions.

Another skill well worth acquiring is learning to read up an octave on the alto. Many second line parts that lie very low on the soprano or even go below its range can be well handled by an alto reading up. The way to acquire this skill is to play simple music that moves mostly stepwise within a limited range. The sixteenth-century four-part dance pieces of Susato et al. provide useful material for this practice. After mastering both fingerings and reading up on the alto, one can progress to learning the bass clef. Then if somebody offers to let you play his bass recorder you will know what to do with it. The alto clef (C on the middle line) not infrequently appears in editions of early music. The tenor recorder is the size usually required, so one should learn to play from alto clef on that instrument. The movable C clef, which can designate any of the five lines of the staff as C, appears in some scholarly editions, and advanced players may find themselves contending with notes in unaccustomed places.

Sight-reading

Sight-reading is mostly a matter of reading rhythms rather than pitch. For the beginner, or anyone who is insecure in reading basic rhythms, there is an excellent book, *Learn to Read Music,* by Howard Shanet (see Appendix, p. 236) that explains rhythmic notation from the very beginning and progresses in a clear, easy, and logical way, with exercises to illustrate every point.

Some amateurs have difficulty reading cut time (the half note gets the beat), which appears often in Renaissance music. Practice for this skill should begin with easy pieces that have simple, straightforward rhythms. Again, sixteenth-century dance music provides excellent practice material. As you play, tap two-to-the-bar; lift your toe precisely in the middle of the beat, down–up, down–up, in four equal movements. This way you subdivide each half note beat into two equal parts, a quarter note for the upbeat and a quarter note for the downbeat. You could think of it as an economical way of tapping 4/4. From easy dance music you can progress to more sophisticated Renaissance rhythms. The two volumes of *Ein Altes Spielbuch,* edited by Franz Giesbert (see Chapter 9, page 212) are a treasury of beautiful music for which the beat, the tactus, the basic, underlying pulse, is almost always the half note. The pieces in this collection represent the golden age of polyphony, and every line is beautiful, flexible, and expressive. As you continue to read from this music you will find yourself forgetting about beats and bar lines and beginning to flow with the ever-changing groupings of notes and rhythms. Sight-reading, like everything else, improves with practice. The more you do it, the better it gets. But you must be sure you are doing it right. At first, it may be necessary to count in quarter notes or even in eighth notes. As the rhythmic figures become familiar you will no longer need to subdivide and you will start to read by gestalt. Each musical period has its vocabulary of rhythmic figures. When the vocabulary becomes familiar it is no longer necessary to spell out the figures note by note, but spelling out is the beginning of the learning process.

High Notes

The top notes on the alto recorder remain difficult long after other notes in the range have been mastered. The fingerings are less obvious in the third register (high E'-flat to G", or A"-flat), and the attack and breath pressure must be very precise. Since these notes are at the upper limit of the alto's normal range they are less frequently called for, so we get less practice in them even though they are the very notes that need the practice most. A solution I have found effective is to play music that consistently goes up to these very high notes, and above. Specifically, I use van Eyck's *De Fluyten Lusthof,* the seventeenth-century Dutch varia- tions for soprano recorder, reading the music an octave higher than written, i.e., in the same range that it would sound on a soprano recorder. From time to time the music ascends to high A", B", and C" above the alto's normal range. These notes do not sound pretty on the alto recorder (unless it is equipped with the anachronistic bell key) but with effort they can be played, and it is indeed this very effort that makes any notes below them easy by comparison. Thus high E', F", and G" come as a positive relief. This is not a very musical exercise, but with a little persistence it will remove the terrors of the normal high register.

HOW MUCH TO PRACTICE,
AND HOW OFTEN

How much time to spend practicing varies according to individual cir- cumstances. Some people have more time to devote than others, some are more strongly motivated, some tire more quickly. When practice becomes tiresome and boring you should stop, since you will no longer be doing good work. Sometimes a seemingly simple problem will elude your most persistent efforts. When this happens, and frustration begins to mount, the thing to do is set it aside for another day and go on to something else. You will be better off physically, musically, and spiritu- ally.

Because playing the recorder is a physical skill, it is good to remem- ber that practice leads toward perfection. The nearer you want to ap- proach that goal, the more you must practice. Practice for beginners is exploratory, full of new things to learn. For the experienced player, practice is more a process of perfecting what he already knows. One moves with great strides at first; later the steps become tinier but much more refined. From the very beginning you should cultivate an attitude of objective self-awareness. Don't become impatient with yourself. You must recognize and realize that you can't do everything you want to on the first try, or the second, or maybe even the tenth. Your muscles are not as quick as your brain. *You* know what you want to do, but your muscles don't until you have trained them. Getting impatient with your- self doesn't help. You are not dumb, but your muscles are, and they need a lot of patient repetition before they begin to wise up. The performer

in the lions' cage is an animal trainer. The performer on the concert stage
is a muscle trainer. Neither of them got where he is by being impatient.
A good teacher is patient because he knows the student is not making
mistakes on purpose. The same knowledge should make the good student patient with himself.

Daily practice is especially important for beginners, since newly
learned skills slip away more easily than those which have become
ingrained. If you don't have time for a solid session of practice on a given
day, play for a few minutes anyway, as a holding action. It is not necessary to make progress every time you sit down to play the recorder. Since
there is such a variety of things to practice and ways to practice them,
it is good to have a schedule and certain goals for each session. An hour
might be divided into ten minutes on tone, fifteen for scales and patterns,
and the rest to work on a piece you are trying to master. If you are taking
lessons ask your teacher's advice on how much time you should spend
on each of the tasks he gives you. You may choose to give an entire
session over to just practicing trills, or sight-reading, or working on high
notes. Set the task to your mood and your energy level. Sometimes it's
good to play just for pleasure and not work on anything. Always begin
with a little practice on tone. As I have emphasized, it calms you and puts
you in the proper frame of mind for whatever will follow. Good practice
is objective self-absorption. It is a discipline of mind and body. It is an
escape from worries and cares into an immediate mental and physical
reality. It is an existential exercise that soothes and refreshes. The rewards of practice reside in the process as well as in the proficiency it
promotes.

Chapter 3

ORNAMENTATION

Improvisation—the performer's addition of ornamental notes and figures to those set down on the page by the composer—has been a part of musical practice from the earliest times in Western art music. It is only since the nineteenth century that composers have come to expect their music to be played exactly as they have written it. Mozart is known to have played brilliant improvisations on the repeats in his piano concertos. Even in the bel canto operas of the early nineteenth century by such composers as Bellini, Donizetti, and Rossini, divas customarily added florid embellishments, a practice currently revived, to our great delight. Improvisatory embellishment has always been a part of folk music and is the heart and soul of jazz, rock, and other contemporary pop music. Since so much of the recorder's repertoire is from periods when ornamentation added by the player was a common part of performance practice, we will want to have some idea of how it was done when we are playing this music.

ORNAMENTATION
IN MEDIEVAL MUSIC

Ideas about how to embellish medieval music can only be developed by informed conjecture since there is virtually no written evidence of how it was done. That it *was* done, there can be no doubt: there is more than one condemnation by the early Church Fathers of various improvisational hijinks in the performance of music for the service. Also, the more florid examples of plainchant are simply written-out versions of what was originally improvised, either in the Western church or in the more ancient Jewish and Arabic cantillation from which plainchant largely derives. Secular music was not even written down until about 1200, and therefore its performance must have been a matter of memory and improvisation. The earliest secular tunes—the monophonic songs of the troubadors and trouvères of France, and the Spanish cantigas—are so minimally notated that we are not even sure of their rhythm, let alone such refinements as their ornamentation. Modern performers of this repertoire choose to embellish it in the manner of Arabian music, which, unlike Western music, has evolved very little over the past millennium. Indeed, it was through the contact with and influence of the Moors that this early secular musical culture sprang up in the West. Thus the close, winding embellishments of Near Eastern music are favored to enliven performances of troubador songs and cantigas, but it must be stressed that in doing so we are only guessing at what can't be known because no concrete information remains.

PROBLEMS OF ORNAMENTATION
IN RENAISSANCE AND BAROQUE MUSIC

Matters are quite different when we come to examine ornamentation in the music of the Renaissance and Baroque periods. We are confronted with a veritable *embarras de richesse.* There are many treatises from the Renaissance that deal with the topic of embellishment in lengthy detail, providing endless examples of the most florid and virtuosic sort. Sylvestro Ganassi's *Opera Intitulata Fontegara* of 1535 is one of the earliest of these, and one of the most formidable. Many Baroque composers prefaced their works with instructions on the form and use of ornaments in their music, providing names and shorthand symbols to denote them. However, some explanations were exact and others vague. Nomenclature and the shorthand symbols were not employed with universal consistency.

There are excellent modern studies of early music performance whose authors view the crosscurrents and apparent inconsistencies from the vantage point of a lifetime of meticulous and sensitive scholarship. A short list of the most important and useful of these works will be found in "For Further Reading," page 252. They are required reading for any player who wants to acquire a really profound grasp of early music performance styles. However, the comprehensive detail necessary to such authoritative studies can become a tangle of confusion to the novice, who may not even be sure just what a trill is. So the material that follows will help you to get your feet wet.

Basically, there are two kinds of ornamentation that we need to know about. One is the free embellishment typical of Renaissance practice which consists of winding around the written notes, filling in leaps in various ways, and jumping to other notes that are concordant with the written part. The other is a relatively small vocabulary of specific ornaments, crystallized in form and use—trills, appoggiaturas, mordents, etc., which evolved in seventeenth-century France, referred to as *agréments.* These were first employed by English and French lutenists as a means of sustaining the quickly fading sound of the lute. They were later taken up by harpsichordists, and eventually their use became pervasive in French Baroque music, and throughout the rest of Europe as well.

The Renaissance manner of free embellishment, known as divisions, diminutions, and various other terms in several languages, all expressive of the method involved, continued in use throughout the Baroque period, being especially favored in Italy. The plain and simple movements of Corelli, Vivaldi, and even Handel, whose sonatas for recorder are written in the Italian style, particularly invite this kind of free embellishment.

In the Baroque period the terms *sonata* and *suite* are instructive as to what kind of embellishment is called for. The sonata is an Italian form, usually consisting of four movements in the sequence of, slow, fast, slow, fast, with the slow movements receiving free embellishment. The suite is a French form, a series of movements based on dances, and these are ornamented with the specific forms of the agréments.

The two kinds of ornamentation are different in many ways. The essential quality of free embellishment, divisions, is decorative, a lacy elaboration of the written notes. The agréments, on the other hand, are more rhetorical in intent, giving a declamatory emphasis to certain notes. Thus divisions generally start by sounding the written note and then proceed to embellish it, whereas the agréments usually change the beginning of the note, either with an unexpected dissonance (the appoggiatura and its various elaborations), or an accent (the mordent, short trill, or slide). Free embellishment does not change the essential movement of a line, but adorns it with a smooth embroidery of smaller notes. The agréments interrupt the progress of the line with dissonance and accent. Free embellishment is the player's invention; the agréments are fixed in form and are applied by convention. Free embellishment is an optional addition. The agréments are often mandatory, either by the presence of

Recorder players by Giovanni Battista Piazetta.

signs indicating them or by the strictures of convention, as with the cadential trill; thus to omit them, especially in French Baroque music, is to fail to fulfill the composer's intention. We can play a Handel largo, or, for that matter a Renaissance dance, virtually unadorned (except for a discreetly placed cadential trill). Such nudity would be shocking and inappropriate in a French sarabande or courante. On the other hand, we can embellish our stately largo with decorations which the French would not find in good taste.

What we must remember is that the intention of all ornamentation, of whatever kind, is to make the music more pleasing and beautiful. This truth is too frequently disregarded, particularly in the realm of free embellishment, where a tendency toward virtuoso display can easily overwhelm aesthetic taste and judgment.

DIVISIONS

Some Renaissance treatises on embellishment are simply compendiums of ornamental formulae. Such is the case with Ganassi's *Opera Intitulata Fontegara* (1535), which, aside from a brief introduction, consists entirely of a great number of ornamental figures of the most daunting complexity, both rhythmically and in the number and speed of their notes. Other treatises offer, as well, fully written-out musical examples to show how the formulae may be applied. The most justly famous of these is the *Tratado de Glosas* of Diego Ortiz (Rome, 1553). After many pages of formulae, Ortiz proceeds to give us pieces illustrating completely free embellishment, embellishment over plainchant, embellishments of the top or bottom lines of a madrigal by Arcadelt and a chanson by Pierre Sandrin, examples of how to improvise an elaborate fifth part to these four-part compositions, and finally, several examples of how to improvise over a ground bass, using one of the standard bass progressions commonly employed in his day as the basis for improvising dance music. All of these pieces are quite beautiful and are great favorites among present-day viol players. The viol was the instrument to which his work was specifically addressed, but players of other instruments can derive great pleasure and instruction from his work as well.

All of these Renaissance instruction books are concerned with a particular kind of ornamental practice, one that is soloistic and usually highly virtuosic. If such pyrotechnics were applied to the melody voice of a chanson, it is likely that the other voices would be filled in by a lute or harpsichord, thus transforming a four-part composition into a dazzling accompanied solo. These are graduate studies in the art of divisions.

We will use much simpler material for our beginner's course, taking a couple of four-part dances of Tielman Susato and mechanically applying a handful of simple formulae wherever the movement of the music dictates. We will apply them only to the top voice, although other voices, of course, could use them as well. There is among voices, however, a hierarchy of suitability for division-making, the top being best, the bass next, and finally, if at all, the middle voices. Division-making in all parts is best arranged in advance to avoid the confusion that can all too easily ensue, and the rule should be that the voices do it by turns, rather than together, which produces a cluttered effect. Keep in mind this Golden Rule of ornamentation: It should enhance the music. If it doesn't make the music sound better, there is no good reason for it—it becomes simply ego display. Pieces in which the top two voices are equal and often imitate each other, as in the five- and six-part dances of William Brade, will, of course, sound best if the two leading voices ornament equally, either imitating each other or, more fun, topping one another.

We will begin with this familiar allemande:

Our first formula will be to transform every stepwise rising pair of quarter notes into a turn:

The result is this:

The repetitions produced in the first and seventh bars are banal and do not enhance the music. However, changing the rhythm of the formula in these spots eliminates the banality:

Now we have:

Another way of avoiding a boring repetitiveness is to start a third below:

which yields:

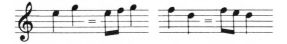

—also a pleasing effect.

Next, let's try filling in the thirds:

This produces:

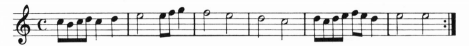

This figure can also be dotted to produce a sprightlier effect:

The next figure, used on stepwise descending quarters, I call a "back step":

Another formula for stepwise descending pairs of quarters is a turn:

The following example uses back steps in one situation and a turn in the other:

(no stepwise desc. ♩'s)

Here is a formula for stepwise descending half notes:

And here is another for two half notes on the same pitch:

Using just these few division formulae, we can ornament the top part of this allemande in a variety of ways. Here are a couple of possibilities:

My favorite of all the Susato dances is the lovely "Hoboeckentanz" given below with two ornamentations. The first consists of stepwise divisions including filling in thirds and fourths, turns, back steps, and a couple of other tricks you will recognize as you play the music. You will notice that as the music goes along, the divisions become more numerous. This provides variety and builds excitement. The second version consists of divisions made by leaping to other concords, that is, all the notes of the division consist of arpeggiations of the chords which are sounding as the division is being played.

I and a group of advanced amateur players whom I was coaching played the "Hoboeckentanz" in a concert, using these divisions to very pretty effect. We played the dance four times. The first time only the top line was played, without ornament, by an alto recorder and glockenspiel. On the repeat, also played simple, the other voices entered one by one at three-bar intervals. The third time all voices played and the top part did the stepwise divisions. And the final time everyone dropped out but

Hoboeckentanz

Stepwise divisions of top line of "Hoboeckentanz"

Divisions by leap of top line of "Hoboeckentanz"

the glockenspiel playing the notes as written while the alto recorder played the arpeggiated divisions. The effect was magical. It was interesting to find that while the stepwise divisions sounded fine and very exciting with the other voices, the arpeggiated version was a soloistic transformation of the piece and sounded best with just the glockenspiel.

Divisions can be put into Renaissance and Baroque music wherever you choose, but it is by no means obligatory to add them. Some pieces sound best just as the composer wrote them, and in others there is simply no room for divisions. The complex polyphonic dances of John Dowland are a good example of music that is best played unadorned. In music with repeats it is best to play the first time plain, saving the ornaments for the repeats. Divisions do not have to be elaborate to be effective. It is surprising to hear how pretty a few simple ornaments can sound.

When you are beginning to devise divisions you will want to practice them first, trying out various figures until you get a scheme that you find pleasing. Then you may want to write it down so you won't forget the good ideas you have come up with. As you gain more experience, you may choose not to write out your embellishments: part of their charm is their spontaneity, and you don't usually forget your best ideas. It's fun to try to come up with something fresh each time.

The few simple formulae I have given you should be enough to get you started, and you can proceed to invent further figures on your own. You can also look in Ortiz, where you will find a wealth of lovely figures. *De Fluyten Lusthof* of Jakob van Eyck is another treasury of divisions written expressly for the soprano recorder. Van Eyck was a blind seventeenth-century Dutch carillon player from Utrecht who entertained the strolling burghers and their wives on Sunday afternoons by sitting in the churchyard playing divisions on familiar tunes on his "little flute," i.e., a soprano recorder. These were found so pleasing that he was urged to set them down, and *De Fluyten Lusthof* was the result. Each tune is first given plain, followed by several divisions of increasing complexity. His divisions are not of the same grace and musicality as those of Ortiz, being somewhat mechanical, but they are great fun to play and they provide lots of ideas for division-making.

THE AGRÉMENTS

In spite of variations of style from early to late Baroque, and from one part of Europe to another, there was a small vocabulary of specific ornaments, the *agréments,* which was employed rather consistently from approximately the last quarter of the seventeenth century through the first half of the eighteenth. It was during these years that most of the solo literature for the recorder was composed: the sonatas, trio sonatas, and larger ensembles employing the recorder as one of the solo instruments, and the florid obbligatos from cantatas of Bach, Handel, and Telemann, as well as a spate of lesser works for altos warbling in twos and threes. A properly stylish performance of these works requires knowledge of the agréments.

As I have mentioned, there is ample information from the composers themselves about the form and use of these specific, crystallized ornamental forms. They were explained again and again, and it makes dizzying reading to go from one composer's explanation to the next because they don't all tell it exactly the same way. Sometimes the words don't match the musical examples. Different terms were used to denote the same ornament, as well as different signs. Still, such differences notwithstanding, there was a general consensus among seventeenth- and eighteenth-century writers as to the form and function of the agréments. I will not undertake a survey of what various individuals said; that information will be found in the books of Dolmetsch and Donington (see "For Further Reading," p. 253). Rather, I will describe only the basic forms and rules for application to the music. Any exceptional forms are purposely omitted in order to present each ornament as simply and clearly as possible, stressing its basic character and what it is supposed to do in the music. These explanations are not to be regarded as infallible or comprehensive. However, they will serve for most situations which the recorder player meets in that part of Baroque musical literature which can be played on his instrument. It is hoped that they will further serve as an introduction to the reading of scholarly and comprehensive works on ornamentation and performance practice.

In the following explanations of specific ornaments, certain terms will be used which may need some explanation. These are: *diatonic, chromatic, main note, upper auxiliary, lower auxiliary, consonance, dissonance, major* and *minor triads,* and *cadence.* To help us understand these terms, we will refer to the piano keyboard.

Diatonic is best understood as referring to the white notes of the piano. If we start on C, a white key, and play only the white keys up to the next C we will have played a diatonic scale in C Major. From C to D we make a whole step, because there is a black key in between. Likewise, from D to E is a whole step. Between E and F there is no black key intervening, so here we are making a half-step. Next come three whole steps, F to G, G to A, and A to B. (Check with the keyboard pictured above to be sure you are in agreement with what I am saying.)

Between B and C, no black key intervening, we play another half-step. Thus, we have just played up a diatonic scale in C Major, two whole steps, a half-step, three whole steps, and a half-step.

To play up a *chromatic* scale we would touch every key, black or white. Both scales sound familiar, but we are, of course, more comfortable with the diatonic sequence of whole steps and half-steps which produces the major scale (and with the related, slightly altered sequence of whole steps and half-steps that produces the minor scale; see Appendix, p. 239) because it is in these diatonic sequences that most of our melodies are written, for example, "My Country, 'Tis of Thee." Some melodies venture, at least part of the time, into the chromatic sequence —for example, the opening notes of the "Habañera" from Bizet's *Carmen.* The melodies we play from the Baroque literature are, with few exceptions, diatonic.

Main note, in the following descriptions, refers to a note as it stands, awaiting adornment, in the written music. Its *upper* and *lower auxiliaries* are a diatonic step above or below it. They may be either a half-step away, or a whole step, depending on where the main note stands in its diatonic scale. In C Major the upper auxiliary of C is D, a whole step. The lower auxiliary is B, a half-step.

So far we have considered notes in sequence, i.e., *melody.* Now we examine notes sounded together, i.e., *harmony.* What makes notes sounded together dissonant or consonant? In the simplest terms, notes a whole or a half-step away from each other are *dissonant.* C and D, a whole step apart, jar with each other. C and B, a half-step apart, jar even more. Try them, and you'll hear. Notes further apart tend to lose their jarring quality and become *consonant.* C and E sound well together, and adding a G above them sounds even better. These three notes, sounding together, form a *triad,* each note separated from its neighbors by more than a whole step. From C to E, it is two whole steps, and from E to G, a step and a half.

It is these triads upon which our whole sense of harmony, of consonance and dissonance, is based. A triad with two whole steps between the bottom note and the middle note, and a step and a half between the middle note and the top note, is termed a *major triad.* A step and a half between the bottom note and the middle note, and two whole steps between the middle note and the top note yields a *minor triad.*

Any of the notes in the triad may be reproduced in higher or lower octaves. It doesn't matter which note of the triad is on the bottom. It just

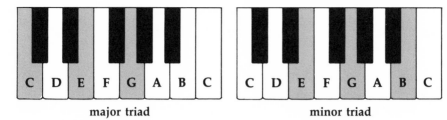

major triad minor triad

has to be the three notes, in any position. The result is a consonant chord, in our example, a C Major chord, C, E, and G. If any of the other notes of the C scale, D, F, A, or B, are added to the chord they will jar with the notes already present, and the chord will become dissonant.

Dissonance is not undesirable. Indeed, it is the driving force of all harmonic movement, since dissonant chords seek resolution into consonant chords. Dissonance and consonance are the yin and the yang of harmony.

This brings us to the term *cadence*. In harmonic terms, *cadence* is the yang, the resolution, at the end of a section or of a piece, to one of the principal chords of the key in which the piece is written.

With these terms clear in our minds, we can proceed to the ornaments. They are presented more or less in their order of importance, starting with the long appoggiatura. Although short appoggiaturas and passing appoggiaturas are less important than trills, their explanation comes next. For someone who wants to read about the most basic ornaments first, I suggest the following sequence:

> The Long Appoggiatura
> The Trill
> The Mordent
> The Port de Voix

The Long Appoggiatura

The long appoggiatura is the standard Baroque appoggiatura. Its function is to alter the written harmony by replacing a main note momentarily with the dissonant note one step above or below. The dissonance is relieved when the appoggiatura is slurred into its main note. It is *always* slurred to its main note. It is not introduced before the main note but starts on the downbeat of that note, thus shortening it. The appoggiatura is stressed and the main note (when it is finally heard) is played more quietly. This ornament provided the Baroque composer and performer with a means of introducing expressive dissonances, which in many cases would otherwise have been forbidden by the harmonic practice of the time. Its usual notation in modern editions, as shown above, is a small note preceding the main note and often connected to it by a slur. The tiny cross ($+$) so often seen above notes in Baroque music, whose meaning is simply to insert an ornament of whatever kind appropriate, can often suggest an appoggiatura, and the ornament can be introduced where there is no sign at all.

The length of the appoggiatura can be varied according to your wishes, but some helpful rules have been given. The long appoggiatura usually takes:

- One-half of a note which is subdivided into two parts.

- Two-thirds of a dotted note, i.e., a note that subdivides into three parts.

- All of a note before a rest, the main note then sounding in place of the rest.

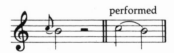

- All of a note which is tied to another note of the same pitch.

There are certain contexts which these rules do not cover. The appoggiatura should resolve to its main note before the harmony changes in order not to lose its character as a dissonance. It might therefore have to move to its main note sooner than the rules above would indicate. An unusually long note may likewise depart from these rules by taking a somewhat shorter appoggiatura. Generally, however, the longer the dissonance is sustained, the greater the expressiveness of the ornament.

If there is no sign indicating whether the main note is to receive an appoggiatura from above or from below, the following rules may be safely applied:

- An appoggiatura from above is used if the preceding note is higher than the main note.

- An appoggiatura from below is used only if the main note is preceded by the note one step below.

This latter rule is conservative, but has an excellent justification—namely, that in the Baroque era dissonances resolving upwards were allowed only if they were prepared, i.e., preceded by the same note.

(The appoggiatura from below frequently appeared in a more elaborate form, explained under "The Port de Voix"; see p. 92.)

The Baroque appoggiatura was not invariably one step away from its main note. Appoggiaturas approaching their main note by leap, though less common, were also possible. They are almost always prepared. Their length is governed by the same rules as stepwise appoggiaturas.

Appoggiaturas can be introduced into the music quite freely even where there are no signs indicating them. For example, if the musical line proceeds entirely in consonant notes, appoggiaturas may be played on the longer notes to liven things up a bit. However, you should avoid putting an appoggiatura on the first note of fresh melodic material. Appoggiaturas can always take the place of trills except at cadences. Such a substitution can solve some vexing problems in technique when trills are called for on very short notes.

The Short Appoggiatura

Appoggiaturas consuming less than half of their main note were standard during most of the early and middle Baroque, but during the later Baroque the long appoggiatura, with its extended and expressive dissonance, was dominant. Toward the very end of the Baroque era, short appoggiaturas reappeared. These short appoggiaturas vary in length from a quarter or a third of their main note at the maximum, to the shortest possible length at the minimum. They are true appoggiaturas nonetheless in that they do not begin before the main note but at its beginning. Their function is not the harmony-altering one of long appoggiaturas, since their dissonance is heard too briefly to affect the harmony. Rather they impart a snapping, rhythmic accent to their main note; the quicker they are played, the crisper the accent. They properly belong to the *galant* period, when they were sprinkled about so liberally as to be a disease. However, some of the more "modern" works of Telemann, J. S. Bach, and others do indicate appoggiaturas which can only be short. They are indicated in modern editions customarily by a tiny eighth note or sometimes a sixteenth. Context will show whether a long or a short appoggiatura should be played. Appoggiaturas in the following situations should be played short:

- Between two notes of the same pitch
- On a note of the shortest value within a given passage
- On a note which is already discordant to the harmony
- On a triplet (where a long appoggiatura would confuse the rhythm).

The Passing Appoggiatura

In passages of descending thirds in equal note values, it was customary in later Baroque practice to fill in the thirds with lightly played, relatively short notes which take their time from the preceding note and are slurred to the following note. These are not true appoggiaturas since they come *before* the note to which they are attached and thus do not alter its harmony. Rather, their function is to make the melodic line smoother and more flowing. Their notation, however, is the same as for a regular appoggiatura from above, a small note to the left of the main note and one step higher. Therefore you must decide by context which ornament is intended. You may feel free to add them yourself even when no sign is present.

The Trill

A trill is a repeated alternation between a main note and its upper auxiliary. Modern trills generally begin on the main note. Baroque trills almost never do, because they are essentially appoggiaturas from above in a more elaborate and arresting form. Thus they start on the upper note, the appoggiatura, which is stressed and held a bit, then they wiggle back and forth before finally settling down on the main note. Except in the briefest contexts, trills always include an ornamental termination—either a turn or a note of anticipation. Both possibilities are shown below, along with the most common notations indicating one or the other:

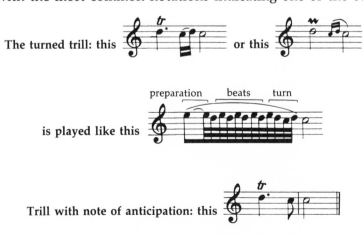

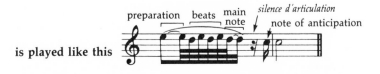

As we look at these written-out interpretations, the first thing to remember is that they are only approximations. All the elements of these trills may be varied in speed or length according to your own expressive purposes. It is precisely because they were flexible that these ornaments were not written out but indicated by signs instead.

Let's examine the turned trill first, since it has a simpler anatomy. The preparation (i.e., appoggiatura) begins on the downbeat, is somewhat stressed, and is sustained. Like the plain appoggiatura, it can be sustained longer for greater expressiveness. This would be appropriate in the context of slower tempos. At very fast tempos the turned trill might be rendered as eight equal notes with no sustaining of the preparation

 , although it is always more stylish to sustain the preparation, if ever so slightly, whenever time will allow.

The number and speed of the beats are up to you. More, and faster, express brilliance and so are appropriate for brighter tempos. The beats may gather speed as they go along. The notes of the turn should be played at the same speed as the beats preceding them. Everything is under a slur, but remember that the note to which the trill resolves must always be tongued.

The trill terminating with a note of anticipation has, as you can see, a much more complicated anatomy. Again, the preparation is sustained and the number and speed of the beats are optional, but you will notice that they come to rest briefly on the main note. Everything so far is under a slur. Next comes a brief moment of silence, the *silence d'articulation,* then the note of anticipation, which is, of course, on the same pitch as the note it anticipates, the note to which the trill resolves. The note of anticipation is generally played much shorter than the conventional notation would indicate. The shorter it is played, the more "kick" it gives into the resolution. As with the turned trill, all of these elements are flexible and allow a great variety of expression. For example, a much sustained preparation, very fast beats, brief pause on the main note, pronounced *silence d'articulation,* and a very short, quick note of anticipation all contribute to a very dramatic delivery of the ornament. On the contrary, a less sustained preparation, slower beats, a longer dwelling on the main note, a less pronounced *silence d'articulation* and a broader note of anticipation, give a softer, gentler interpretation. Thus you can understand that al-

though the anatomies of these trills are very closely defined, their interpretation can be very flexible and expressive.

Turned trills, with their smoother, more melodic form, are most
often encountered within a musical phrase. Trills ending with a note of
anticipation are more dramatic in character and are usually employed to
announce a cadence, either at the end of a phrase or at the end of a piece,
although turned trills may also perform this function in a less emphatic
way.

Often notes receiving cadential trills are preceded by a note one step
above which is identical with the first note, the appoggiatura, of the trill.
The trill nonetheless begins on the upper auxiliary, the note being simply
rearticulated. Another possibility is to connect this preceding note to the
upper auxiliary by a tie, thus giving a trill with a particularly long
preparation. A tie written in the music indicates this practice:

Very short trills, usually consisting of only four notes without ter-

mination , occur in contexts where they add sparkle and accent,

usually short notes at quicker tempos, or on the second of two repeated
notes, especially if the second is on a strong beat.

When a descending scale passage with trills is moving at a lively clip
there is no time to articulate between the upbeat notes and the upper
auxiliaries of the ensuing trilled notes. Thus they can be connected with
ties, as in the example below:

The Mordent

performed

The mordent is a rapid movement from the main note to its lower auxiliary and back again. It is played on the downbeat of the note it embellishes, not before, and is accented. Its function is to give emphasis and bite to the main note, therefore it should be played very quickly and sharply. It may consist of more than one alternation, though increasing the number of beats diminishes its bite. In addition to the sign given above, the small cross may be interpreted as a mordent, and, of course, you can also introduce it yourself. Mordents are effective on notes approached from below by step or leap, but are less effective when approached from above by leap; they are never played on notes approached by step from above.

The Port de Voix

performed

The *port de voix* is a compound ornament combining an appoggiatura from below with a mordent. The appoggiatura follows the normal rules regarding its length. This combination of mordent and appoggiatura was so common that some writers, particularly in France, gave it as the invariable interpretation. This is an exaggeration, but certainly any appoggiatura from below may be so elaborated.

The Slide

performed

The slide consists of a run of two consecutive notes beginning a third above or below the main note. They are lightly accented, quickly played, and are slurred to the main note. They take their time from the beginning of the main note, consuming approximately half of undotted notes and a third of dotted ones. The slide is usually notated by two tiny notes on the actual pitches to be played. This graceful ornament may be introduced almost anywhere; it gives a mild accent to its main note. The more quickly it is played, the stronger the accent.

The Turn

The most common Baroque turn is the upper turn consisting of four equal notes, the upper auxiliary, main note, lower auxiliary, and again the main note. The notes are all slurred. The first note of the turn is accented and thus behaves like an appoggiatura or trill in replacing a consonant note with a dissonance. Thus the upper turn can be freely used in place of a trill on notes that are too short to allow the more elaborate form of the turned trill to be clearly executed.

The lower turn begins on the lower auxiliary, then moves to the main note, the upper auxiliary, and back to the main note.

The lower turn is much less frequent than the upper turn. Notice that the sign for both of these ornaments is the same, so the choice must be decided upon by context.

If the turn sign is placed slightly to the right of its main note, the main note is to be sounded before beginning the turn. In this situation it is the main note which receives the accent and the turn becomes merely a bit of increased melodic activity as the main note passes to the following note. The rhythmic interpretation of these melodic and unstressed turns can be greatly varied. Since almost every eighteenth-century writer resorts to a different rhythmic structure to notate them, this suggests that their performance must have been very free.

The Double Cadence

The double cadence is a compound ornament consisting of a cadential trill preceded by a dotted note which takes a turn and sometimes a mordent as well. This is a standard ornamental formula at important cadences, which display a pair of dotted eighth notes. Eighteenth-century explanations of its performance show a great variety of rhythmic schemes. Two possibilities are given in the example above.

Conclusion

The preceding descriptions demonstrate what precise entities these Baroque ornaments were, clearly defined in both form and function. Every detail of the simplest or most elaborate ornament can be varied either in length or stress, articulation, or number of repetitions; the smallest variation brings a subtle change of expression and meaning. Baroque ornaments are as flexible as the player who performs them. Further variety can be obtained by interchanging ornaments which perform analogous functions. For example, the upper turn, the trill without termination, and the trill with termination are all members of the same family whose prototype is the upper appoggiatura, and to some degree they may be thought of as increasingly elaborate versions of that basic form. A similar relationship exists between the appoggiatura from below, the *port de voix,* and the lower turn. The substitution of one ornament for another can greatly change the expression of a passage.

There are other reasons for altering or substituting ornaments. Quantz suggests that the size and resonance of a room should affect the speed of a trill (a strong resonance will blur a fast trill). Higher, more clearly speaking notes can take faster and more brilliantly performed ornaments which would sound indistinct and garbled in the quieter low register. In addition, alteration can solve otherwise impossible technical problems, for example, the trill between low A and B-flat on the alto recorder. This trill is repeatedly demanded at cadences in the key of G Minor (Handel's Sonata in G Minor, Op. 1, No. 2; Vivaldi's Sonata No.

6 in G Minor from *Il Pastor Fido*; Corelli's Variations on *La Follía,* Op. 5, No. 12; etc.). A possible solution is to extend the preparation and curtail the beats to the minimum of two.

Some general suggestions by Quantz and other writers will conclude this discussion. Ornaments should not be introduced at the beginning of a piece; a melody must first be heard unadorned if the embellishment is to be fully appreciated. A corollary to this rule is that in sequential patterns the ornamentation increases as the repetitions continue. One should never ornament the first phrase and leave subsequent repetitions plain. At the very least, they must receive the same ornamentation. Ornaments provide drama, increase melodic activity, and heighten expression. If they are sensitively employed in relation to the music's structure they contribute immeasurably toward a vibrant and meaningful performance.

Chapter 4

ALTERNATE FINGERINGS, TRILLS, AND FAST FINGERS

GENERAL PRINCIPLES

Alternate fingerings are available in great abundance on the recorder. Almost every note can be fingered in more than one way. Some notes have three or even more possible fingerings. These alternates are useful in several ways. They can be used to correct intonation if the regular fingering is out of tune. They can be used to achieve dynamic effects, a sharp alternate blown softly for a piano, or a flat alternate blown harder for a forte. They can also be used for their difference in timbre from the normal fingering. Their greatest usefulness, however, is in easing moments of technical duress.

As for correcting intonation, I feel the player should generally learn to do that with his breath, and if a particular note is so far out that this is not feasible, the recorder should be retuned or replaced. Seeking dynamic and tone-color effects is a matter for very advanced players who already have their basic technique well under control. Therefore we will examine alternate fingerings simply as a means of easing bits of complicated fingering in playing trills and related quick ornaments.

The rapid back-and-forth movement of trills is possible if all the fingers go up and down together in moving from one note to the other. They are well-nigh impossible if some fingers must lift simultaneously as others fall. Thus alternate fingerings are designed so that all fingers lift and fall together in going from one note to the other. There are three ways of achieving this. The most common is to take the regular fingering for the upper note and then drop one or more additional fingers to lower the pitch a half-tone or a whole tone, whichever is required. A familiar example of this method is the alternate E in the lower register of the alto recorder. F', the upper note of a trill on E, is lowered a half-step to E by adding the third finger:

$$0 \;\; 2$$
$$\underline{3} \;\; \leftarrow$$

Another, but less frequent, way is to take the regular fingering for the lower note and lift finger, or fingers, to produce the upper note. An alternate F'-sharp, for the trill from E to F'-sharp in the lower register of the alto, is an example of this method. E is transformed into a perfectly satisfactory F'-sharp by lifting the first finger:

$$1 \;\; \leftarrow$$
$$0$$

$$-$$

A third method involves alternates for both notes, as in the frequently encountered trill across the alto's break from the first register to the second, G' to A':

$$1$$
$$2$$
$$\underline{3}$$
$$4$$
$$5 \;\; \leftarrow$$
$$6$$
$$7$$

The break is avoided, along with its nasty clicks, by using an alternate G' that is in the second register; put seven fingers down in front (no thumb) and lift the fifth finger to produce an alternate A'.

In these three ways the recorder player can find neat and possible trills for most of the notes on his instrument. The alternate fingerings which I present, given in terms of fingering for the alto recorder, work on most standard "neo-Baroque," or "English-fingered," instruments. The same fingerings will work for the comparable notes of standard sopranos and sopraninos. Alternate fingerings on larger sizes, however, are more various, and if you need them you may have to discover the appropriate modifications for yourself.

·   ·   ·

The method I present for learning the alternate fingerings had its genesis some years ago when I was practicing a Sonata in D Minor by the French Baroque composer Anne Danican-Philidor. The second movement, a Courante, is liberally sprinkled with short trills; and at a certain point I realized that instead of learning these trills as part of the movement itself, I would be more efficient if I taught myself the trills, practicing all possible trills in D Minor before trying to insert them into the actual movement. So I started going up and down the D Minor scale, short-trilling on every note four times. I had a delightful revelation: not only could I be aware of the appropriate light action of my fingers, and think ahead about what fingerings were coming up, including necessary alternates; I could also look out the window. I have a fine, unobstructed view of lower Manhattan, and there are always plenty of things to look at. My fingers went about their mechanical tasks with minimum attention from me. All I had to think about was: Are they light and relaxed; and, what note is coming up next?

By following my scheme you, too, can become a carefree automaton. We go up and down a scale, repeating each of the ornaments I present (short trill, mordent, *port de voix,* and turned trill) four times on each note, then thrice, twice, and finally, once. Once we have gotten things in order in C Major, we can move outward, to F, G, B-flat, D, etc. Alternate fingerings, as they are required, appear in a logical order. We don't have to read any notes, so our attention is free to observe that we are making the right, light finger action. This, as it has turned out, is the greatest virtue of these exercises: They let us think about our finger action. It should be quick and relaxed, from the third knuckle where the finger is hinged to the hand. These are exercises for fast finger action. That they also teach you alternate fingerings, and put four ubiquitous Baroque ornamental figures into your fingers, comes as a bonus.

The repetitive format of these exercises is the key to their success. Doing the same ornament four times in a row on the same note is what allows you to think about your finger action, *and* to think ahead about what fingering is coming up. After the first time, the three remaining repetitions are automatic movement. When you go on to do the ornaments three times per note your thinking has to get a bit faster, but only a little bit. Most of the action will still be automatic. As you proceed to two repetitions, and finally one on each note of the scale, you may at first lose the desired lightness of finger action, being preoccupied with novelties of fingering. But with daily practice, the routines become ever more familiar, and you will soon find that you can skip through them quite quickly with full awareness of the light finger action which they promote.

The explanations that follow are admittedly rather dense, and I suggest you approach them the same way that you would a recipe that you are trying for the first time—that is, read them through carefully two or three times before picking up your recorder and putting them into action. You may want to go back to the chapter on ornamentation and reread the explanations of each of these ornaments to be sure you understand them.

THE EXERCISES

The Short Trill in C Major

The scheme for short trills in C Major is shown both by the notes with the trill sign (∿) above them, and fully written out to be sure that you understand them. The two trills requiring alternate fingerings (those on E and G′) are indicated by brackets written above them. The special fingerings for these notes are shown with arrows next to the finger or fingers which move up and down to perform the trill. In all the examples that follow, brackets above a note are meant to remind you that an alternate fingering is involved.

Played as:

etc.

Alternate fingerings for E in the E/F′ trill:

0   2

<u>3</u> ←

Alternate fingering for G'/A' trill:

1
2
3
‾4
5 ←
6
7

I suggest you first play this exercise and all those that follow in slow motion, to be sure your fingers know exactly what they are doing. Play the four notes of the trill as eighth notes and leave plenty of time between one repetition and the next.

Once your fingers know the movements involved they can begin to move faster, although you may still want to put a fair amount of space between each repetition to give yourself more time to think about what's coming next, and to preserve your awareness of lightness of finger action. Eventually, when the movements have become automatic, the ornament should be played as fast as possible, for the short trill is indeed a very quick little ornament and often appears on very short notes where there is little time in which to do it. The short trill gives a bit of sparkle to the note it embellishes. Also, you are training your fingers to move with great rapidity, and this they can do only if they move lightly. Gripping fingers can't perform the short trill.

Things to keep in mind:

- The four notes of the trill should be absolutely equal. There are musical contexts, such as short trills on longer notes, where the first note might be slightly held, but for the purposes of these exercises we want the crispest delivery, *presto possibile!*

- The ornament begins *on* the downbeat, not before. This takes some concentration. You may find it helpful to use a metronome to keep yourself from jumping the gun. The ornament should commence precisely with the tick of the metronome. If you do use a metronome, start slow. Confusion and frustration will follow if you set it at too fast a tempo.

- The ornament is under a slur. Your tongue should be present only at the beginning of the act.

- Play the repetitions *in tempo.* Don't pause going from one note to the next. If you need to pause, you need a slower tempo.

The Mordent in C Major

The mordent is the sharpest of all Baroque ornaments. It is beyond glitter; it gives bite. Its very name comes from the Italian *mordere,* to bite. Remember that it consists of the note, the note below, and back to the note, on the downbeat, accent on the first note of the ornament, and all under a slur.

The trick in playing the mordent is to get the breath accent on the first note of the ornament, and that on the downbeat, not before. Thus the breath accent on the very short first note of the ornament teaches our breath to be very prompt. If the breath accent isn't right on the button, the note is gone already and the accent lands on the main note, making *it* sound like the downbeat preceded by two very fast pick-up notes, and the mordent is deprived of its bite. Again, the metronome can be a useful monitor. The ornament must start with the tick, not before. Once you've got it right you will get the feel of the ornament. It is delicate, but decisive. It is for accent. The fingers must be light because the movement is very quick. The breath must be lively and alert enough to hit a tiny and swift-moving target. The mordent is very instructive to the breath.

Performed as:

Alternate E for F'/E mordent:

0 2

3 ←

Alternate G for A'/G' mordent:

1
2
3
‾
4
5
6 ← ⎫
7 ← ⎬

Note that the mordent on A' (A'–G'–A') offers a different way of avoiding the register break. This is so we arrive on the main note with a more usual and reliable fingering (123/45) than the alternate A' (123/4 67), which on some instruments is weaker and sharper.

Things to keep in mind:

• Deliver, with accent, *on the beat.*

• Though the breath gives a quick dart of air for the accent, finger action must remain light. An instant of stress from the breath must not encourage stress in the fingers.

• Do it first in slow motion and spaced, to be sure you've got it right, then gradually faster; and on, swift automaton!

• Don't do a double mordent.

Double and more extended mordents exist, but we are at present training our fingers to make the quickest, lightest action possible, which is exemplified by the single mordent.

The Port de Voix in C Major

As you will recall, we refer to the *port de voix* as a compound ornament since it combines an appoggiatura from below with a mordent as you slur to the main note. Here is the scheme for the *port de voix* in C Major:

Note that to perform a *port de voix* on F, you take the regular E for the appoggiatura from below and only use the alternate E for the mordent. An arrow above indicates the note of the ornament that requires an alternate.

Alternate E for mordent in *port de voix* on F':

Similarly, for a *port de voix* on A' you use the regular G' for the appoggiatura, slurring across the register break to the A', and using the alternate G' only for the mordent.

Alternate G' for mordent in *port de voix* on A':

The *port de voix* introduces certain nuances in the use of alternate fingerings since we want to use the standard, more solid fingering for the appoggiatura, which is to receive the accent, and reserve the alternate only for the mordent. An example of this is seen in the *port de voix* on F'. We use the regular fingering of E for the appoggiatura and the alternate E only for the mordent.

Things to remember:

- The ornament is simply an elaborated version of a simple appoggiatura from below. The appoggiatura begins on the downbeat, receives the accent, and follows all other rules for a normal appoggiatura.

- The mordent does not receive any accent. It is merely a bit of melodic activity at the moment of slurring to the main note.

The Turned Trill in C Major

performed

In quick contexts, all the notes of the ornament are performed equally, and that is the interpretation to be used for this exercise. The entire ornament is, of course, under a slur. Here is the scheme for turned trills in C Major:

Performed as:

etc.

Note that in the turned trill on E you only use the alternate for the first two E's, since the third and fourth E's are connected with the D below in making the turn. The example below indicates the alternate notes with arrows above.

Alternate E for turned trill on E:

Note that the lowest note, E, for the turned trill on F' is taken with the alternate fingering, as indicated by an arrow above it.

As with the turned trill on E, the turned trill on G' uses the alternate on only the first two G's. The three A's all use the alternate.

Alternate A' and G' for turned trill on G':

The trill on A' uses an alternate G' for the turn, in this case the second alternate which we employed for playing a mordent on A'.

Alternate G' for turn on A' trill:

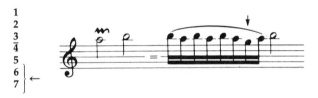

Note that in playing this alternate G' the thumb, which has been in rolled position for the B's and A's, must come off entirely. Otherwise you will get an uneasy F'-sharp instead of the G' you want.

Things to remember:

- All the notes of the ornament should be played as smoothly and evenly as possible and slurred. I advise that you begin playing this ornament quite slowly to get the fingerings straight, especially when it is required to change from an alternate fingering to a regular one midway through. It is helpful to break the ornament into two parts and practice each separately before putting it all together.

- Although all eight notes of the ornament are slurred, the note to which they resolve is to be tongued.

- The turned trill can be resolved to the note next above (as in the exercises) or the note next below, but never to the same note as is receiving the ornament.

MOVING TO OTHER KEYS

When you can perform any or all of these exercises in C Major, you can begin to proceed outward into adjacent keys, consulting the charts that follow. In these, only new alternate fingerings are described. Notes requiring alternate fingerings that have already been described are simply indicated by a bracket.

The Short Trill in F Major

There is no trill sign on the high F″, since there is no way of performing this trill. New alternate fingerings introduced in F Major are:

Alternate B-flat for A/B-flat trill:

Note that you start with a normal B-flat, using the "fake" fingering only for the second B-flat.

Alternate A' for A'/B'-flat trill:

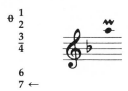

Alternate D' for D'/E' trill:

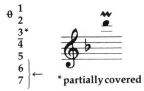

* partially covered

Note that to get the alternate D' properly in tune, you must partially cover the third hole. Comparing the alternate with the normal D' will tell you just how much the third hole needs to be covered.

The Mordent in F Major

There is no mordent, obviously, on low F. Note that the mordent on

B-flat  is performed with normal fingerings.

Alternate for A' for mordent on B'-flat:

Alternate fingering for D' for mordent on E':

The Port de Voix in F Major

There is no *port de voix* on low F.

Alternate A' for *port de voix* on B'-flat:

Note that we use the normal A' for the appoggiatura, and the alternate for the mordent.

Alternate D' for *port de voix* on E':

See note above.

The Turned Trill in F Major

As you can see, more alternates are required in the fingering of turned trills than in the other three ornaments. Sometimes an alternate is needed for the trill, sometimes for the turn, and sometimes for both. Novelties

of fingering introduced in F Major are the following:
Alternate B-flat for A/B-flat trill:

Note that, as with the short trill on this note, you begin with the regular
fingering for B-flat and then switch to the "fake" B-flat for subsequent
beats of the trill.
The trill from A' to B'-flat uses both an alternate A' for the trill and an
alternate G' for the turn:

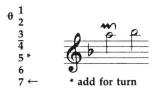

Note: Don't forget to take your thumb off when you add finger five to
make the turn.
The trill from B'-flat to C' uses an alternate A' for the turn:

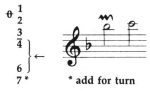

The trill from D' to E' requires "shading" (or leaking) the third hole, and
the third finger must slide very quickly to cover the entire hole to make
the turn on C':

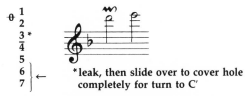

The trill from E' to F" uses the alternate D' for its turn:

The Short Trill in B-Flat Major

Two new alternate fingerings are introduced: An alternate D for the
D/E-flat trill. Two ways of manipulating the same fingering are shown.
I prefer the second way since it only requires trilling one finger:

An alternate E-flat for the E-flat/F' trill:

The Mordent in B-Flat Major

The same two fingerings we have just met appear in a different context
for the mordent:

Alternate D for mordent on E-flat:

Alternate E-flat for mordent on F':

The Port de Voix in B-Flat Major

As in previous situations, we take the regular fingering for the appoggiatura and only use the alternate for the mordent as we are slurring to the main note. These alternates, for D and E-flat, are the same as for the mordent, above, and don't need to be repeated.

The Turned Trill in B-Flat Major

The trills on D and on E-flat once again present us with the uneasy problem of having to change from alternate to regular fingerings in the middle of the ornament. The trill on F′ uses an alternate E-flat for its turn. Alternate D for turned trill on D:

Note: Use alternates as shown below.

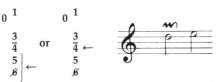

Alternate E-flat for turned trill on E-flat:

Note: Use alternates as shown below.

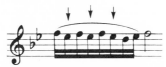

Alternate E-flat for turn of trill on F':

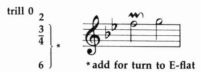

The Short Trill in E-Flat Major

We encounter three new alternates in the key of E-flat—G' to A'-flat, A'-flat to B'-flat, and D' to E'-flat:

Alternate G' for G'/A'-flat trill:

Alternate B'-flat for A'-flat/B'-flat trill:

Note: Start with the normal B'-flat, and use the fake fingering for the second B'-flat. The fake fingering is raw, but in tune.

Alternate D' for D'/E'-flat trill: This is the same alternate D' that we met before, requiring tuning by partially covering hole 3, but here we are coming at it from an E'-flat instead of an E'. Thus we only have to trill one finger, 7, instead of both 6 and 7:

The Mordent in E-Flat Major

By now I think the format will be clear enough that I can streamline a bit. We use only two of the new fingerings: the alternate G' for the mordent on A'-flat, and the alternate D' for the mordent on E'-flat. Note that the mordent on B'-flat (descending to A'-flat) uses standard fingerings.

The Port de Voix in E-flat Major

Again, the alternate fingerings are employed as with the mordent, above; but remember, we should always play the appoggiatura with the normal fingering.

The Turned Trill in E-Flat Major

If I tell you that the scheme for turned trills in E-flat Major requires no new information beyond what I have already given and that you could figure them out for yourselves, there is the distinct possibility that you might not bother to do so, and I wouldn't mind in the least if you didn't. By the time we have gotten this far into flats the fingerings become so esoteric that their usefulness for training your fingers to move faster diminishes. There are useful alternate fingerings to be encountered among the sharp keys, however, which I will review briefly, leaving it to you to put them into the repetitive practice schemes I have recommended.

Alternate Fingerings in G Major

There are two: First an alternate F'-sharp, already mentioned, produced by covering just the thumbhole. The note is clear and usually very well in tune. It provides an easy trill from E to F'-sharp, and an easy mordent from F'-sharp to E. The other useful alternate is a third way of fingering an E by covering holes 1 through 4, with no thumb. This E provides a neat way of making the turn on an F'-sharp/G' trill. I should also mention the trill from low A to B. Start with the regular fingering for B (0 123/ 56) but on subsequent repetitions use a fake B (0 123/ 5) to avoid lifting and dropping fingers at the same time in going back and forth between the A and the B. You will recall that we used a similar ruse for the A/B-flat trill.

Alternate Fingerings in D Major

The important new alternate we meet in D Major is an alternate B' for trilling from B' to C'-sharp, or for making the turn on a C'-sharp/D' trill:

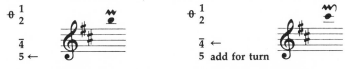

Alternate Fingerings in A Major and Beyond

At this point in the sharp keys we once again arrive at the point of diminishing returns. The fingerings, though technically possible, are not really feasible for any except very advanced players, whereas the purpose of these exercises is to show amateurs how to develop lightness and speed in their fingers. If, indeed, the material in this chapter is mostly new to you, don't try to encompass it all at once. Stick to short trills in C Major, and follow the scheme of repetition I describe. Remember that the point of these exercises is to regulate your finger action, and this requires much repetition to become automatic. You're not supposed to think while you are doing these exercises; they are designed to *avoid* thinking. Instead, they should allow you to contemplate, to observe your fingers as they pursue their busy, mindless, repetitive tasks. You don't want them to think, the little dears, you just want them to be happy and secure and obedient, and not to strain themselves as they play. Ask nothing more from them than that. When they have learned one game and know it so well that they are in danger of getting bored, introduce a new game. Don't try to teach them turned trills if they are still confused about what to do and where to go in playing short trills or mordents. And be sure all the rules are familiar in C Major before changing the field to F, or G, or B-flat.

There are more alternate fingerings, and more ways of using them, than I have shown, but I suspect that by the time you need them you will know how to find them yourself. If there's one you can't find, then you have a wonderful question with which to perplex an expert.

Chapter 5

COMPOUND
ARTICULATION

Compound articulation means the use of different parts of the tongue to articulate a succession of notes, double-tonguing and triple-tonguing. For the recorder player there are two aspects to compound articulation: the modern method and historical techniques. They are different in almost every way. The primary purpose of modern compound tonguing is speed. Modern double- and triple-tonguing, as practiced by brass players, flutists, and recorder players, consists of alternately using the tip of the tongue and the back, represented verbally as "di-ga, di-ga, di-ga" for double-tonguing or "di-ga-da, di-ga-da" for triple-tonguing. In perfecting these tonguings one strives for absolute equality between the front stroke and the back stroke.

Compound articulation of the Baroque and Renaissance sought just the opposite effects. It strove for variety, not speed. The various tongue strokes were used to make the succession of notes sound different from each other, not equal. Use of the back stroke, "ke" or "ge," was eschewed in the Baroque period as having too harsh a sound. Rather, they used a variety of strokes with the tip of the tongue represented by the letters "t," "d," "r," and "l," or for very fast articulations a combination of the tip and the sides of the tongue represented by "did-le" and "did-l-de." Compound articulations were often used on notes of moderate speed and were closely associated with the French Baroque practice of *notes inégales,* the playing of stepwise progressions of eighth or sixteenth notes in pieces of a moderate tempo, somewhat unequally, generally in pairs of long-short even though the notes are written as equal. This practice has its modern counterpart in jazz, where notes are played unequally to impart a rhythmic swing and drive to the music. The practice of *notes inégales* has a very similar musical goal, and the use of dissimilar tongue strokes enhances the rhythmic inequality by providing a difference in accent between the pairs of notes.

MODERN COMPOUND ARTICULATION

We will start with a discussion of the modern practice, since it is easier to understand and thus easier to acquire. There are various ways of representing the action of double-tonguing with syllables, "tiki," "taka"; "diga," "duga"; but none of these provides the perfect verbal analogue, for there is none. We have to discover the action by the way the sound comes out of the recorder. What most people find when they first try double-tonguing on the recorder is that it comes out with a limping, uneven rhythm. The first note is longer than the second, and the back stroke, the "ga," will sound too explosive; but of course, for the modern technique, we want both articulations to sound absolutely equal in rhythm and attack. At first, it will seem hard to believe that the back of the tongue can articulate just as neatly and delicately as the tip, but your tongue already knows how to do it, as you will be reminded if you think of the old song "K-K-K-Katy, Beautiful Katy." If you sing it to yourself, you will hear how lightly and crisply the back of the tongue can move. The tongue stroke you are making when you say "K-K-K-Katy," of course, is too strong and explosive for the recorder. "G-G-G-Gwendolyn" might be a little more like it. The point is that the facility is there. Getting it under control, so that it is rhythmically equal with the tip stroke, and getting it light enough to suit the recorder is the problem.

The way to solve this is to play exercises from some book of practice material such as that by Rooda (see Appendix, page 205). Moving at a very moderate tempo, even slowly if necessary, make each articulation as light and legato as possible, and, of course, listen very carefully to be sure your back stroke articulation is indistinguishable from the tip stroke. This is how to practice for equality. The ultimate goal of the technique is speed, but you will never acquire smooth, even control if you start out practicing double-tonguing fast. Notice that in this moderato practice, I have recommended that you articulate as smoothly and legato as possible. The reason for doing so is that very legato playing requires the quickest, lightest, most delicate tongue strokes and thus promotes the most refined control.

At the same time you are practicing slowly for perfect control and evenness, you can also be doing some simple little verbal exercises to develop speed. These do not require a recorder in your mouth. All that's needed is that you talk to yourself; you can decide when and where you want to do them. Say the syllables "digadoo" quickly and lightly in the

♫ ♪

rhythm of two sixteenth notes and an eighth: di ga doo. The feeling is bouncy and fun and a little silly. When "digadoo" is coming out lightly and crisply, lengthen it to "digadiga*doo,*" four sixteenth notes and an eighth. When you have gotten your tongue around that one proceed to "digadigadiga*doo,*" and when you can produce that trippingly, on to "digadigadigadiga*doo.*" By the time you can double-tongue eight sixteenths in a row you can probably go on "digadoo-ing" indefinitely. Then, for more fun and profit, you can start "digadoo-ing" your way through some tune. I found "Polly Wolly Doodle" quite suitable for the purpose.

By the combination of these two techniques you will very quickly find yourself in command of modern double-tonguing. I know they work because this is precisely how I taught myself to double-tongue during one compulsive weekend. The process was fun for me but the person I was living with at the time didn't enjoy it. When you have got your "digadoos" and legato exercises running smoothly, you can turn to the back of the Rooda book for some useful musical examples upon which to try speedy double-tonguing. There you will find a number of charming English country dance tunes that proceed mostly in eighth notes with occasional flurries of two, four, six, or more sixteenths. These move mostly stepwise and are thus easy to finger. They will provide you with excellent opportunities to put your new skill to the test.

Once you have mastered double-tonguing, you should find that triple-tonguing comes very easily. The tongue strokes can be more or less indicated by "digada." Triple-tonguing is for articulating very fast triplets. Some modern flute and brass players advocate alternating patterns of "tikete, ketike." I find this confusing and tongue-tying, and since articulation is so light on the recorder it seems easy enough to repeat the single pattern of "digada." As I have said, all attempts to transcribe verbal equivalents to the actual movements of the tongue in compound articulations are approximate at best. However, it can be said that the faster the articulations go, the closer the tongue gets to the roof of the mouth, rather in the position of pronouncing a short "i." This position minimizes the movement of the tongue, which of course makes it easier to move it faster.

HISTORICAL COMPOUND ARTICULATION

If verbal analogues for the tongue's action are difficult to find for modern compound articulations, the situation is even murkier with historical compound articulations. We peer at the matter through several glasses darkly. Did the writer choose his syllables correctly to represent the tongue action he was trying to describe? What was the pronunciation of the language at the time? How are we to understand instructions that are often brief and enigmatic?

Quantz, in his treatise on flute-playing published in 1752 in Berlin, gives the most complete and understandable instructions. He recommends the articulation "ti" for notes that are to be played sharply, with separation, or for notes with wide leaps between them; "di" for smoother, slower notes; and a combination of either of these two with "ri" in quick-moving stepwise passages. The "ri," curiously enough, is used for downbeat notes, although it is never used on the first note of a passage. "Ti-ri" and "di-ri" are a Baroque form of double-tonguing, and to understand them I suggest you imagine a little boy marching around imitating the sound of a drum, "ta-Rum, ta-Rum, ta-Rum Tum Tum." To make this "Rum," the boy's tongue is flicking against his hard palate a little further back from the teeth than his "ta." Also, the "ta" is serving as an upbeat and the "Rum" as a distinctly accented downbeat. The "Rum" stroke is rather like a single repercussion of a trilled "r." Try imitating a drum yourself and you will discover that your tongue is striking your palate in different places. This is Quantz's compound articulation for a stepwise series of sixteenth notes. It produces a series of slight accents on the "ri" syllables and the notes come out slightly unequal, the "ri" being somewhat longer. It is for both of these reasons that the "ri" is used on the downbeat notes. Quantz instructs us to tongue a series of four sixteenths with the following articulation: "ti di ri di." He also gives us several pages of examples of how to use these three tongue strokes in various musical configurations. The difference between his compound articulation and the modern practice is that he is not using a different part of the tongue for the various strokes but using the tip in different ways, striking different parts of the palate.

For very fast notes Quantz gives an articulation that does use different parts of the tongue, although it is not the modern front and back technique. He describes it with the syllables "did-ll" for double-tonguing and "did-ll-di" for triple. This is indeed a marvelously quick and light articulation once you have got the hang of it. To get the feel I advise you to say "feedle-de dee" the same way that Vivien Leigh said it as Scarlett O'Hara in *Gone with the Wind.* Then progress to "deedle" and "deedle-de." Precisely what is happening is as follows: First you make a "deed," very short and quick, then the second part, "ll," comes from the sides of the tongue because the tip, of course, is back against the palate. The trick is to make a very sharp "eeee" sound as you say it, which keeps the tongue very close to the roof of the mouth. The movement is not at all like the way we Americans say "fiddle" or "diddle." Some people get this tonguing quite readily, while it eludes others totally —possibly because it requires pronouncing the word in an affected manner. It's worth working on, though, because it imparts a delightfully lively expression to the notes, and it certainly can keep up with the fastest of fingers.

Jacques Hotteterre's *Principes de la Flûte Traversière* was published in Paris in 1707. His advice on articulation is briefer than Quantz's, but similar in content. He gives only the syllables "turu," which correspond to Quant's "diri" and "tiri." Like Quantz, he tells us that the "ru" stroke comes on the downbeat notes but is never used on the first of a series of notes. Thus a series of four sixteenths starting on the downbeat should be tongued "tuturutu." For very fast passages he suggests an articulation which reverses the usual accent of "tu*ru*" in which the "tu" serves as an upbeat to the "ru's" accented downbeat, suggesting instead *"tu*ru," with the "tu" on the downbeat note and the "ru" on the upbeat note. This is a sort of double-tonguing designed for speed.

The earliest instruction book for the recorder, *Opera Intitulata Fontegara,* was written and published by Sylvestro Ganassi in Venice in 1535. Indeed, aside from a couple of German treatises on improvising on the organ published in the late fifteenth century, this is the earliest instruction book for any kind of instrument. Ganassi was a virtuoso performer on the recorder and the viola da gamba. His treatise consists mainly of a great number of examples of divisions (ornamentations) which are extremely elaborate and complicated.

In his introduction he offers us some advice on articulation which is both elaborate and somewhat enigmatic. Basically, he describes three modes of articulation: hard, intermediate, and smooth. For the hard, he gives the syllables "teke teke teke," which are of course the same front and back strokes of modern double-tonguing. The intermediate articulation is shown by "tere tere tere." This would seem to correspond to Hotteterre's "*tu*ru," recommended for very fast tonguing. Ganassi's third kind of articulation, the smooth variety, is shown by "lere lere lere." What he has in mind here is a little difficult to understand, since he does not describe how and where to place the tongue to make the "le" stroke. Presumably it is similar to the "re," but perhaps striking a little further back on the palate. Ganassi then goes on to show various combinations within these three categories of articulation, using the five vowels—for example, "taka teke tiki toko tuku." He advises that you try all the vowels to discover which one suits you best. In his intermediate category, in addition to "tere," he gives "dere," and even "kere." Unfortunately, Ganassi offers no musical examples for the application of his articulations. Altogether, his instructions present us with a mystery as much as an explanation. What is clear is that he employed the front and back strokes of modern double-tonguing and used great variety in his articulation.

As we know, a competent recorder player uses his tongue and breath together in a variety of ways to create subtle differences of attack, from the lightest and smoothest to the sharpest and most explosive. The delicacy of these movements almost defies description, and certainly resists any meaningful transcription into verbal equivalents. Perhaps Ganassi was trying to describe the indescribable, and perhaps what a competent player does is very similar to what Ganassi was trying to tell him how to do.

Chapter 6

ENSEMBLE PLAYING

Making music with congenial company is one of the most delightful pastimes known to man. The recorder by its nature leads you to this cheerful prospect. Pianists and harpsichordists are self-sufficient; most of their repertoire is in the solo literature. But while a lone recorder player can certainly take solitary delight in unaccompanied preludes and dance tunes, the real joys of his musical experience will be found in playing the ensemble literature. There is a vast amount, from the Middle Ages through the Baroque, but it is particularly the Renaissance, the period from 1450 to 1600, that supplies most fodder for recorder consorts—the chansons, canzonas, fantasias, and dances among which groups of amateur recorder players seek their pleasures.

How exciting it is the first time you get together with a friend to play duets! And if that goes well, as it usually does, you find yourselves looking around for a third, then a fourth, maybe even somebody with a bass, and suddenly you have a consort of recorder players who now have the challenge not only of playing their instruments but of playing *together*.

Playing music together is teamwork in that the participants must do separate things together in order to achieve a common goal. The same description holds true for any team sport, although what is done, how much together, and to what end varies. What does not vary is team spirit, a sense of ensemble, a community of endeavor. Most teams do not mark time with the precision that musicians do, although crews of rowers in shells or lines of one-legged paddlers perched on the sides of African dugouts are notable timekeepers. (Interestingly, large ensembles of rowers, such as propelled triremes and other monster galleys, required a conductor to keep time from the podium with a cat-o'-nine-tails.) To get things right, musicians must move with the precision of a surgical team or a high-wire act. Fortunately, even when things go wrong no one expires and the musicians seldom fall off their chairs. The goal of musical teamwork is different from that of team sports; it begins with the first note and ends with the last. It's the performance that counts. There is no winning. This teamwork is not mock war, but mock peace. The effort is not to struggle with one another but to cooperate. What a fine, civilized activity music making is!

There are many things to consider in ensemble playing: finding a convenient, comfortable place to meet, deciding how to conduct the playing session and what the program will be, deciding who, if anyone, will direct the group, learning how to tune up, and learning to play together in time. Further refinements include matters of articulation, dynamics, instrumentation. As a final celebration of your experience together, you may wish to prepare and present a program of your best pieces. Each of these elements will be examined in turn, but first we should consider the primary requirement for happy ensemble playing— that is, a benevolent attitude.

Professional players are supposed to be able to do what they want with their instruments. The professional says to the listener, whether it be just one other person or an entire audience, "What you hear is what I intend." The amateur, on the other hand, knowing that he will not succeed perfectly in the execution of the music, says, "What we hear, you and I, is not precisely what I intend." Even though he may have a very sophisticated idea of the sounds he wants to make, the limitations of his technique thwart him. A certain amount of frustration, accordingly, is inevitably part of the amateur player's lot. His ego is tentative and vulnerable, capable of being bruised. He is his own severest critic, cursing his fumbling fingers or flagging attention for leading him to make "stupid" mistakes.

It thus behooves participants in the ensemble endeavor to behave towards one another with tact and consideration. This obvious point is too often ignored. It is true that an atmosphere of good-natured tolerance and forbearance does not always exist in professional ensembles. Members of a highly respected, world-famous string quartet, for example, were known not to speak to one another except in rehearsal and even there with a great deal of vituperation. Perhaps this mode of contention was necessary for the achievement of their exalted effects. For my own part, I have always found that rehearsals are most successful when conducted with good humor and patience. For amateur ensembles this should be regarded as an absolute necessity. More tact is required for ensemble playing than for most of life's transactions. Thus the very act of playing music together is, or should be, civilizing.

WHERE TO PLAY

Choose a spot that is quiet, with sufficient space for everyone to manage chairs, music stand, and instruments. A "live" room with a bare floor and relatively few furnishings is preferable to one with heavy carpeting, drapes, and overstuffed furniture, all of which absorb sound instead of reflecting it. A big, sunny kitchen can be a lovely place to play, especially if there is some bread baking in the oven. You should be cautioned, however, against eating and drinking while you play. Saliva inevitably will flow and can lead to an unwanted buildup of residue in the windway of your recorders. This is not my imagination. I have been assured by an expert repairman that when he revoices recorders he can tell who has been eating cheese and crackers and drinking wine while playing. So it's best to save the refreshments for the break.

The idea of playing out of doors has a certain pastoral charm, but it usually turns out not to be practical. For one thing, there is always at least *some* wind, enough to blow the pages around in a bothersome way. They must be fastened with clothespins or clips, thus complicating page turns. Also, a breeze blowing against the window of the recorder interferes with the air exiting from the windway, thereby muffling the tone and sometimes carrying it away altogether. In addition, when playing out of doors, you do not have the desirable acoustical effect of sound reflecting from the walls, floor, and ceiling of an enclosed space. Playing in the sunshine gets too hot and uncomfortable; there is also likely to be glare reflected from the music. All in all, I recommend playing indoors.

Have enough light! Peering at the music causes mistakes in reading. For the same reason, be sure that you have enough copies of the music. Two persons reading from one stand is comfortable; more is not. It is not usually necessary for each player to have his own stand. Playing two to a stand reduces clutter, allows the players to sit closer to one another, which makes it easier to listen to each other, and facilitates page turns. However, unless you know in advance that there will be enough stands, it is always a good idea to bring your own along. For any ensemble larger

Detail from The Banquet *by Hans Mielich, 1548. Wadsworth Atheneum, Hartford.*

than three, I recommend sitting in a circle. The closer the circle, within the limits of comfort, the better you will be able to hear one another. If you are preparing a performance, however, it is best, at least at the later rehearsals, to sit in a half-circle, as you probably will when you perform. Before you leave for a playing session, it is wise to check to be sure you have all parts of all the instruments you will need (I have been embarrassed more than once by arriving at a rehearsal with only two-thirds of one recorder or another), your music, and a pencil.

Getting together informally to play music is a social occasion and sociability is certainly in order, but a certain amount of discipline is also required for the sake of the enterprise. The players should arrive on time, preferably in a cheerful frame of mind and not too tired. "On time" should be understood to mean sufficiently before the time that playing is to begin to get set up, put your instruments together, and begin tuning. Tuning is the first item on the agenda and cannot really be effectively accomplished until everyone is present. The procedure for tuning will be given in detail below.

It is best if everyone agrees to concentrate on the musical task for a certain length of time and to save social chatter for the breaks. The larger the group, the more necessary this rule becomes. One annoying habit that is very easy to fall into is to noodle or practice your own part while others are tuning or rehearsing. The key word here is courtesy; the courteous ensemble-player, after he has finished his own tuning, does not warm up his rauschpfeife or krummhorn!

There are a couple of other points of ensemble courtesy that I really feel should be mentioned: We shouldn't play others' instruments without being sure that we have their permission to do so. Instruments are very personal possessions, and people may prefer not to share them. Among my own collection of recorders, there are three that I would never lend to anyone; permission even to blow on them is bestowed as an honor. When I lent one once to a professional colleague, it came back without the special quality that I esteemed in it, and it took me a while to coax it back to its former self. I have been more cautious about both lending and borrowing ever since. When you borrow music from other people be sure the owner's name is on it, and make a special effort to remember to return it, especially if it is a single part of a set. I'm sure I am not alone in possessing music in score and parts for which some of the parts are missing, and thus the music is unplayable. It is so easy to scoop up a part from someone else's music along with your own and then discover it months or years later and wonder where it came from. If there is no name on it, you may never know, so it is prudent to have your name on music before lending it, or to write the owner's name on music you have borrowed. The problem of straying music will never be eradicated, but perhaps if we give it some priority in our thoughts it can be ameliorated. Every time I look up Telemann's "Six Partitas" in my file and find four copies of the bass part, two of the score, and one of the solo part I shake my head and wonder: how, why, who, where?

Even if our music is returned to us, it is disheartening to find it marked with pen, magic marker, or heavily engraved pencil. These *souvenirs d'occasion* are less welcome than a light, and erasable, pencil-marking. Don't inscribe permanent graffiti!

The group should have a program for the session, however informal it may be. If it is an ongoing ensemble, which is the situation I am addressing, this should comprise a mixture of the familiar and the new. It is best to begin with a familiar piece by way of a warm-up, which helps to get the ensemble spirit going. Then proceed to the *pièce de résistance,* some challenging piece the group is working on. After a solid session of work on that, a break is in order, and then the group might go on to reading something new. It is usually satisfying to end the session with a few familiar favorites. This format works well for informal playing sessions, since it conforms to the expected energy curve. Even when you're rehearsing for a program, it is advisable to put the hardest piece second on the agenda. An evening devoted entirely to sight-reading should likewise end with something easy in order to finish with a satisfying musical experience.

WHO LEADS?

Who directs the ensemble? Ideally, I suppose, suggestions should come equally from all members. That would be the balanced approach, assuming that each member was equal in skill and experience. This, however, is not usually the case, and so the less experienced members gratefully accept direction from the more experienced. Some people are fond of the role of director; others shun it out of shyness or modesty. Oddly enough, the one who likes it most may not be the one who does it best, and the member with the greatest musical skills and knowledge may not have much interest in telling other people what to do.

If one person *is* to be in charge—for a piece, for an evening, or forever—it should be by mutual consent. Having given that consent, the other players should be prepared to listen to what the leader says. It is annoying to have things come to grief because someone was not listening to instructions and therefore starts in the wrong place, does not take the repeat, or whatever. It is also unsettling to have two members of the group struggling to be the leader at the same time. If there is to be a leader, let him or her be it, and the others can await their turns on subsequent pieces. As a matter of fact, the idea of rotating direction is a very good one, and each person in turn should be encouraged to undertake the role to the extent of his abilities. Leading the group is, after all, an aspect of ensemble skill, and everyone should be allowed to develop it.

TUNING

When you are playing a recorder by yourself, playing in tune is a matter of hearing intervals correctly as you proceed from one note to the next. It is a skill that develops as you become more familiar with what the correct intervals are. It is like whistling or humming a tune by yourself and trying to get the intervals right, although with the recorder things are much easier since the correct fingering yields a very close approximation of the right note. When playing the recorder with others, however, you no longer need to rely on subjective perceptions of what is or is not in tune. Instead, you have the objective results of your sound in conjunction with that of other players. When you are attempting to match the same pitch (unison) with someone else, you listen for *beats* and attempt to eliminate them and achieve a *beatless unison.* When tuning perfect intervals with other players (perfect fourths, fifths, major thirds), you direct your attention to *difference tones.* Both of these phenomena are difficult to describe in words alone, without a physical, aural demonstration, but since they are both very helpful in ensemble tuning, I will do my best. I ask for your close attention.

Beats and Difference Tones

Beats are not difficult to hear and understand, and are very helpful in getting perfect unisons. Therefore, every reader should try to struggle through this explanation. Difference tones are more problematical and some readers may choose to skip over the topic, coming back to it when their musical skills and knowledge are developed to the point that they can perceive and understand these less obvious, but useful and instructive aural phenomena.

All sounds are composed of vibrations; many speeds of vibration arriving at the ear at once give the characteristic signature of a particular recognizable sound. Musical sound, or *tone,* is recognized by the slowest of its "recipe" of vibrations, its basic *mode of vibration.* We perceive this as the *pitch* of a given musical tone. Although there will be a complex of faster vibrations above it, it is this basic mode of vibration to which we tune. *A–440,* for example, is the common, agreed upon standard note to which modern ensembles generally tune. Why A–440 should be chosen is of less interest to us than precisely what the terms mean. The *A* in question is the A above middle C, the lowest A on the alto recorder. *440* means that 440 sound waves impinging on our ears per second give the impression of this pitch. It's an arbitrary standard. It could just as well be 415 pulses per second, and very few of us would have cause to object. People gifted, or blighted, with "absolute pitch," perceive differences in the pitch of notes absolutely. When they hear a note vibrating at 440 they recognize it as an A, and 415 is for them, unequivocably, A-flat. Although useful in many ways, absolute pitch can be a curse. I remember a gifted but unhappy oboist from high school who had learned her absolute pitches from a piano that was a half-tone flat. Thus, everything she played sounded to her ears a half-tone higher than it should have. She eventually gave up music, although she had a very good talent for it, because she couldn't reconcile the discrepancy.

If, indeed, we happen to be trying to tune to someone's A–440, we try to match this A with our own; we try to blow it at 440 pulses (of the sound wave) per second. The same fingering should give the same note —right? Not quite. If our note is slightly sharp to the one we are trying to match, it will be vibrating somewhat faster, say A–445; and if we are slightly flat, our note will be vibrating slightly slower, say A–435. In either case we will perceive a sensation of throbbing between the two slightly mismatched pitches. The speed of these throbs, or beats, will be the difference between the vibrations of the two notes. Thus, both of the examples above would produce five beats per second (440 minus 435 equals 5 beats per second; 445 minus 440 equals 5 beats per second). If the pitches are farther apart, the beats will be faster; if they are closer, the beats will be slower. It is only when the two pitches are vibrating exactly together that we have the impression of a single sound, a pure, beatless unison.

Beats are relatively easy to hear, and they are very useful in getting instruments exactly in tune on the same pitch. I use the following procedure: One person is appointed as "anchor" and is assigned to hold his note as steady and even as possible. The other person must find this steady anchor tone by changing his breath, blowing harder or softer and listening to the speed of the beats that result. If there are beats at the outset, as there usually are, the "finder" has two choices; he can blow harder or softer. Without knowing whether he is sharp or flat, he has a fifty-percent chance of making the right choice. If the beats get slower, he has chosen to move his breath in the appropriate direction and can proceed to achieve a beatless unison with his fellow. If the first guess was wrong and the beats get faster, then the second try has a one hundred percent chance of success. If he blew harder and the beats got faster, then he *knows* he must blow softer, and vice versa.

When people are first introduced to this concept of tuning by making the beats go away, several things might happen. The finder, hearing beats, may choose the wrong direction, and then hearing faster beats, may panic and move even further away, resulting in momentary trauma and confusion. The initial blow might yield a beatless unison from which the finder then departs in search of what he is supposed to hear, i.e., beats. The anchor may be less than steady and move in sympathetic pursuit of his finder, the two thus blowing ever harder or softer as they seek the desired union. An objective third pair of ears helps sort out such initial confusions. Eventually, everyone calms down and comes to realize that making the beats go away is a method of achieving perfect in-tuneness that completely bypasses those terrifying decisions as to whether we are sharp or flat. Beats are easy to hear, and when we understand how to use them they lead us quickly to the desired unison, which, itself, has a palpable, recognizable sonority that we find more easily each time we seek it.

Blowing octaves in tune is akin to making beatless unisons. If we blow an A–440, the A' one octave higher will vibrate exactly twice as fast, A–880. By the same token, the A one octave *below* A–440 vibrates at 220. This is the meaning of *octave* in music: twice as fast is the octave above, and half as fast is the octave below. It so happens that in the recipe of vibrations that make up a musical sound, or tone, especially for the recorder, the second most prominent ingredient is a vibration *twice* as fast as the basic mode of vibration. We use the basic mode of vibration to tune beatless unisons. We use the second mode of vibration to tune octaves. This second mode of the lower tone, 880, must coincide with the basic mode, 880, of the upper tone, without beats. These beats between octaves, however, are less obvious to the ear than are beats between unisons. Therefore I suggest that to get octaves in tune the upper note should try to "disappear" into the lower note, which indeed it will when its vibrations match those of the lower note's second mode of vibration. Again, like the beatless unison, it's a matter of sonority. In tune, octaves have a silvery rightness, one sound, enriched in its upper modes of vibration.

Difference tones are more elusive to our perception than either beating unisons or octaves. It's not that they are so hard to hear, but rather that they're hard to *notice.* We hear difference tones, usually quite annoyingly, when we are playing duets on two altos or sopranos. They are that buzzing in the ear that we try to ignore as we tootle along. When they are in tune with the intervals we play, as they should be, they are less noticeable. Difference tones are manufactured by our ears. Their description, but not explanation, is as follows: When two different pitches arrive at the ear, the ear creates a buzzing tone whose speed of vibration is the difference between that of the upper pitch and the lower pitch.

Does this description have a familiar ring to it? It should, because it is the same as that describing the throbbing phenomenon of beats, except that here the two pitches are much farther apart and thus the beats between them are much faster, so fast indeed that we begin to perceive their rapid hum as a distinct pitch. Here is the routine I use to demonstrate to my students the relationship between beats and difference tones:

I and another person begin, on altos, by getting a perfect beatless unison on open G' (second finger of left hand only). When we have gotten this, and while the other person holds his pitch, I begin to flatten by gradually sliding my first finger onto the first hole, my third finger onto the third hole, and finally the fourth finger onto its hole, thus producing an alternate-fingered E below my partner's G'. What happens between the two notes is as follows: First we begin to hear beating, which gets faster as my note gets lower. This turns into a jarring buzz, then an indefinite hum, and when I finally settle on my E, the hum assumes an identifiable pitch, a C two octaves plus a major third below my E.

difference tone

When this difference tone has been perceived and identified, we begin again on G' and E (I use the standard fingering at this point, thumb and first finger), and I gradually slide on my second finger to produce a D, which makes the hum of the difference tone rise to a G two octaves below my partner's open G'.

difference tone

Sliding my third finger onto its hole to make a C causes the difference tone to rise again, this time to a C one octave below the C I am playing.

difference tone

Difference tones, or for that matter, beats, are easier to perceive if the two players producing them sit with their instruments at right angles to one another. Also, one player might sway slightly from side to side, which helps to bring these differential vibrations in and out of the ears.

If difference tones are so tricky to hear, why, you might ask, do we bother with them at all? There are two answers to this question. First, they serve as fine-tuning devices for getting intervals perfectly in tune. When the difference tone is vibrating at its appropriate speed, and is therefore at its most inconspicuous, the two notes that produce it will be in exactly the right relationship, and the interval they are sounding together will have its clearest, brightest, most characteristic sonority. A

perfect fifth between two tones, C to G' for example , is so

solid that it can be mistaken for a single sound. If the fifth is less than perfect, the two tones will produce faint beats, and the difference tone will growl indistinctly down below. The sonority will be unclear. Listening for difference tones trains our hearing acuity; they lead us to a perception of what perfect intervals should sound like. The most important intervals and the difference tones which result from them are shown below as they occur in a C major chord. (In the following examples the actual *sounding* pitches are shown by white notes, and the difference tones that result from them are shown as black notes.)

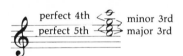

A perfect fifth produces a difference tone an octave below the lower sounding note.

A perfect fourth produces a difference tone an octave and a fifth below the lower sounding note.

A major third produces a difference tone two octaves below the lower sounding note.

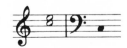

A minor third produces a difference tone two octaves and a major third below the lower sounding note.

The interesting fact that these examples illustrate is that all the difference tones produced between the notes of a major chord reproduce the root note of the chord (in C Major the root is C), at the distance of either one or two octaves below it. This is why major chords, when they are perfectly in tune, sound so solid and clear. The difference tones provide a reconfirming foundation to the chord.

The other reason why we should concern ourselves with difference tones—a corollary of what has already been said—is that they are there, whether we want them or not; so we may as well get to know them, tame them, and let them teach us what they can. We don't listen for difference tones in ensemble playing; we listen for the correct, distinctive sound of the intervals which they have taught us to perceive.

One final admonition before we go on to the method of tuning a group of recorders: At any stage of tuning, whether you use the scientific procedures just described or the practical suggestions to follow, you should always blow a perfectly straight, even tone. I am appalled when I hear someone blow a tuning note that contains a vibrato. It's like getting your balance on a tightrope by doing a shimmy. It may work all right for the individual, but it makes me reluctant to be on his team.

Playing in tune is the most basic skill of any ensemble. A pianist gets his instrument tuned by a professional tuner, and then is no longer responsible. All he has to do, all he *can* do, is strike the keys and accept the pitches that ensue. We who play instruments over whose pitch we have immediate control have a much greater responsibility. We must tune together at the outset and then listen and correct throughout our playing. Our task is not easy, but it can be very rewarding because we have the possibility of playing *perfectly* in tune, something that even a well-tempered keyboard can never do. We often seek help from each other in deciding if a note that is almost right is too high or too low. Usually someone else's ear can hear whether a note is sharp or flat more easily than the player himself can. When in doubt, we should ask one of our fellow ensemble players. It is a fact that on some days one can hear better than on others. Our ears are keener when we are well rested and alert. When we are tired, our attention flags in hearing as in all other things. We help one another in the ensemble endeavor of playing in tune. It is not easy. It is never easy, but working together we can do it.

The first question to decide is whether to tune to standard pitch, A–440, obtained from a tuning fork or electronic tuner, or simply to tune the recorders to each other. Since recorders vary so much in their relation to standard pitch I recommend the latter procedure, except when playing with a keyboard instrument, when, obviously, one must tune to it.

When one's recorder is sharp, one separates the head and middle joints a bit, thereby lengthening the tube and lowering the pitch. When the recorder is flat, one pushes them back together again. The flattest recorder, with the joints pushed all the way together, is the instrument that all the others must tune to. If someone has a recorder that is particularly flat, it is unfair to inflict it on the others and it should be set aside until it has been retuned.

Separating the joints, or pulling out, on a recorder affects the open notes the most (e.g., D's on sopranos and tenors, and G's on altos and basses) so these notes are not the best to tune on. The notes that are affected the least are also best avoided (second-octave E on sopranos and tenors, and second-octave A on altos and basses). So beware of tuning to A, even though that is often the first note that comes to mind. Good notes for tuning, on any recorder, are the notes played with the three fingers and thumb of the left hand. These are solid notes which must be in tune without using any special fingerings; if they are not in tune the instrument is probably at fault. These are the notes that we adjust, by pulling out or pushing in, to get the ensemble's intonation together.

When two musical companions are getting together for some easy duetting, they will tune their altos' E's or D's together, or their sopranos' B's or A's, or some mutual unison between two different sizes, and proceed to warble. They may choose to observe or to ignore difference tones as they go their happy way. But for ensemble playing, a more thorough tuning routine is required. I recommend the following:

1. Begin with tenors, tuning for a beatless unison on low G. Have everyone pull or push until the unison is perfect.

2. While the tenors continue to play the G thus agreed upon, the altos tune their lower-register C to a perfect fourth above the tenors.

3. Now the basses tune their C's, in octaves with the altos, in fifths below the tenors, and in unison with themselves.

4. Finally, the sopranos tune their G's, in octaves with the tenors, in fifths above the altos, and in unison with each other.

You can use similar schemes with A's and D's, the "two-finger and thumb" tuning. Something to keep in mind is that by the time the tuning has spread out to sopranos and basses, it may be necessary to recheck the original tenor unison.

This system tunes the solid, basic notes, but each player must discover by himself any notes on his instrument that require special adjustments of breath or fingering to get them in tune. Most recorders are not perfectly in tune with themselves or anything else, so it is useful to know when one has to make adjustments with one's breath or with one's fingering. For example, the bottom two notes on many instruments tend to be sharp and must be blown gently. Octaves are found to be wide, and must be adjusted with either breath or fingering. Careful practice and careful listening will help the player to make decisions concerning the tuning of individual notes on his instrument.

Once the recorders have been tuned, strings, if there are any, may be tuned to the pitch the recorders have arrived at. There is, however, a real danger here. Unless recorders are *really* warmed up, they rise in pitch almost immediately as they are played, and the pitch keeps rising. A wise string player takes a pitch slightly higher than that of the recorders to tune to; I have heard many a disaster occur when that rule was not followed. The recorders all rise together, but the strings are left behind. They, of course, find this very upsetting. The same thing happens to reed players, who are likely to become more and more fatigued as they strain to "lip up" to a rising pitch. My advice here is: When you are fortunate enough to have other instruments in your ensemble, keep retuning the recorders to bring the level of pitch back down to where you started. Usually this will mean pulling out a bit more on everyone's part.

If everyone starts together, it is logical to tune the first chord. In early music this will always be a concord. If the chord does not sound in tune, the way to correct it is as follows:

1. Tune the root (lowest note) of the chord with its octaves.

2. Tune the lowest fifth to the root and then any of its octaves.

3. Tune the thirds.

Other likely tuning chords are: the last chord of the piece, the last chord of a given section, or consonant chords at the ends of phrases. An example of the latter might be found in a Bach chorale, which proceeds phrase by phrase, each phrase ending in a consonant chord under a fermata ⌒ (hold sign). The procedure for working on intonation in such a piece is to tune, in turn, the opening chord, the chord under each fermata, and the final chord. Once this has been accomplished go back and play the sequence of chords in time, four beats per chord at a moderate tempo. When this can be done with all the chords in tune, play the piece as written. You will find the intonation much improved, since your ears will expect the series of modulations upon which the chorale is based.

In dance music the first and last chords of each section will often be the same, but in a different position, that is, the same notes will be there, but in different octaves. Playing two versions of the same chord, which happens in this situation, is very helpful and revealing.

Whenever two voices come into a unison or an octave there is an opportunity to check intonation, and if there is a problem the players involved should make a note to listen for each other at that spot. Fifths and fourths between voices are almost as good; the perfect intervals are the easiest to hear. Getting a piece nicely in tune involves much of this sort of lapidary work, polishing each interval in turn until the intonation sparkles.

PLAYING IN TIME

Playing in time has two interrelated aspects: keeping the beat together and getting the individual rhythms right. Rushing or dragging the tempo (usually rushing, from nervousness) can throw the others off and ruin the ensemble; actual rhythmic mistakes are of course problems that must be dealt with. Much of the music facing an amateur recorder consort is quite challenging rhythmically. I have seen more than one trained musician, unfamiliar with the style, founder on rhythms which an experienced amateur recorder player could toss off with scarcely the blink of an eye. The rhythmic complexity of Renaissance and earlier music is much greater than that of the music that follows it in time. Only with the advent of the modern era have rhythms again approached the complexity of earlier times. This rhythmic complexity presents difficulties for the amateur ensemble, especially for those members who have only recently learned to read music at all.

I will offer several ways of getting the ensemble's rhythm together that I have found to be effective and enjoyable. One obvious way to deal with the problem is to "speak" the rhythms out loud, unencumbered by the distractions of playing one's instrument. If the rhythms are particularly complex, the whole ensemble can speak each line in turn together, perhaps at the same time keeping a beat together by snapping fingers or tapping lightly with pencils on their music stands. I have never seen a group fail to enjoy this. It's such a pleasure to get it right for a change without having to worry about fingerings. You will notice I suggest speaking the rhythm, using "da" or some such syllable, not singing it. I always present the exercise as "speaking," although I myself may then fall into singing the pitches as well. But I would never want to frighten anybody by suggesting that he had to sing. It is nice if the pitches come along with the rhythms, and I am sure they help, but the exercise is just as valuable without them.

If the problem is not in the individual rhythms themselves but in getting the various rhythms of all parts to fit together, then everyone might try speaking the rhythm, each of his own part. This is a delightful effect, a sort of rhythmic chant with figures popping out from one voice after another. It is a technique that invariably brings to light who is having problems where, and so leads to solutions.

Another and more difficult exercise is to speak the composite rhythm by watching all the parts at once and speaking every beat and subdivision that appears in any of the voices. This is, of course, an excellent way to get everyone to notice the other parts as well as his own. It is also quite tricky and usually cannot be done well without a certain amount of practice.

It is useful to have everyone play each part together in turn, using any instrument that will fit. Next, you could divide the group in half, each half playing one voice, and play various combinations of two voices only. A further development of this idea is a technique I call "add-a-part," which works especially well on sectional pieces such as the polyphonic dances of John Dowland and Anthony Holborne. In "add-a-part," everyone always plays on the instrument required for his own part. First we all play the top part; then we make a repeat, *in tempo,* and everyone drops to the second line except the sopranos, who continue playing their own part, thus producing a lopsided duet. Repeat once again and everyone drops to the third line except top- and second-line people, who repeat their own parts. Continue repeating until everyone has dropped down to his own part. Add-a-part requires as many repetitions as there are voices in the composition. Its virtue is in allowing the players to hear the texture of the piece as it is put together layer by layer. Players of lower parts become familiar with the parts above them before they come to play their own line, and upper-part players, through repetition, become increasingly secure with their own notes. Their attention is freed and they can be aware of what is going on below them. Of course the whole process can be reversed and, starting with the bass, add-a-part can be played by adding the lines above. This is a mechanical process, to be sure, but it is an efficient and effective way of getting things together.

ARTICULATION

Some basic principles of articulation are presented on page 39. These rules of course apply equally in solo and in ensemble music. When your ensemble is working on a piece of music one of the things you must consider is what scheme of articulation you are going to use. When you have agreed on the articulation of a particular figure or phrase, everyone should articulate it the same way when it comes his turn to play it. This will enhance the clarity and coherence of the music, and it will also encourage you to listen more carefully to yourselves and to each other.

Often in Renaissance music (and earlier and later) various voices will be playing in different meters at the same time. 6/8 against 3/4 is a frequent juxtaposition. It is employed constantly in the charming dance "Mvylinda" by Anthony Holborne. ("Mvylinda," i.e., *muy linda,* is Spanish, meaning "very pretty," which this piece certainly is.) "Mvylinda" is a five-part piece with three repeated sections. Each voice changes almost from bar to bar from 3/4 to 6/8, and rarely are all five voices playing in the same meter at once. The resulting texture has great sparkle and life, and it is much enhanced by the proper articulation. In the opening section of "Mvylinda," given below, I have added articulation signs of two kinds. Above some quarter notes I have placed a line with a dot over it: ♩̇. This is to indicate that these notes are to be played somewhat separated and with a slight breath accent. Over some eighth notes I have placed a dot which means that the note is to be played very short, but

with no breath accent: 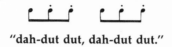. The principle here is that in 6/8, eighth notes
are articulated to sound as two groups of three:

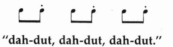

"dah-dut dut, dah-dut dut."

In 3/4 they are articulated to produce three groups of two:

"dah-dut, dah-dut, dah-dut."

Note that in a 6/8 bar, when the rhythm of eighth-quarter appears, ♪ ♩
the eighth note should be played very short; thus a dot appears above
it. First try playing each line ignoring the articulation marks. Then play
it again with the accent and spacing the marks imply. You will hear how
they clarify which measures are 6/8 and which are 3/4, and you will
hear how the parts play against one another as you put all five voices
together.

    In polyphonic fantasias, canzonas, chansons, and so forth, the
rhythmic groupings are subtler. Unlike dance music, which has a strong
beat and recurring rhythmic patterns corresponding to the steps of the
dance, and therefore fits easily into measures, the independently moving lines of a polyphonic fantasia are composed of rhythmic figures
that have little to do with the bar lines of modern transcription. Bar
lines were not employed in the original notation; and although bar
lines help us to read the rhythm, they tend to obscure the ever-changing rhythmic structure of the music. It's like looking at the flowing
contours of a landscape through a barred window. This is why many
present-day players are learning to read from the original unbarred notation, and modern editions of early music in original notation are beginning to appear.

    Renaissance polyphony does have an underlying pulse, or *tactus,* but
it lies very deep and is unobtrusive, so that the lines above it move with
a changeable freedom that defies meaningful transcription into barred
notation. When you play this music, you must learn to ignore the bar line
and seek instead to perceive and articulate the shape of the lines as they
really are.

Mvylinda

DYNAMICS

The natural tendency of phrases to get louder as they rise and softer as they descend, which corresponds to the dynamics inherent in the recorder, has already been mentioned. This concept is particularly appropriate for the interweaving voices of Renaissance polyphony, and it is good to keep it in mind as you play. There are other ways of creating dynamic effects, particularly in dance music. You can play the repeats with more spaced articulation to create the illusion of playing softer. Another way is by means of instrumentation, adding and subtracting parts to create the effect of crescendo and decrescendo. Start with the melody line alone and bring the other voices in, one by one, at the beginning of new phrases in the music. This creates the excitement of a crescendo. Dropping voices one by one until only the melody remains produces the effect of a decrescendo. This scheme, of course, only works with pieces that have a clear melody in one part for which the others provide counter-melodies and harmonization, such as the sixteenth-century dance settings of Susato, Attaingnant, et al. The tune, a pop song, is on top, with more or less lively alto, tenor, and bass parts below. Polyphonic pieces, wherein all parts are equal in melodic importance are not susceptible to such add-a-part, subtract-a-part dynamic effects.

INSTRUMENTATION

When you play from music arranged specifically for recorders, instrumentation is no problem since, in effect, it has been done already by the editor. What this usually entails is that the music has been set an octave higher to fit the recorder consort. If we examine the actual ranges of the instruments, this will be easier to understand. The soprano recorder's actual sounding range is from the third space C in the treble clef up two octaves and a whole step to the D six ledger lines above the treble clef. To read the notes at their actual sounding pitches would be inconvenient for the player, who would be confronted with an undue number of ledger lines above the staff, and for the printer, who would have to set these awkward ledger lines. Therefore the common expedient is to notate soprano parts one octave below where they actually sound. The correct editorial procedure to show this transposition is to put a tiny

8 above the clefs of parts so transposed 𝄞 to indicate that the notes will sound an octave higher. Alto and tenor parts are notated at their actual sounding pitch. This is why when you look at a score of recorder music the soprano appears to be lower than the alto.

The actual sounding pitch of the bass recorder's lowest note is the F three ledger lines below the treble clef, or the fourth line of the bass clef. Thus the bass recorder's range straddles the two clefs, and to notate its music at actual sounding pitch would involve using many ledger lines, whatever clef were used. Therefore it is also customary to notate bass parts an octave lower than they actually sound, thus putting them nicely within the bass clef. Again, a tiny 8 above the clef sign indicates this transposition 𝄢. The following illustration shows the recorders' actual ranges and the customary transpositions.

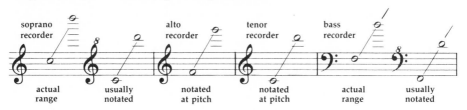

When a consort of recorders is playing from vocal music, i.e., music that has not been arranged for recorders, the soprano and bass read the notes in their customary way; the alto must play his notes an octave higher than written. Since it is the usual practice in vocal music to notate the tenor part an octave *above* where the tenor voice is actually singing, again to avoid ledger lines, the tenor recorder plays the notes as written. These transposed tenor voice lines have an 8 *below* their treble clefs 𝄞. Of course the result is that the recorders will be playing the music an octave higher than it would sound if sung by voices, or played by a consort of krummhorns or viols. Playing music at the actual pitch at which it is notated is referred to as playing at *8-foot pitch.* 8-foot pitch is a term derived from the organ, on which an open pipe eight feet long yields a C two octaves below middle C. Playing the music an octave higher than notated is termed playing at 4-foot pitch, since an open organ pipe four feet long gives a C one octave above that of an eight-foot long pipe. If a harpsichord has three sets of strings, two sets will sound at actual pitch and the third will sound an octave higher. Thus the sets are described as *two eights and a four.* The recorder consort plays at 4-foot pitch.

When a group of recorder players gets together simply to play for their own amusement, the fact that they are playing at 4-foot pitch most of the time is of little consequence since everyone is into the fun of making music. It is when you are preparing a program for an audience that the constant high chirping becomes a problem, and ways must be found to bring variety into the sound by changes of instrumentation. One way has already been described under "Dynamics": gradually building from one voice up to four and then back down again.

The most gratifying change of instrumentation is to get out of the

4-foot octave and down into the 8-foot, and for this some kind of *real* bass instrument, antique or modern, is required. Among modern instruments the guitar sounds very well as the bass for a consort of low recorders. The timbres enhance each other and the guitar's pluck adds rhythmic vitality. A cello played softly and with a minimum of vibrato works well, as does a discreetly played bassoon. Morris Newman is the only bassoonist I have heard displaying such discretion. As a member of the Trio Flauto Dolce (now defunct) he played so delicately that his bassoon matched an alto and a tenor recorder perfectly. Since he also plays recorder, he understands the problem. Modern instruments are built to play much louder than recorders and must be willing to play down all the time if they wish to consort with them.

On the antique side, a bass krummhorn fills the bill if the part doesn't go too high and exceed the instrument's limited range (only up to B-flat below middle C). The same may be said of the bass cornamuse, which is after all merely a krummhorn without the "krumm," i.e., the upward curving tail. The Renaissance rackett (basset or bass) is very successful as a bass for low recorders; as Praetorius observed, this is indeed its best use. It's an ornery little rascal, but when it is under control its soft buzz adds a lush, buttery smoothness to the sound.

The ranges of bass krummhorns and cornamuses, basset and bass racketts, are:

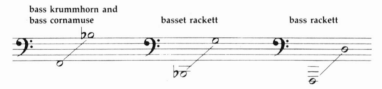

A bass viol, of course, is wonderful, but isn't so easy to find. Viol players prefer to play with other viol players whenever possible. Of course if there aren't any others around, then a viol player might have to play with us. Viol players should be treated with great respect. Somewhat more remote possibilities are the bass dulcian and the sackbut, but both instruments are difficult to control. Few people play them, and fewer still play them well.

Once you've got your real bass instrument, you can use bass recorders for tenor and alto parts. There is much music with tenor parts that fit on a bass recorder, such as the music of the German Renaissance published in Schott's series *Antiqua Chorbuch.* And you can use tenors for the top parts. The lush, dark sound is a wonderful contrast to the silvery

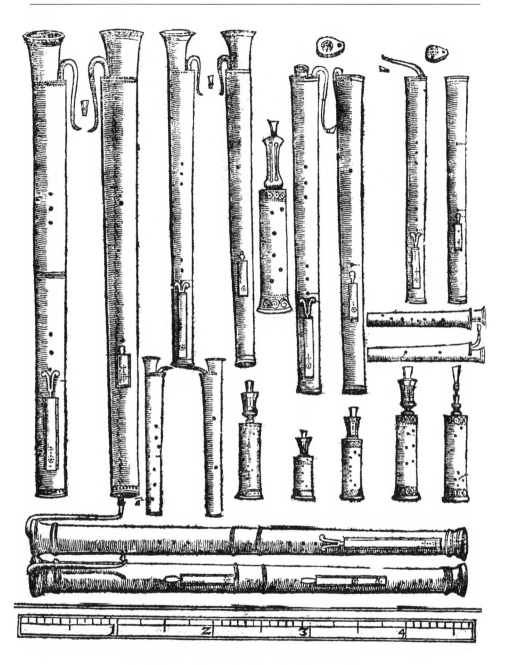

Various sizes of dulcians and racketts, and a bass sordun,
from Praetorius's Syntagmum Musicum.

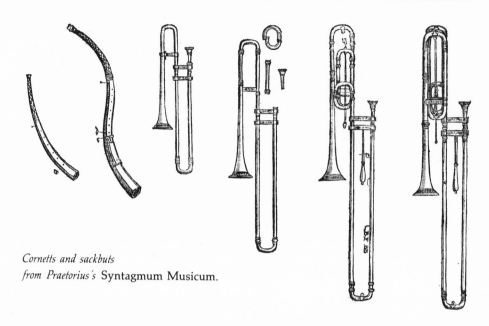

Cornetts and sackbuts
from Praetorius's Syntagmum Musicum.

pipings of the 4-foot choir. A delightful effect is to repeat a section or the whole piece with the top two voices doubled an octave higher by soprano or alto recorders. All of this suggests expanded forces, at least six instruments, including lots of bass and tenor recorders.

Another, and more direct, way to the 8-foot octave is to sing. Much of the music we recorder players use is written in a basically vocal idiom. This is so for virtually all Renaissance music with the obvious exception of music for keyboard, lute, viol consorts, instrumental canzonas, etc. Certainly if the music is supplied with words, singing it is a possibility. Most chansons, lieder, frottole, and such do not demand trained voices for their performance. In fact, they often sound better sung with the relatively straight sound of untrained voices than with the lush, overripe, vibrato-laden sound with which the modern vocalist is trained to sing.

It goes without saying that the lines must be sung in tune, but this is not so difficult as the inexperienced singer might think. For someone who has done little or no singing but is willing to give it a whirl, I offer the following advice:

1. Choose simple music; that is, music which is homophonic (all parts moving together in the same rhythm) with a limited range

in each voice. The previously mentioned collection *Antiqua Chorbuch,* published by Schott, provides much suitable and lovely material for the fledgling chorister.

2. Play your part first on your recorder. No one expects a tyro to be able to sing his part at sight.

3. For best results, memorize your part. This can be done by alternately playing and singing. Also, of course, you must memorize the words. If they are in an unfamiliar foreign language, get someone to help you with the pronunciation. Picking the part out on a keyboard as you sing it is a good way to check your pitches and intonation.

4. Remember that singing requires more support than playing the recorder. "Support" is not a mysterious word: it is the difference between speaking in a loud voice (singing) and in a soft one (playing the recorder). Don't be afraid of singing the wrong note or off-key. These things can be corrected with repetition and application of the rules above, but trying to run your voice with the same minimal pressure appropriate to the recorder will result in frustration.

Once the group has gotten a couple of pieces down, it all becomes much easier and more fun. Part-singing is a much more common musical pastime in England than in America, where so many amateurs labor under the delusion that they are tone-deaf and thus turn to instruments for their musical outlet.

People who claim they are tone-deaf are committing a solecism because if they were tone-deaf they wouldn't be able to notice the difference between what they sing and what the true notes should be. And why would a tone-deaf person have any interest in music at all? It is my opinion that the only tone-deaf person is a deaf person.

In some amateur recorder groups all the members have singing experience, and in many at least one member does, but in some groups no one does, or at least so they believe. But what about in summer camp sitting around the campfire singing "Row, Row, Row Your Boat" or "The Canoe Song" or "She'll Be Comin' Round the Mountain"? What about the uproarious belting out of "Ninety-nine Bottles of Beer on the Wall" with or without a beer in hand, or roaring out one's school song at a football game? What about the national anthem or "America" or "America the Beautiful"? No, I think there are few indeed who have never swelled their vocal cords in song. Here are a couple of ways to begin to use singing along with your recorders.

The famous thirteenth-century English canon "Sumer is icumen in" is a good piece for beginning singers. This canon, or round, is for four voices entering at intervals of two bars (although up to twelve entering at two-bar intervals is perfectly possible). Beneath the canon is a *burden*, or *pes*, a simple two-bar motif which is itself a tiny two-part canon.

The Sumer Canon

Pes (Ground)

Since the pes consists of only eight notes using only four pitches, it's a good place to put the shyest singers.

There are several ways of presenting this charming canon:

1. Begin by having everyone sing the canon together in unison, then after one repetition of the pes let the voices enter one by one until everyone is in. At the end the voices will drop out one by one, the last to enter being the last to end. Just when to drop the pes is a matter of choice. Usually, it is most effective to let the last voice sing his final segment unaccompanied.

2. Do it first on instruments, each person playing the part he will sing, and as each person completes his part on his recorder he immediately returns to the beginning and sings his part through, then once again to the beginning to play the canon on a recorder for the third and final time through. This scheme produces a delightful texture of first all instruments which are gradually supplanted by voices which once again yield to the instruments. Just how to manage the pes in this scheme is again a matter of choice.

To present the canon and the pes completely requires six persons, four for the melody and two for the pes, but it can sound very effective with a minimum of four, two for the pes and two for the canon. There are many early canons and rounds that can receive similar treatment.

Percussion

Percussion instruments, in great variety, have always been used in Western music just as they are used in all of the world's musical cultures. From the earliest times there are depictions of drums of all shapes and sizes, tambourines, bells, clackers, all sorts of noisemakers that keep time and accent the beat. Such rhythmic instruments are so natural to music that it is no surprise to find pictures of angels, peasants, and court musicians hammering bells, beating drums with finger or stick, and clapping hands. This ubiquitous percussive activity is, of course, associated with a certain kind of music. In many cases the pictures make it quite clear what sort of music was being played. We often see scenes of dancers with musicians standing to one side providing the accompaniment, either a single figure playing a three-holed pipe with one hand and a tabor (drum) with

Violas da gamba from Praetorius's Syntagmum Musicum.

the other, or a group of three or four, one of whom is playing a drum. Drums go with the dance, as we all know. To what music an angel is playing a tambourine is less certain, but a medieval gowned figure hammering bells might well be sounding out the slow-moving tenor of a motet. With the exception of a couple of patterns to accompany particular dances, we don't know exactly what these many percussion instruments played, and so we must make our own choices. Music built upon a strong recurring beat invites the use of percussion. The flow of a polyphonic composition generally does not. Wherever percussion seems appropriate and sounds effective we should feel free to use it. I would urge one rule of taste: Less is more. A simple repeated pattern does more for the music than an elaborated tattoo full of improvised riffs and syncopations, which draws too much attention to itself. In a large ensemble of loud instruments, shawms, cornetti, sackbuts, etc., an elaborate percussion part adds to the excitement and is welcome. In a quiet ensemble we need just a touch to provide that extra rhythmic spark.

Orchesography by Thoinot Arbeau, first published in 1589, is a treatise on sixteenth-century social dances which gives the steps, some tunes, and in the case of two dances, a part for the drum. It's a pity that Arbeau wasn't a little more generous in the social dances, since he gives numerous examples of tattoos for "war dances," that is, marching steps.

These two patterns are the only specific percussion parts that we have from the Renaissance, but they are revealing and suggestive in their simplicity.

For the pavane: ♩ ♩ ♩ | ♩ ♩ ♩ |

For the basse danse: ♩ ♩ ♩ ♩ ♩ | ♩ ♩ ♩ ♩ ♩ |

For the pavane, Arbeau supplies music in a four-part setting; for the basse danse, a single melodic line. In both cases the drum part is notated throughout and consists of an unvarying repetition of the appropriate pattern. Obviously Arbeau felt that simple percussion is most effective and useful for the dancers. It is safe to assume that for the dances not supplied with percussion parts, the drum's beat should follow the patterns of the steps. The steps and music of the galliard, for example, have the same rhythmic pattern as "America,"

and the drum enhances both dance and music by following the same pattern.

A good guideline to follow in devising percussion patterns for dance music is to avoid anything that would be confusing to dancers if you were playing for them. An unsteady percussion has no value and it is hard enough for an inexperienced percussion player to play a simple pattern evenly and steadily, so keep it simple and solid. Always bear in mind that the function of percussion is to enhance the music, and if you do choose to venture into elaborations be sure that they serve the music.

The sections that follow offer suggestions to stimulate your percussive muse with different instruments.

DRUMS Any size will do. Smaller, higher-pitched drums go better on fast pieces played by high instruments. Slow pieces on low choirs like a deep, hollow sound from the drum. Experiment with the different sounds produced by striking with a stick, a padded mallet, or the fingers. Different timbres result from striking in the center of the drumhead or to the side. Striking the rim of the drum, especially if the body is made of clay, often yields a pleasing and useful sound.

TAMBOURINES A tambourine is a very flat drum with jingles set into the hoop and a drum skin stretched over one side. It can be played by striking the head with the fingers, which gives both a drum sound and the clashing sound of the jingles. According to how you strike it, you will get more or less of the jingles' jangle. You can also hold it by the rim and strike it against your leg or other hand, on the rim rather than the head, if you want just the sound of the jingles. Professional percussionists produce a shivering "trill" by slowly rubbing a moistened or rosined thumb around the edge of the head, a thrilling effect well worth mastering.

FINGER CYMBALS The trick is to hold one cymbal steady in one hand and strike it on the edge with the other. The fingers should never touch the metal, grasping only the elasticized cloth loops to which the cymbals are attached. The adept can manipulate finger cymbals attached to forefinger and thumb of one hand, but for the novice the two-hand method is easier to control. One-to-a-bar on the downbeat is usually enough for finger cymbals.

GLOCKENSPIEL A gradated set of metal bars set over a sound box, either diatonic (the C scale) or chromatic (with additional bars for the sharps and flats), struck by hard mallets. The chromatic version is more versatile. Doubling the melodic line on the glockenspiel produces a marvelous silvery effect, a pretty surprise for repeats. It is also good as a drone, playing tonic and fifth on the downbeat of each measure. This is good for fleshing out a monophonic medieval tune such as a cantiga or troubador song. Small glockenspiels, such as are used in elementary school music classes, are easily obtained and relatively inexpensive. Use the mallet to strike the bars with a slight flick of the wrist, as you would with other percussion instruments. If the mallet is allowed to rest on the bar for an instant, the vibrations are dampened and you will get a clank instead of a ringing sound.

There are other percussive sounds suitable for early music, but I would exclude maracas, claves, and gourd scrapers.

HARPS AND PSALTERIES These are widely depicted in the hands of medieval and early Renaissance musicians. In the musical iconography of the time the harp symbolized a king (from the biblical King David, who is invariably depicted in medieval manuscripts with harp in hand), and the psaltery was the instrumental symbol of a queen. Aside from their regal implications, both instruments are wonderful additions to a consort of recorders. It is easy to pluck a simple melody on them, or a drone of tonic and fifth. They both share the limitation of being diatonic instruments, so you must find parts for them that do not include chromatic alterations. It was not until the sixteenth century that attempts were made to develop chromatic harps, and these were complicated double- and triple-strung affairs. In the seventeenth century hooks were attached to the crossbar at the top of the harp which when turned to press against a string raised the pitch a half-step. I have seen players using harps of earlier design, without hooks, achieve the same effect by pressing the string against the crossbar with a fingernail or a bit of metal. This is a technique requiring some practice. With a little searching you can find parts for harp and psaltery that do not require incidental sharps or flats. The strings can, of course, be pretuned at will for whatever key you are playing in, but, short of stopping the strings as described above (only possible with harps), once you have tuned to a given key, that's it.

Harps are usually strung with nylon or, rarely, with gut, which is

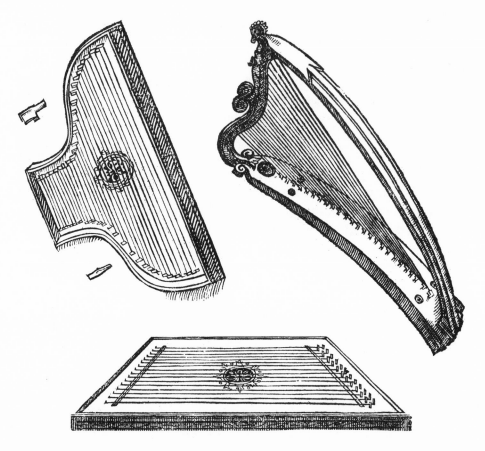

Harp and two forms of psaltery, from Praetorius's Syntagmum Musicum.

the authentic material. Nylon is perfectly satisfactory and more stable than gut, although the specialist may choose gut for its softer, smoother tone color. Metal-strung harps give a sharper, brighter sound. Wire strings are more typical of the traditional Irish harp, whereas Gothic and Renaissance harps were generally strung with gut. For the purposes of an amateur group, such historical niceties are irrelevant and the sounds of wire, gut, or nylon are all equally welcome.

Psalteries are strung with wire and give out a sharp, clear, bright, ringing, and yet ethereal sound very congenial to angels, in whose hands they are often seen, presumably ringing paeans to the Queen of Heaven. Psalteries come in a variety of shapes and with a varying number of strings; to be useful they should have no fewer than ten. The strings, stretched over two bridges, are too high above the sound board to allow stopping against the wood of the instrument as is possible with the strings of a harp, so the psaltery is a strictly diatonic instrument. Nonetheless it is very useful, especially in medieval music.

Harps and psalteries must be tuned by the player, either with the aid of an electronic tuner (there are excellent small, lightweight, battery-operated tuners available by Korg and other manufacturers), a tuning fork, or from a pitch upon which the recorders agree. Get the recorders in tune together before tuning your harps and psalteries. Then take their A or other convenient note upon which there is agreement and proceed to tuning the rest of the strings in fourths, fifths, and octaves. Tuning the strings is not difficult and gets easier with practice. It also provides excellent ear-training. If you find, as is so often the case, that the recorder consort gets noticeably sharper as the instruments warm up in playing, you will want to tune the strings slightly sharp to accommodate to the gradual rise in pitch of the recorders. Winds rise in pitch as they get warmer, and strings drop with a rise in temperature. This is a perennial tuning problem with which mixed ensembles of strings and winds must contend.

There are many individual craftsmen and small workshops producing harps and psalteries in a variety of sizes, shapes, and prices. Their advertisements will be found in such early-music journals as *The American Recorder*. These instruments add visual as well as aural charm to your ensemble. One final word of advice: Guard your tuning wrench as you do your wallet or purse. It is easy to lose and difficult to replace. If you lend it, demand a receipt signed in blood.

PREPARING A PROGRAM

There is nothing that brings an ensemble's skills together better than preparing a program to present for an audience. When we are playing for our own pleasure things can be loose and easy, but when we know that people are going to be listening to what we play, we are stimulated to devote care and attention to our intonation, phrasing, attacks and cutoffs, and to assemble a program that is well balanced and pleasing. However informal the occasion, playing for others encourages us to do our very best. We can play for a group of invited friends, with refreshments to follow, in a church or temple, club or organization, or even present a formal concert with admission fees, depending on the skill, ambition, and experience of the group. A concert is fun to prepare and exciting to perform, and there is no better discipline for getting it all together.

Some people claim they would be much too nervous to be able to play before others. But if you prepare properly, practice your parts thoroughly, and rehearse carefully, you will almost surely please, and as a result of the experience you will learn a good deal. It is a mistake to be afraid of audiences; they generally arrive with pleasant expectations and will not be nearly as critical of your efforts as you are yourselves. When it's all over you can bask in praise and admiration. If there are genuinely critical listeners among your audience, their comments will probably prove instructive. Purely negative remarks such as "That sounded awful" are boorish and should be ignored.

A number of things must be taken into consideration in preparing a successful program. The first is always to choose music that is well within your ability. I have heard many a group founder trying to present a piece that was at the extreme limits of their ability. Even if they got through it, the effect on the audience was more of relief than of pleasure. By the same token, it is wiser to play music that you know well rather than new pieces, unless they are simple. Minor slips are then easily corrected and can pass without notice, instead of causing the music to falter into confusion or even come to a halt. An easy piece played well evokes more pleasure than a difficult one barely gotten through. Your goal is to please, not to astonish.

The program should always begin with a sure winner, which puts both you and your audience at ease and in a positive frame of mind. This rule is forgotten so often that I repeat it: Start with a piece that is sure to please and that you are sure to play well. It may be an old chestnut and maybe everyone in the audience knows it already. So much the better; hearing something familiar is never a bad beginning so long as it's a good tune, such as "Pastime with Good Company" or even "Greensleeves." It should also be a cheerful, positive piece unless your programmatic theme is exclusively tears and melancholy, which is inadvisable in any case.

The major piece on the program, in terms of length, seriousness, and complexity, should come at the end of the first part, if there is an intermission, or two-thirds to three-quarters of the way through an uninterrupted concert. The part after the "big" piece should consist of lighter pieces, and you should end with the lightest, brightest, jolliest piece in your repertoire.

You should group pieces: three fantasias, four villancicos, five chansons, a dance suite, etc. These groupings can be made clear on the printed program, if there is one, or in the oral announcement. Medieval and Renaissance musical forms are short compared to those of the Classical and Romantic periods, so you should, in effect, make longer pieces by making groups of smaller pieces. It is ridiculous to have applause after every one- or two-minute piece. This concept of grouping encourages you to select pieces that are relevant to one another in terms of similarity or contrast of mood, tempo, key, and instrumentation. For example, you might choose a grave fantasia in a minor key followed by a light one in a major key, or two chansons of a moderate character followed by one which is solemn and ending with one which is lighthearted and gay. When you are grouping pieces you should try minimizing the space between one and the next, leaving just time enough for the effect of one to sink in before beginning the next, but not so much time that your hearers' attention begins to wander. Achieving this should be part of your rehearsal routine.

Dance suites are best presented *segue,* that is, the galliard should follow immediately after the pavane with perhaps a measure of percussion to establish the new tempo, with the branle or some other very quick dance bursting out after the galliard. A dance suite can be assembled from many sources so long as they are of the same period and character. For example, dances from Attaingnant, Susato, de Tertre, and Moderne, Franco-Flemish mid-sixteenth century, all go very well together, but a dance by Holborne or Dowland wouldn't fit with them. The dances of an assembled suite do not all have to be in the same key. Indeed, a change of key is refreshing, but the new key should be related to that of the preceding piece, for example, a sequence of pieces in C Major, G Major, G Minor, C Major. Changes of instrumentation from one dance to the next also provide pleasing contrast: perhaps a pavane on low recorders, galliard same with top voices doubled an octave higher, a branle on four krummhorns (if you're lucky enough to have them), and a final branle on high recorders. For the final branle, you might use the technique of starting with a single melody line and gradually introducing the other parts, described above. Of course, percussion of all sorts—drum, cymbals, tambourine, glockenspiel—can be added freely as a cook adds spices. Instrumenting a dance suite for contrast and variety is fun, and a great way to exercise your imagination and taste. If, however, your forces are limited to four recorders—soprano, alto, tenor, bass—don't be dismayed. A dance suite played through with just those instruments will be nonetheless pleasing if the segues are crisp and secure.

What kind of a program to present? Essentially there are two kinds: a potpourri and a thematic program. A potpourri program consists of music drawn from various periods, styles, and countries. The topic of a thematic program may be broad or it may be quite specific; it may be, e.g., the music of Spain, or Spanish music of the sixteenth century, or the *Cantigas de Santa Maria.* In any case, it must all relate to the stated theme. A group that is just beginning to give concerts will of necessity offer a potpourri, since their repertoire will be too limited to permit them to assemble an entire program with a single theme. However, even within such a program it is wise to make groups of pieces that do have thematic unity, e.g., two motets and an estampie can comprise a medieval group, followed by, say, some pieces of Josquin and his contemporaries; then perhaps a Baroque piece if you have the forces for it, and ending with a group of Elizabethan songs and dances.

Chronological sequence is less important here than a balance of sonorities and forms. Thus in this hypothetical program I suggest putting the Baroque piece—a sonata, trio sonata, or chamber cantata—in the third spot, since it is likely to be the longest and weightiest item on the program. It should appear when both audience and players are warmed up and ready for something substantial. And after that comes "dessert." These rules are not hard and fast; the Baroque piece may well come last as the culmination of all that went before. The point is that a good program should be planned like a menu, a menu for a musical feast.

A thematic program can be built on an infinite number of ideas, but should be guided by two principles. The first has just been discussed, that of a well-planned feast balancing light and heavy, serious and gay, in a satisfying sequence. The second principle is that the material should as much as possible really illuminate the topic. "Music for Spring" should show how composers depict the joys of springtime in music. A program built on *cantus firmus* compositions should illuminate the various ways composers have utilized this musical form. A program billed as "Music for Christmas" should, in my opinion, include some items that are familiar and traditional. "Christmas Music from Czechoslovakia," on the other hand, doesn't raise false expectations of "Lo How a Rose Ere Blooming" or "The First Nowell." Assembling music for a thematic program is a great educational experience because you will surely have to go to reference books and card catalogues to find enough music to fill out your program. And you will have a good time doing it.

I will end with a few admonitions about the length of your program. In a word: avoid long programs. It is far preferable to leave your audience wanting more than to have them wondering when the performance will be over. The more inexperienced the group, the more this applies. Forty to forty-five minutes is a good length for a concert without intermission, an hour and twenty minutes to an hour and a half with intermission. You should time your pieces. Figure twenty to twenty-five minutes of solid music if there is to be no intermission, and forty to forty-five if there is one. The rest of the time will be filled with changing instruments, seatings, explanatory remarks to the audience or reading of texts (if you choose to do so), and, let us hope, applause.

In all but the most formal situations, addressing a few words to your audience is helpful in establishing rapport and setting people at ease. Such remarks should be brief, concise, friendly, and informative. If you have nothing to say, don't. If you have a lot to say, edit. If you do speak, be sure you are clearly audible. Oral commentary should add to the experience; otherwise skip it. Never, never, never turn a concert into a lecture.

Don't lengthen your concert unnecessarily with time spent looking for the next piece of music or the next instrument you are going to play. The music should be in the proper order, with penciled reminders where necessary. Instruments should be tuned in advance and if a tuning chord is required, that should be practiced in rehearsal as an integral part of the piece. Establish who is to give starts and cutoffs for each piece, and be sure everyone has this marked in his music so everyone will know whom to watch. The person who is to give the downbeat, or whatever gesture he will use to begin a piece, should be sure he has everyone's eye before making it. This gesture should be established and its clarity assured in rehearsal. When preparing a concert, you should rehearse not only the music but everything you will be doing on stage. You will convey conviction if you look as though you know what you're doing and the best way to achieve this is to know what you're going to do. Preparation of this sort is an excellent hedge against nervousness and stage fright.

Stage fright, performance nerves, or whatever you want to call it, deserves a comment. I don't believe there is anyone with such sangfroid as not to feel excitement in some form when performing. It may be pleasurable exhilaration or fearful anxiety. In any case, the adrenals are pumping and this is the one thing for which you cannot rehearse. It takes an audience to get the adrenaline up. But you can prepare for this unique experience in advance by knowing what to expect, especially at the beginning. Because you are very excited, whether pleasurably or fearfully, it is easy for your attention to wander. Therefore concentrate very hard on what you are doing. After the first couple of numbers you will settle down a bit, but even then you must keep your concentration on your music. Distraction is a very powerful force when one is before an audience. If you have the security of careful preparation, and you keep your concentration, the stimulus of performance will make you play better than you ever have before. Ill-prepared spots will be fraught with anxiety and will probably go wrong. So prepare! If you cannot play something consistently well in rehearsal, don't attempt to perform it. Miracles don't happen. One can simulate to some degree the excitement of the performance in rehearsal by pretending that it is the performance, saying you will go on no matter what happens. It is surprising how often this game of "let's pretend" will actually induce an instructive degree of nervousness and distraction. Expect to be nervous, expect to be excited, expect to be distracted, and practice concentration. Then, when the big moment arrives, you will be prepared.

When you perform, you are bringing a gift of music to your audience. Make it the best you can possibly offer. Prepare it thoughtfully and well and you will be gratefully received.

Chapter 7

SELECTING
AND CARING FOR
YOUR RECORDER

PLASTIC RECORDERS

In recent years the problem of choosing one's first recorder has been much simplified by the advent of good and inexpensive plastic instruments. One can buy sopraninos, sopranos, and altos in plastic which are comparable in appearance and playing qualities to wooden instruments that cost many times their price. Not all plastic instruments are good, but there are three firms whose products I do recommend: Aulos, Dolmetsch, and Zen-On. Aulos makes sopraninos and sopranos in both two- and three-piece (separate foot-joint) models, and they are all good, as is their three-piece alto. The Dolmetsch plastic soprano is excellent, with a clear, bright tone. Also, it is the most nearly indestructible instrument on the market. Dolmetsch altos are less successful than the Aulos or the Zen-On products. The Zen-On soprano (Stanesby Jr. model) and alto (Bressan model) were designed by the distinguished Boston maker of fine recorders, Friedrich von Huene. Both are excellent and beautifully finished.

Both Aulos and Dolmetsch produce a plastic tenor, but neither instrument is successful. The Aulos is quite heavy to hold and tends to overall sharpness as well as other intonation faults. The Dolmetsch plastic tenor is even more out of tune with itself. Both instruments are inexpensive, but their intonational shortcomings cause much grief to a consort seeking to play in tune, and so, regretfully, I do not recommend them. In future models these makers may succeed in eliminating the design flaws and be able to provide us with a much-needed inexpensive tenor recorder.

As of this writing, no maker has produced a plastic bass. An instrument of such size may approach the point of diminishing returns, being too heavy in plastic and more easily made of wood.

No plastic, mass-produced recorder is as good as a fine wooden one, but plastic has certain advantages, especially for the novice. Plastic instruments do not shrink and swell as wooden ones do, and thus never need revoicing. If the windway becomes clogged with cracker crumbs or other residues, it can be flushed out with soap and water. Plastic will not crack in cold weather or hot sun. You can take it to the shore and even drop it in the water with no harm done. If it is lost, you need not be distraught, for there is another just like it waiting to be bought at the music store for a modest sum. And since they all come from the exact same mold, you don't need to select. They are more alike than peas in a pod. The chief disadvantage of plastic is that it does not absorb moisture as does the cedar plug of a wooden instrument. Therefore the windway of plastic recorders is much more prone to clogging. This can be considerably alleviated by the occasional application to the windway of a dilute solution of a mild detergent such as Ivory Liquid. One drop to a tablespoon of water is about right. Dribble this solution through the windway so that all surfaces are thoroughly wetted as well as the blade, then blow out the excess and wipe. The detergent's wetting action reduces surface tension, causing moisture to flow away rather than to stand in droplets on the plastic's shiny surface. This treatment usually lasts for several days and can be repeated ad infinitum.

Plastic instruments are ideal for beginners. Children (ages seven to nine) should start on soprano, since their small hands usually cannot accommodate the wider stretch required by the alto. For adult beginners, however, the alto is usually best. The lower tone is mellower and easier to control, and it is for the alto that most of the authentic literature specifically for recorder is written. Playing Baroque music is usually the adult beginner's first interest, and almost all of it is for the alto recorder.

Some people object to plastic on aesthetic grounds; wood is more beautiful, it's warmer, it's more natural. All quite true, but for musical purposes an instrument, regardless of its appearance or the materials of its construction, is a tool and not an *objet d'art.* It is what it does that counts, not what it looks like, and one doesn't put a very fine tool in someone's hands before he has learned to use it. The fact is that a beginner who starts on a wooden recorder usually ruins it in the process of learning how to play, and the better and more refined the instrument the more surely this is so. A beginner shouldn't get a wooden recorder until he has earned it, and in the meantime should be grateful that there are such good plastic instruments as those mentioned above to learn on. There are ugly plastic instruments (though none among those I recommend), just as there are ugly wooden ones. Both are usually inferior musical instruments, but a pretty instrument is not necessarily a good musical tool.

WOODEN RECORDERS

If you are a beginner who has somehow acquired a cheap wooden instrument, in most cases you will be better off to replace it with a good plastic to learn on. But at a certain point in your progress you will want to graduate to a good wooden recorder, and here things become more difficult because, unlike plastic, wooden instruments are *not* all alike. Even from the same maker and in the same wood, recorders vary widely in quality from one instrument to the next, and so you must select. If there is no music store in your area which has a number of instruments from which to choose and you therefore must order by mail, be sure that you can return the instrument if you are not satisfied with it. Any reputable dealer will do this as a matter of course. Naturally it is better if you can make your own choice since dealers, in spite of kind words to the contrary, do not have time to sit down and test a number of instruments before wrapping one up and sending it out. They will simply go to their stock and pull out a recorder of the model and wood you have ordered, so you are buying a pig in a poke. It may be a wonderful pig, but it may not.

Recorders are made from a great variety of woods, ranging from the exotic hardwoods, grenadilla, boxwood, ironwood, bubinga, olivewood, and rosewood, to the more mundane softer woods such as maple, cherry, plum, and pear. One sees advertisements in which different qualities of tone, response, and loudness are ascribed to instruments made of these various woods. Such claims are ninety percent hogwash. There is more variation from one instrument to the next in the same wood than in instruments made of different woods. Recorders made of exotic woods have a more striking appearance and, being made of rarer materials, they are more expensive, but the higher price does not guarantee a better instrument. Wood of any kind, being a natural substance, is as variable as Nature herself, and fashioning a fine recorder out of it involves the balancing of many dimensions. Subtle variations in the bore or thickness of the wall, the size, placement, and possible undercutting of tone holes, thickness of the blade, the distance between blade and windway (cut-up), chamfers cut into the wood at the top and bottom of the exit of the windway, and the extremely delicate dimensions of the windway itself to create the optimum focus of the breath stream against the tone-producing blade—all of these variables and more must be juggled against one another. Success is not easy to achieve. There is always an element of chance in making a recorder. Friedrich von Huene, whose instruments are among the most highly prized (and priced) recorders in the world, has summed up the matter nicely: "If I knew how to make a perfect recorder, I would make a perfect recorder every time."

While the true test of a recorder comes in the playing, there are things you can check with your eye. It is not desirable to have a heavy lacquered finish on either the outside or in the bore, since this prevents the wood from "breathing," that is, responding to humidity changes. A thick, heavy finish, especially in the bore, prevents bore oil from penetrating the wood to fill and preserve the tiny tubules of the wood fibers. Such heavy lacquer or epoxy finishes also change the vibrational characteristics of the wood, transforming it in effect into plastic. These heavy finishes are easy to perceive. If as you peer down the bore you see an extremely smooth and shiny surface that is glassy to the touch, chances are that it has been plasticized with too heavy a finish. A light, thin coat of lacquer has a dull, uneven shininess, and is acceptable. An oil finish, which is the most desirable, has a dull, smooth, matte appearance. Many recorders appear to have no finish at all. The wood in the bore looks perfectly dry. So long as the surface is smooth and free of any tiny slivers

Carved ivory alto recorder by I. B. Gahn, Nuremberg, c 1700.
The Crosby Brown Collection of the Metropolitan Museum of Art

or gouges, this is all right, but the first thing you will want to do with such an instrument when you get it home is to apply bore oil (about which more later). In general, the surfaces of the instrument should be smooth, clean, and even; it should be a very nicely turned and finished piece of wood. A carefully finished instrument which nonetheless has many tiny pores on the surface of the wood is less desirable than one that is perfectly smooth; in other words, the wood is too porous, less airtight than a smoother wood, and yields a duller tone. Also, a pore might occur just where the maker has cut the edge of the blade, creating a little nick that is very difficult to remove. The various kinds of rosewood often display pores.

There are some visual checks you can make on the head joint. Holding the instrument up against a bright source of light, squint through the windway from the beak end. You should see a very thin line of light at the nether end. If there is no line of light the plug is too high and the instrument probably will not play well. Conversely, if the line is too thick the plug is too low and again the tone will be adversely affected.

Looking at the lower end of the windway, you should see a narrow exit slot of uniform height all the way across. In the best of the old instruments and good modern copies of them, this exit slot will be anywhere from .6 to .9 millimeter high. In most modern mass-produced instruments the slot will vary from .9 to 1.2 millimeters in height. Both the upper and lower edges of the exit slot should have chamfers cut at about a 45-degree angle and of a width somewhat less than the thickness of a nickel. These chamfers should be smooth and even all the way across, with no nicks or bumps. Examine the edge of the blade. It should be evenly and sharply cut with no nicks or gouges, and it should be exactly parallel with the exit of the windway. Tone holes should be neatly and roundly cut. Undercutting to make the holes larger on the bore side than on the exterior, especially when neatly done, is a sign of careful handwork performed with sharp tools, and usually betokens a superior instrument.

Ivory trim is in general more decorative than functional. Actually, most makers these days eschew the use of real ivory out of concern over the depredations of poaching ivory hunters on the few remaining herds of elephants, and so resort instead to plastic with the appearance of ivory. Ivory or ivory-like rings at the joints supposedly strengthen them, but in fact the wood beneath must be turned so thin to accommodate the rings that it is made more fragile, particularly if the ring itself should crack, as not infrequently happens. Nonetheless, most better instruments have them, so don't worry; just handle your instrument carefully. A thick ring added to the bottom of the foot joint may have a positive structural function, lengthening an instrument which in the finishing is discovered to have too short a bore. My favorite alto, a von Huene in ironwood, has a fat turning at the bottom in the proscribed ivory. It's beautiful, and I confess I'm grateful that it is there. Sleeving of the mouthpiece with ivory acts as a prosthesis for a cracked head joint. Without a crack the sleeve is mere embellishment. My ironwood alto is so embellished. I chose it from among a group of others on musical grounds, but I was glad that it was the most gorgeous as well as the best playing instrument. With use ivory mouthpieces tend to discolor where the mouth touches them. An ivory bushing on the thumbhole is a very good thing, since the ivory or other, very hard ivory-like substance resists the abrasive action of the thumbnails of those players who use the pinching action to crack the thumbhole to get the upper registers. Even the hardest woods, however, are eventually gouged out by constant pinching, and the response of the high notes suffers. The cure is to insert a bushing if one wasn't there in the first place.

The first playing test should be to blow long tones on each note of the instrument. See how much air each can take and how softly you can blow without a radical drop in pitch. Pay special attention to the next to the bottom note (low G on altos and basses, low D on sopranos and tenors). This note is notoriously prone to burble. If it burbles at normal breath pressure, reject the instrument. If a burble appears only with strong pressure it is acceptable, and no burble at all means the instrument should receive strong consideration. The gamut of tones should be relatively even in volume if not in timbre. The highest notes should come clearly and evenly without undue breath pressure, and they should be free of extraneous fizzy sounds. The beau ideal we seek is an instrument that is both full at the bottom and limpid and easy at the top. Usually a compromise must be struck.

If we are satisfied with the gamut, we proceed to check for intonation. The first check is to see if the instrument plays at standard concert pitch, A–440. You must bear in mind that recorders, like all wind instruments, play sharper as they warm up; so warm an instrument before testing, or expect it to blow a little flat to A–440. A tuning fork is not ideal for this test, since the fork itself changes pitch slightly with changes in temperature. It is better to use an electronic tuner, such as the small, battery-operated model by Korg. These devices have the added advantage of allowing you to check every note of the chromatic scale rather than the single tone of a tuning fork. You can either set the tuner to "meter" and observe the response of the needle as you blow, or switch the tuner to produce tones and listen for beatless unisons. The danger in either case is that you accommodate your breath to try to match the tuner. The safest method is to start blowing the recorder first, then turn on the tuner to see how closely they match. An instrument that tends overall to be slightly sharp, and in my experience most do, will probably not cause you problems. One that is flat will be a continuing liability, since others will always have to tune down to you. A distinctly sharp instrument, even if lovely and nicely in tune with itself, should be rejected unless you expect to play only by yourself.

Once you are satisfied that an instrument is in tune to standard pitch, you should check its octaves, C to C', A to A', etc. This can be done by ear, but if an electronic tuner is at hand it provides a safer and more accurate check. Also check fifths, C to G, G to D, etc. A dealer once told me of a teacher who in testing an instrument made a practice of running through the circle of fifths, playing arpeggios in each successive key with astonishing rapidity. But, aside from the fact that this is an overly rigorous test for the average amateur to perform, I would question any routine that is performed too quickly. Go slow so you really have time to listen.

When an instrument has passed the tuning tests, you should check it for ease of articulation, trying various degrees of attack with both single- and double-tonguing. If the lowest and highest notes respond only with the lightest of tonguings, or the high notes must be attacked strongly to sound, do not choose this instrument.

When you have found an instrument that looks right, sounds right, and plays right, try it with a few familiar tunes and technical passages, just to see how it feels to you. If it feels congenial or if, as is more likely, you find yourself falling in love with it, then it is the instrument to choose. Selecting a fine recorder is an exacting and time-consuming process. If you feel unsure of your own ability to judge, take along a more experienced player or your teacher to help you. If you take your teacher, you should offer to pay for the service, and whoever helps you should be taken out for a celebratory treat once the selection has been made. Don't buy an instrument just because it's the best of the lot if you are not genuinely satisfied. It's foolish to spend time and money getting a recorder that doesn't make you happy.

Playing a New Wooden Recorder

By and large, a new recorder does not improve as you play it, although one often has the illusion that this is so. In reality, you are gradually learning the characteristics of your new instrument and how to handle them, so more than likely it is you who are improving, not the instrument. A good maker voices his instruments for optimum results. How else could he balance the variables? When someone tells me he is having trouble with a new instrument because "it isn't broken in yet," I think, nonsense! Either he hasn't learned to play it yet, or the instrument is faulty.

There are conflicting opinions about beginning to play a new recorder. The general wisdom is that this should be done slowly, with fifteen minutes of playing a day for the first week, twenty the next, and so on, in order to let the wood adjust gradually to the humidifying effect of the breath, and thus avoid cracking the instrument. There is, however, a contrary opinion that suggests longer playing from the start, say half an hour the first day and increasing playing time more rapidly, the idea being that if the wood has an inherent flaw that will lead to cracking, you may as well find out while the warranty is still in effect. I favor this latter view. This is not to imply that you should abuse a new instrument by playing it for hours when you first get it. You should warm it carefully, especially the head joint, by putting it in your pocket or holding it under your arm for a few minutes. This reduces condensation of moisture from the breath onto the instrument. Dry the bore thoroughly after playing and leave the disassembled instrument in a spot where it will not be chilled by cold air. The function of the cedar plug is to absorb moisture and reduce clogging in the windway. The plug indeed does absorb more than the wood which surrounds it. If the instrument is chilled after playing, the surrounding wood contracts more than the moisture-laden plug, and the resulting stresses can easily lead to cracking. This is as true of old recorders as it is of new ones, which is why when you go out into the wintry night after a session of playing, you should keep the head joints of your recorders inside your coat. A thoroughly seasoned piece of wood has a moisture content of 6 percent or less. Getting wood to this state is a time-consuming process. In the old days the sawed wood was first dried, then left out in the wind and the rain, then brought in and dried again for a number of years, at which point it was completely stabilized and ready to be made into an instrument. Today, with the vast amounts of wood being consumed in the manufacture of recorders, there isn't time for this laborious process, so quicker methods of kiln-drying under controlled humidity have been used, with varying success: New England maple responds well to this treatment and is favored by American makers, but exotic hardwoods are trickier to handle. The sad fact is that most mass-produced recorders are made from imperfectly dried and seasoned woods. Sooner or later, checks, cracks, and splits are likely to occur, so playing such an instrument for a few minutes a day when it is new, and increasing the time very slowly, may well be just postponing the inevitable.

Swabbing Out the Recorder

Do not use those pretty swabs consisting of fluff on a twisted wire stick that are usually supplied with a new recorder. The fluff comes off easily and gets caught in the bore. A length of string with a small weight on one end and a piece of clean cotton or linen cloth on the other makes a good fluff-free swab. Just drop the weight down the bore and draw the cloth through. This doesn't serve for the head joint, so you can use the wire swab, draping a piece of cloth over the offending fluff. Swabbing of any kind should be a gentle action. Repeated forcing of a bulky swab through the bore will eventually alter its dimensions, and in effect ream it out. Particular care should be taken with the foot end of the center joint where on fine instruments the bore contracts imperceptibly.

In addition to moisture from condensation, recorders can and frequently do get wet from actual saliva drooling from the player's mouth into the instrument. Some people drool more readily than others, but we all should try as much as possible to prevent saliva from getting on our instruments. Besides the obvious clogging problem, saliva contains chemicals that over time build up a residue on the surfaces of the windway to the detriment of the voicing.

Here, a strong cautionary note about clearing a moisture-clogged windway: The common procedure is to place a finger over the window to prevent the instrument from shrieking, and then to blow a strong blast of air through the windway. This practice is bad for several reasons. First, the fingers should never touch the blade, since there are oils and chemicals on the fingers which are deleterious to the wood. Second, repeated finger pressure against the thin and delicate blade will distort it and ruin the voicing. Third, blowing air at high pressure through the instrument is not good for its response. And fourth, humid air from the breath has less clearing effect than drawing in the drier surrounding air. Thus the correct way to clear the windway is to suck air in through the windway with a sharp intake of breath. This method is more effective, is quieter, and can be combined with catching a breath between phrases. *This is important, so I repeat: do not blow out to clear the windway; suck in!* Never touch the blade with your finger. If you have any doubt, a glance at the discoloration of the wood around the finger holes will convince you that there is chemical action of the fingers on the wood.

When the weather is muggy or it is raining and the atmospheric humidity is very high, instruments get wet and stay wet, and clogging windways become a great problem. One solution is the drop of mild detergent in a tablespoon of water mentioned above. Another is the use of an electric hair dryer switched to "cold" (no heat) and directed to send a stream of air through the head joint at the bottom end. This method works very well and does not harm the recorder, but I feel trepidation in recommending it: *Heated* air will certainly harm it. If your hair dryer does not have an adjustment for blowing unheated air (but I believe they all do), do not use it for this purpose. It should only be used as a portable fan, and indeed a fan does the job almost as well, though it does not provide as focused a stream of air. Do you understand, dear reader? A hair dryer blowing *unheated* air helps cloggy windways on soggy days.

Revoicing

As an instrument is played, the wood responds to the moisture of the breath, slightly swelling and distorting, especially at the windway, where the moisture is greatest. Thus the voicing changes, usually for the worse, so recorders after being played for a time need to be revoiced. The most likely change is that the plug will swell and expand upward into the free space of the windway. Likewise the wood of the head joint itself may swell downward into the windway. Or the woods may simply distort. These changes are minute and may not be perceptible to the inexperienced eye, but what will be perceived is that the instrument is not playing as well as when you first got it. The high notes become elusive, the low notes weak, the tone is stuffy, and the instrument clogs up frequently. All of these are signs that it is time for a revoicing. It is not generally understood that recorders need revoicing from time to time in the natural course of things. We tend to think that once we've bought an instrument, that's it. Revoicing is not a radical operation. A moment's thought about the changeable nature of wood will disabuse us of this fearful notion. A new instrument may benefit from revoicing twice in its first year and perhaps annually for the next couple of years. Then the wood will become more stable and subsequent revoicings will be more of a cleaning operation rather than any actual altering of the wood.

Revoicing is *not* a project for the amateur. Even an expert repairman is learning on the first one hundred to one hundred fifty recorders he voices. The dimensions involved are numerous and extremely delicate. To know them and control them requires long experience and a very sharp and well-trained eye. Any amateur attempts are likely to botch the job irreparably, so hands off! Where, then, does one send a recorder when it begins to show signs of unwelcome change? Back to the maker, or to a repairman authorized by him. Some makers will not accept their own instruments back for revoicing if the instruments show signs of having been worked on by somebody else. Good repairmen are aware of this and will refuse to work on such instruments. Most American makers of quality instruments willingly take their instruments back for revoicing and other adjustments or repairs.

If you have an instrument whose maker is obscure or unknown, then you must apply to one of the handful of competent craftsmen who offer the service of revoicing. They are often recorder makers themselves, but not all makers are willing to service instruments other than their own. A good repairman will restore your recorder to its original state with little if any change. Indeed, the instrument may come back better than ever. If it truly is in need of revoicing, it will certainly be improved. Recorders don't get played out, but they do need adjustments, as do all musical instruments.

Oiling the Bore

Wood, even the hardest and most dense, is somewhat porous, not entirely airtight. Thus bore oil. Bore oil—usually raw (unboiled) linseed oil —conditions, preserves, and seals the wood. It makes the bore smooth, even, and uniform, and tone and response are improved. If the bore looks and feels dry, it is in need of oiling. If a drop of oil placed on the surface of the wood is absorbed almost immediately, the wood is thirsty and needs oiling. Some bores have been coated with varnish or epoxy, and if this is heavy, oil simply cannot penetrate it. With a thinner coat the oil will eventually get through, but it will take longer. Don't play on an instrument for a day or so before oiling it so it will be relatively dry. The oil is applied with a swab, as described under "Swabbing Out the Recorder," that is reserved for this purpose. All of the bore of the foot joint and the center section should receive oil, but in the head joint you should oil no higher than half an inch below the window. Oil should never touch any part of the plug, the windway, or the blade, since moisture tends to form droplets on an oily surface—just what we do not want in the sound-producing part of the instrument. Do not sop the bore with oil but put on enough to produce a glistening surface. The oil should be left on for several hours, up to a day or more, so that the wood has a chance to absorb as much as it can. Then thoroughly wipe out the excess. If all the oil has disappeared and the wood still appears dry, it would probably be wise to give it a second application. A successful job of oiling and wiping will leave the bore smooth but not oily to the touch. A new instrument can be oiled every six weeks or so, as long as the wood continues to absorb the oil. Eventually every six months to a year may be sufficient. Bores with heavy finishes and wax-impregnated instruments which do not absorb oil benefit from an occasional application, nonetheless, just as a cleansing treatment.

The exterior of the recorder, if not varnished or otherwise rendered impervious, will also benefit from an occasional light application of oil, again left on for a while before a thorough wiping and polishing. It's good for the wood, which will be penetrated from both sides, and its appearance will be enhanced. Of course one must be careful not to let any oil touch the plug, windway, or blade.

Loose Joints

The tenons at either end of the middle joint of a recorder are lapped with a thin layer of cork so they will make a snug and airtight fit in the corresponding sockets of foot and head joints. The cork should be lubricated lightly with cork grease, not only so that the sections will slide together easily but also to avoid excessive friction between cork and socket, which will tend to pull the cork away from the tenon.

Eventually, of course, the cork will either tear or become so com-

pressed that the joint becomes loose and wobbly. A radical—and temporary—solution for this problem is to swell the cork by moistening it
thoroughly and then subjecting it to the heat of a match briefly until the
moisture has dried, revolving the barrel and trying to keep the heat of
the flame only near the cork. The dangers of this procedure are obvious:
it is all too easy to char the cork or even the wood, although the cork does
swell quite miraculously. I perform this fire-and-water-make-steam act
from time to time as a quick expedient, but I feel uneasy while doing it
and I don't recommend it. Better to take the instrument to a repairman
for a relapping of fresh cork. Or do as the ancients did, and wrap the
tenons with fine cotton or linen thread. Two or three layers may be
required to get enough thickness for a snug fit. The thread should be
wrapped tight enough to hold its place but not so tight as to put undue
constricting pressure on the tenon. There is a neat trick of starting with
a vertical loop of thread, the loop extending beyond the tenon toward
the center of the joint and the free end hanging below the tenon. You
then proceed to wrap over this loop, contriving to finish the wrapping
on the loop side of the tenon. Then put the final free end of the thread
through the loop and pull the initial free end of the thread which is on
the other side of the wrapping, thus drawing both the loop and the final
free end under the wrapped thread. Snip off the excess bit of thread and
both ends will be securely held beneath the wrapping. (See illustration.)
Thread-wrapping, like cork, should be kept lubricated. In assembling a
recorder you should screw the joints together rather than push them
together vertically, always moving in the same direction as the thread is
wrapped or the cork is overlapped.

Wrapping the tenons with thread

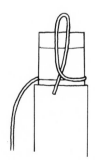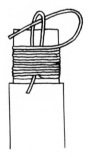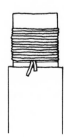

Tuning and Retuning

In the tuning of a consort of recorders, the usual procedure is to determine who has the lowest instrument and have everyone else pull out their recorders' head joints to be more or less in agreement with it. This is a less than perfect expedient for a couple of reasons. First, pulling out the head joint has considerably more flattening effect on open notes (G, F, E, and D on the alto) than on the notes with more fingers down. The vibrating column of air inside the instrument is shorter for the open notes and therefore pulling out to lengthen it will have a proportionally greater effect than doing so would on the longer vibrating column we are making when we have more fingers down. Also, when the head joint and center joint are fitted snugly together the bore is continuous from head joint to center joint. As the tenon of the center joint is pulled out from the socket of the head joint, a space is created in the bore. This extra space in the bore has a disconcerting effect on the intonation of the instrument because it is not the same for the lower register as it is for the upper register. Specifically, this ring of extra space in the bore *increases* the flattening effect of pulling out for the lower register, but *decreases* the flattening effect of pulling out for the upper register, especially for the notes A, C, and D in the upper register. Thus if we pull out enough to get the lower register in tune we are likely to wind up with an upper register that is sharp. If the octaves between lower and upper registers are in tune with the joints fully pushed together, they will get wider as the joints are pulled apart, and if the upper register is sharp to the lower to start with, pulling out will only make it sharper still. This extra ring of space indeed is a devil for intonation.

The solution is to eliminate it by filling it in with a ring of wood or plastic of the same size as the space. Many professional recorder players have such rings of various thicknesses which either singly or in combination fill in the gremlin space, restore the bore's continuity, and equalize the effect of pulling out on the upper and lower registers. Such tuning rings should be standard accessories, provided by every maker to fit the recorders of his manufacture. Indeed, a set should be included with every Baroque-style recorder with any pretensions to quality that is sold. Alas, this is not the case, so we must improvise, looking for washers and bushings of the right dimensions or making slices from bits of tubing of the appropriate thickness and diameter. It's a bother, but the beneficial effects for tuning make it worthwhile searching around for something that will serve. Perhaps a few letters to the makers would encourage them to supply this need. They are the logical persons to do so, since they have created the bore dimensions and tenon thicknesses of their instruments. They have the appropriate measurements and could easily supply rings of the correct size, thereby saving us a lot of running around and trial and error.

There is another way of flattening a sharp recorder more or less uniformly, but it is considerably more cumbersome and unaesthetic than the invisible and easily slipped-in tuning rings. Nonetheless, it is an effective expedient and should be described. Lining the top and sides of the window with strips of Plasticine (a children's modeling compound) flattens all the notes, open and closed, almost equally. It doesn't look pretty but it can transform a hopelessly sharp recorder into a usable instrument. The compound should be affixed to the exterior surface only. None should impinge on the inner surfaces of the windway. Experimentation will tell you how much is needed.

When a recorder is out of tune with itself, we generally send it to an expert repairman for retuning. By altering the tone holes or making adjustments in the bore, many faults can be corrected, though by no means all, since changing a single hole may affect more than one note, and in opposite ways. In a simple situation where only one note will be affected, the general rule is to enlarge the first open hole below if the note is flat and to make the hole smaller if the note is sharp. Undercutting a hole may also solve a problem. It is unwise for the amateur to remove any wood from his recorder; that irrevocable step should be undertaken only by an experienced craftsman. But if the problem involves filling in tone holes, the amateur may experiment with impunity since the added material can be easily removed. For a temporary job, Plasticine may be employed. A more permanent material is wax, and specifically a combination of carnauba wax and beeswax melted together in equal proportions. The method of applying either material is similar. First you must apply a very thin layer on the part of the hole to be filled in. This helps a subsequent thicker application to adhere better. For Plasticine, the applying instrument is a wooden dowel that is thinner than the diameter of the hole. Smear a thin film of Plasticine on one end of the dowel and transfer that onto the part of the hole that is to receive further filling, then add Plasticine as needed in an even layer that is equal from the bore side to the exterior wall. It can be sculpted smooth with a toothpick. Wax must be heated to a molten state and is applied with a hot metal rod, so a spirit lamp, gas flame, or other source of heat is necessary for this operation. Heat the rod, then apply it to the hole to warm the surface which is to receive the wax. Again, for better adhesion, lay down a very thin film of wax first. Reheat the rod, take up a bit of wax, and apply it to the preheated and coated area. Further sculpting can be done with a sharp metal tool after the wax has cooled. Beeswax is soft, sticky, and malleable. Adding carnauba wax, which is hard and brittle, produces a substance that is both hard and sculptable. When applying the wax you should hold the instrument vertically to avoid the melted wax's running into the bore.

Having discussed how to apply filling material, we must examine where to put it in order to solve various problems. First it must be understood that we are only undertaking to flatten notes that are too sharp. Correcting a note that is flat involves removing wood, requiring the skill of the repairman. An important basic principle to remember when filling in the tone holes, is that material added to the upper side of the hole has a greater flattening effect on notes in the *lower* register. Conversely, filling in the lower side of the hole mostly affects the *upper* register. The reasons for this are as follows: filling in the upper side of a hole in effect slightly lowers its position on the tube; filling in the lower side increases impedence of the vibrating column of air, that is, the first open hole below the fingered note defines the lower end of the vibrating column and makes that vent hole smaller. This has a flattening effect on the column of air. Constricting a vent hole by filling in has approximately three times as much flattening effect on notes in the upper register as in the lower. If this makes sense to you, fine. If not, take it on faith: Filling in on the lower side of a hole flattens the *upper* register; filling in on the upper side flattens the *lower* register.

Now to specifics. The tuning modifications that follow are presented for an alto recorder.

Low F: To flatten a low F that is sharp, either add material within the bore at the very bottom, thus constricting it, or lengthen the bore by adding a ring of material to the bottom of the instrument. Either method is likely to affect the low B-flat as well, so be sure to check the B-flat with its upper register octave. Oddly enough, this procedure may have a sharpening effect on very high notes in the third register (high E-flat, E, F, and G) so you should check those notes as well.

Low G: Fill in the upper side of hole 7. For most recorders this is a double hole, so start with the larger of the two holes, and be sure you do not muffle and flatten the G-flat/F-sharp out of usable existence in the process of flattening the G.

Low A-flat: Again, a double hole on 6. Fill in the upper side of the one hole of the pair that is left uncovered.

Low A: Fill in the upper side of both holes on 6. Check to be sure you are not ruining A-flat/G-sharp.

Low B-flat: Fill in the upper side of hole 5, but check upper B-flat since cross-fingered notes in the upper register are especially sensitive to filling in. If the low F is also sharp, work on the bottom of the recorder as described above.

Low C: Fill in hole 4 on the upper side.

Low C-sharp: Better to refinger the note if it is too sharp, i.e., 0/12   456 rather than the usual 0/12   45$\cancel{6}$.

Low D: Fill in upper side of hole 3.

Low E-flat: Unless the E is also sharp, it is better to correct this note by fingering, adding the sixth finger.

Low E: Fill in the upper side of hole 2. Check that there is not an undue flattening effect on E-flat and high F".

Middle F': Upper side of hole 1. This will also affect middle G', so check.

Middle G': Upper side of hole 1, or possibly the lower side of the thumb-hole. It is best to avoid filling in the thumbhole, particularly on the upper side, as this may affect response in the upper registers when the thumbhole is cracked.

A'-flat: Lower side of hole 7. Actually, the larger of the two double holes, the one on your right as you are holding the instrument in playing position. Make sure you are not flattening low G in the process.

High (second register) A': Lower side of the larger, righthand double hole on 6.

High B'-Flat: Lower side of hole 5. Check for undue flattening of low B-flat.

High B': Lower side of hole 4. Check low B and high C'-sharp.

High C': Lower side of hole 4.

High C'-sharp: Lower side of hole 3.

High D': Ditto.

High E'-flat and upward: These notes are usually best treated by constricting or lengthening the bore at the bottom, of course checking low F and B-flat as you do so. For all of these notes, if hole 7 is closed by a key, as is usual on tenors and basses, the height of the key pad above the hole has an effect. Adjusting the key so that the pad is a tiny bit closer to the hole may produce the desired flattening effect.

As is evident from the preceding instructions, filling in holes to correct intonation is not a simple task. Although it is true that filling the upper side has more effect on the lower register and filling the lower side has more effect on the upper register, any filling in does have some effect on both, so constant checking should be part of any retuning operation. Also, it should be borne in mind that intonation difficulties may be the result of a voicing problem, which is why it is inadvisable to alter your recorder in any irreversible way, i.e., by removing wood. It is probably best to make your retuning experiments first with Plasticine. Once you are sure of what you want to do, you can make a more permanent retuning with wax.

I will conclude this section with a few words about how you might carry your recorders about with you. If you have just one there is no problem, but as you acquire more sizes you begin to cast about for some convenient carryall. What I use myself is a large canvas bag. I put the smaller recorders into it in their individual cloth cases, and I carry the bass in pieces, each piece inside a heavy sock, the kind one wears mountain-climbing. The more precious recorders travel in their own hard cases inside the canvas bag. The bag is very large and very sturdy, and, as you can imagine, it gets very full and heavy at times.

Some people prefer to use a gun case. (Yes, a *gun* case!) These are long, relatively flat, molded cases of light-weight plastic and are lined with sheets of Styrofoam with wide and deep corrugations running lengthwise. These grooves provide neat places for various recorders to nestle in.

Everyone, of course, finds his own solution according to his own needs. We just want to be sure that we protect our instruments from the cold, the rain, or hard knocks as we tote them about with us. It is convenient if we can find a solution that provides space for music and a stand as well. If we begin to feel weighted down by all our paraphernalia, we can take comfort in the fact that we don't play a string bass or a sousaphone.

Chapter 8

REPERTORY
OF THE RECORDER:
A HISTORICAL SURVEY

BY COLIN C. STERNE

One of the joys of playing the recorder is the joy of discovery. To delight in reviving the sounds of a piece of old music, to sense the closeness of a composer remote in time, to take pleasure in the gradual comprehension of an unfamiliar musical form—all of these are a part of the satisfaction of playing the instrument. There is a danger, of course. It is the "antique collector syndrome": the mistaken idea that anything old must of necessity be good. Unfortunately, even with music, age is no guarantee of quality. But then, the disappointing discoveries only tend to sharpen the pleasure derived from those that are successful. Eventually, the serious player will want to make his own discoveries, without being confined to the output of publishers of recorder music and without the intervention of recorder editors. Scholarly editions of early music, including complete works of individual composers, have become readily available through any substantial music library, and it is there that the most satisfying finds can be made. The survey which follows is intended to assist in the making of these finds. And for the less venturesome player, the one who feels more comfortable playing from edited versions, the information provided can serve to increase his understanding of the music he plays, making him a more confident and more intelligent performer. Not that the survey pretends to be a history of Western music.

There are already enough of those, many of them excellent. Rather is it intended as a series of historical guideposts for the serious player who wishes to explore the rich repertory that is available to his instrument.

THE MEDIEVAL PERIOD

Literary and pictorial evidence suggests the existence of the recorder long before there are specific indications as to the music it played. Illustrations of the twelfth century show that the instrument was already in use by that time, but it is not until several centuries later that composers begin to specify its use in their music. This situation is not peculiar to the recorder, of course. Since the medieval composer chose to retain only minimal control over the "orchestration" of his music, permitting the performer to make most of the decisions in that area, the role played by instruments in the period must of necessity remain somewhat indistinct.

There is no evidence of the use of instruments in the earliest music of the Christian church. But the middle of the twelfth century, which ushers in the Gothic period, brings with it the first flowering of an extraordinary body of secular music in which instruments did indeed play a part: the songs of the troubadours and trouvères. Joined later by the German minnesingers, these poet-musicians, the troubadours from the south of France and the trouvères from the north, created melodies which retain a freshness and grace even to twentieth-century ears. Although the poetic texts deal most frequently with the relationship between the poet and his lady in the tradition of courtly love, there are topical and moral songs as well. In contemporary illustrations an instrument is often depicted assisting the singer. Since the melodies come down to us without accompaniment, it has been conjectured that an instrument was used to double the vocal line or else to provide improvised preludes and interludes. A recorder may appropriately assume that role. Many of the melodies, in fact, would seem to lend themselves to a completely instrumental performance. An account of the origin of "Kalenda Maya," a famous song by the troubadour Raimbault de Vaqueiras, describes how the composer put words to an already-existing instrumental dance. In a modern performance of the songs, the addition of percussion to those that are dancelike, and of a drone, supplied by a plucked psaltery or bowed vielle, to the more lyric examples would not be out of place. Similar in style to the troubadour songs are the Spanish

Cantigas de Santa Maria, collected by Alfonso el Sabio ("the Wise"), King of Castile and León (1252–1284).

Some medieval dance music has come down to us, but not in great quantity. Perhaps, like his twentieth-century counterpart, the medieval dance musician played by ear, with little reason to write out what he performed, and possibly little ability to do so. The *estampie* was the principal medieval dance form. Jongleurs seem to have preferred the vielle for performing estampies, but this has not kept recorder players from playing them, nor should it. The music of an estampie is set forth in a chain of musical statements. Each statement consists of a melodic unit, or *punctum,* which is repeated, each time with a different ending. The first ending is called *ouvert* and the second *clos.* Often the same endings are used for each of the various statements in the chain, suggesting a sort of musical rhyme scheme. Once again percussion parts and drones may be added in modern performance.

Music consisting of nothing more than a single line of melody is said to be monophonic in texture. Such was the texture of the music of early Christianity, Gregorian chant. The secular songs of the troubadours and trouvères were monophonic as well. But already by the year 1000 or so, the revolutionary idea that music might consist, not just of a single melody, but of two or more separate, independent melodic lines woven together had begun to occur to Western composers. Using the existing melodies of chant, they began to add new melodic lines to them. *Polyphony* is the term for a texture consisting of two or more independent melodies, and this early form of polyphony is called *organum.* Notre Dame in Paris was at the center of its development. At first organum had the same free rhythmic flow as the chant melodies that formed its basis, but eventually its musical time began to be measured with an underlying beat and the organization of that beat into units of meter. Certainly the problems of synchronizing part music in a performance situation must have been a factor in bringing about this change.

Organum was a purely vocal art, but by the middle of the thirteenth century the new technical procedures had resulted in a new form in which instruments evidently participated. That form was the *motet.* The bottom voice of the motet, its foundation, was again derived from Gregorian chant. Called the *tenor,* it consisted of pitches derived from chant and organized into a rhythmic pattern which was constantly repeated. Above it a new melody was added. This melody had its own separate text, that text being, in the earlier motets, a commentary on the text of the tenor. *Motetus* was the name given to this added part. If a third part was added, also with its own text, it was called the *triplum.* The tenor was often performed instrumentally. Motets were originally sacred compositions, but eventually there were secular ones as well, their upper parts being in the vernacular and frequently celebrating such worldly activities as love-making and drinking. And all this above a Gregorian tenor! Under the circumstances, it is not surprising that the motetus and triplum frequently took on a folk or dance flavor. Some thirteenth-century motets exist without texts and would seem to be instrumental compositions entirely, quite playable by recorders. Even in motets which do have texts, recorders may double the voice parts or may substitute for missing voices.

The fourteenth century was the time of Dante, Petrarch, Boccaccio, Chaucer, and Giotto. It was also the century of the great French poet-composer Guillaume de Machaut (about 1300–1377). Machaut becomes the first musical "personality" for us because of the autobiographical information he includes in his poetry. We know that he took pride in the music he wrote and in the position he held as a composer of the *Ars nova,* or new art. That term was invented in the early years of the century by Philippe de Vitry, another poet-composer. An important aspect of the new art was its new rhythmic freedom. Indeed, Machaut's rhythms are extremely varied and often fascinatingly complicated. But beyond that, Machaut also freed himself from the earlier reliance on chant as the foundation for musical composition and substituted the melodic motive and its development as the principal unifying element, something that marks him as modern. The fourteenth century saw a new emphasis upon secular music, too, and Machaut's secular compositions form the bulk of his output. The primary forms of the period, forms closely allied with poetry, were the *ballade,* the *virelai,* and the *rondeau.* Within these fixed forms with their strict schemes of repetition, Machaut was able to create sensitive, elegant chamber music for voices and instruments. His typical polyphonic compositions involve one or two singers (lines with texts) supported by one or two solo instruments (lines without texts). Unfortunately, the supporting instrumental lines usually need more weight than recorders can give. Machaut, writing to his young mistress, mentions the bagpipe or organ as being particularly appropriate for accompanying the love song he has just written for her. None of this means that recorders are excluded from performing Machaut's music. Recorders may double or replace a voice part. And even completely instrumental performances of Machaut's songs can be successful, but with the instrumental colors mixed and in strong contrast. An ensemble of recorders is quite inappropriate. Indeed, Machaut's melodic ideas and textures are at times so tenuous as to need the kind of presence that a singer brings to a performance. Only then is completely successful contact made with the listener. Trying to perform such works without a singer often causes instrumentalists to adopt a breakneck tempo in the hope that energy will replace expression. Unfortunately, it seldom does.

Machaut's great Italian contemporary was the blind organist Francesco Landini (c. 1325–1397). Less angular melodies, sweeter harmonies, and more gentle rhythms mark Landini's music in comparison with that of Machaut. As with Machaut, textless supporting lines suggest instruments plus voice in Landini's *ballate,* and many of the compositions lend themselves to a totally instrumental performance with instruments of mixed colors.

Toward the end of the century, the new rhythmic freedom is carried to an extreme to produce music of extraordinary rhythmic complexity. Although the forms used are basically those used by Machaut, composers such as the French Jacob de Senleches and the Italian Anthonello de Caserto produce an extremely mannered music intended for skilled performers and a highly sophisticated audience. It is music that serves as a transition between Machaut and the major composer of the fifteenth century, Guillaume Dufay.

THE RENAISSANCE

The Renaissance brought with it, as one might expect, an increased emphasis upon secular music. Instrumental participation in ensemble music that would seem to be exclusively for voices was frequent, and the great bulk of secular vocal music from the Renaissance is fair game for players of the recorder. Polyphony was the principal texture of Renaissance music, and composers developed incredible skill in its use. But they turned their attention, too, to the vertical aspects of their music, writing at times in a chordal texture. Stylistic performances of Renaissance music will necessitate some knowledge of Renaissance ornamentation. We know that the instrumentalists used it, and we even have treatises from the period describing its application. That by Sylvestro Ganassi, *Opera Intitulata Fontegara,* published in 1535, is the most familiar to recorder players, since it is the first treatise on the recorder that we have. But the examples for viola da gamba given by Diego Ortiz in his *Tratado de glosas,* published in 1553, are more musically sensitive. One interesting aspect of Ganassi's treatise, however, is the stress he places on expressive playing. Proposing the human voice as the supremely expressive musical medium, Ganassi insists that recorder playing must imitate singing. Further, he instructs the player to determine the expressive quality of a particular piece of music and to project that quality in his playing. A variety of articulation syllables are provided as the "words" of recorder performance. And, with some pride, he even reveals the fingerings for seven extra notes on the instrument which were unknown to the other players of his time.

Another challenge to the performer of both medieval and Renaissance music is that of the application of *musica ficta.* The term refers to pitches which were chromatically altered in performance even though no indication of the alterations occurs in the music. The problem is complicated, too much so to be investigated here. But the serious player will certainly want to gather as much information on the subject as he can.

Although we are apt to associate the glories of the Renaissance with Italy, the period in music has its beginnings farther to the north. "They have discovered a new way," wrote the poet Martin le Franc, in 1442. Thus did he announce another period of "new music" and tender a salute to the two composers, Guillaume Dufay (about 1400–1474) and Gilles Binchois (about 1400–1460), who best represented it. Both Dufay and Binchois were associated with the court of Philip the Good, Duke of Burgundy. It was a court of elegance and taste. The painter Jan van Eyck and the sculptor Claus Sluter were also active there. What we know today as Holland, Belgium, northeastern France, Luxembourg, and Lorraine were all under the control of the Burgundian dukes. It is convenient for us to mark the beginning of the Renaissance in music with the music of the Burgundian composers.

One important aspect of this "new way" was in the sound of the music. Medieval music theory had classified the octave, fourth, and fifth as consonances, with thirds and sixths as dissonances. The distinctive harmonies of the medieval motet—bare, open sounds—resulted from this practice. Machaut's harmonic vocabulary admitted many more thirds and sixths. But with the Burgundians, these intervals occur with even greater frequency, and the result is a new warmth and sweetness. As characteristically Burgundian as this sound is, however, it seems highly likely that it did not originate with the Burgundian composers, but was rather an import from England. English music had emphasized thirds and sixths long before the taste for them developed on the Continent. It may have been the music of John Dunstable (about 1370–1453), English composer, astronomer, and mathematician, which brought the new sonority to the attention of Continental composers. But Dufay and Binchois quickly made it their own.

The principal form of secular vocal music cultivated by Dufay and Binchois was the *chanson*. With a text in French, the chanson was essentially a solo song with instrumental accompaniment. Some are quite effective as instrumental pieces, although the appropriate ensemble is still one of mixed colors.

The role of instruments in the sacred music of the early Renaissance is still somewhat problematic. Some of Dufay's sacred compositions are in *treble-dominated* or *cantilena* style, where an active top voice, with text, is supported by less active lower voices which are textless, and therefore assumed to be instrumental. This procedure was already in evidence in the secular music of Machaut. But others of Dufay's sacred compositions are for voices of equal activity, each of them with texts. Did instruments double the voices in this situation? We are still not certain. Certainly the masses and motets of the period will provide less repertory for recorder players than will the love songs.

Johannes Ockeghem (about 1430–1497) and Jacob Obrecht (about 1452–1505) were important Flemish composers who carried forward the discoveries of the Burgundians. In their music we observe a more consistent use of a device that Dufay had already used to a lesser degree: imitative polyphony. Polyphony is, as we have already observed, the conception of a piece of music as a series of interwoven melodic lines, each line having a certain independence, but each making its contribution to the whole. *Imitative polyphony* involves cutting each of those lines from the same cloth. They resemble one another. They may even, as in a canon, be identical. But they retain their independence by their temporal relationship to one another, each voice making its statement of the material at its own point in time. Imitation is one way of integrating the various lines of music that make up a polyphonic composition. And both

Ockeghem and Obrecht handled the device with great skill. Delighting as they did in the challenges of the new discoveries, neither composer, however, permitted expression to be overwhelmed by technique.

A distinctive feature of Flemish music is the downward extension of the bass range. The result is that the light, bright sonority of Burgundian music gives way to a richer, darker sound. The chansons of Ockeghem and Obrecht emphasize emotional content: the austerity of Machaut and the restraint of Dufay are replaced with a new intensity. All the voices share equally in the musical statement. And finally, the secular vocal repertory becomes the province of the instrumental performer as well: Flemish chansons were both sung and played.

The procedures of the Burgundian and Flemish composers came to full flower in the music of Josquin des Près (about 1440–1521). Perhaps the greatest composer of the Renaissance, Josquin, a native of Flanders, grew up under the influence of Ockeghem and Obrecht. He may, in fact, have been a pupil of Ockeghem. Certainly his music demonstrates a command of the Flemish procedures. But around 1470 Josquin traveled to Italy to serve professionally there as both singer and composer. It was not unusual for Flemish musicians to make such a trip; they were highly sought after for positions at Italian courts because of their reputation for excellence and because, following the death of Landini, Italian music had failed to keep pace with the new technical advances of the North. Nevertheless, the light, simple, direct quality of Italian music must have charmed Josquin, for his own music reflects these qualities along with its complete mastery of Flemish polyphony. It is this fusion of North and South in Josquin's music which is an important source of its strength. The *frottola,* the Italian form of secular song, was light in mood and texture and simple in design. Furthermore, its composers had little use for the polyphonic complexities of the chanson, preferring instead textures which actually seem chordal. Josquin even tried his hand at writing some; but, of more importance, in his more serious music he learned how to mix polyphonic and homophonic textures. His melodies, too, show a simplicity and grace. And he developed more skill in using music to intensify the meaning of a text than anyone had done before him.

It was during Josquin's lifetime that the first part-music was printed from movable type. In Venice, in 1501, Ottaviano dei Petrucci brought out such a collection, the *Harmonice Musices Odhecaton.* The Franco-Flemish chansons that the book contains were printed in choir-book form, that is, with all the parts in a single volume. Later publications were to make use of the more familiar part-book procedure, where each part is printed separately, and a full set of part-books is necessary for performance. Composers, however, used a score when writing their music. They also began in this period to fashion the various lines of a composition at more or less the same time. The earlier procedure had been to complete one line before starting on another. The taste for mixed colors in the instrumental ensemble began to give way during Josquin's lifetime to a preference for homogeneous sound—for four viols, for instance, or four recorders. And in vocal music, four voices (soprano, alto, tenor, and bass) became the norm in texture and range.

A particularly intriguing contemporary of Josquin des Près was the Netherlander Heinrich Isaac (*ca.* 1450–1517). Isaac was a most cosmopolitan composer, serving at several courts, and comfortable with the Italian, French, and German musical styles. A small but impressive part of his output consists of compositions for unspecified instruments. Their rhythms are particularly fresh and appealing.

The impact of the Flemish style was felt throughout Europe, with varying results. In Italy, for example, the frottola, in its simplicity, may have influenced Josquin des Près and his Flemish contemporaries, but the reverse happened as well. Italian composers began to incorporate the intricacies of Flemish polyphony into their textures. They began, too, to choose texts of more consequence and to match their music more carefully to those texts. The frottola form of brief, repeated sections of music then no longer sufficed, and the form adopted was that of the Flemish motet. Although a sacred composition for voices, this form was quite different from the medieval motet. Basically, the procedure in the Flemish motet was to create a melodic idea for the opening portion of text and to allow each of the voice parts to present it in imitative polyphony. Each succeeding portion of text was subjected to the same procedure, but with its own melodic idea. The result was a succession of polyphonic sections. Occasionally a section might come to a complete close before the beginning of the next section, but more frequently there was an overlapping of these units.

Motet form, outfitted with a secular text, resulted in the Italian madrigal. The first madrigals began to appear around 1530 and were written by Flemish composers living in Italy—Philippe Verdelot (died about 1550), for example, and Jacob Arcadelt (about 1505–1560), and

Adrian Willaert (about 1490–1562). Close alliance of music with text was a characteristic of the madrigal, but this did not prevent them from being performed with a mixture of instruments and voices or even by instruments alone. Cipriano de Rore (1516–1565), Orlando di Lasso (1532–1594), and Philippe de Monte (1521–1603) all contributed to the development of the madrigal.

In France, the Italian madrigal seemed to have little appeal. Perhaps the very freedom of its form, so dependent on its text, was not in keeping with the French inclination toward clarity in structure. At any rate, French composers developed a secular song of their own with a more clearly defined form, a tendency toward homophonic texture, the inclusion of repeated sections of music, and rhythms that were influenced by the dance. This was the French *chanson.* But the new chanson, first appearing around 1530, was not of the type composed a century earlier by Dufay. Clément Jannequin (about 1485–1560), Claude de Sermisy (about 1490–1562), and Pierre Certon (about 1510–1572) were important contributors to the development of the chanson. By its very nature the chanson lent itself to instrumental performance better than did the madrigal. This was primarily because the text of the chanson had less influence on the form of the music. It also had to do with the clearer texture of the chanson and its more concise rhythms. Instrumentalists not only performed chansons frequently, but they decorated the vocal lines with intricate ornamentation. Italian instrumentalists, subjecting chansons to this treatment, called the result a *canzona.* Eventually instrumental canzonas came to be written that were not based upon a preexistent vocal chanson, but merely retained the flavor.

The German secular song, the *lied,* combined Flemish polyphony with characteristically German melodic material. Heinrich Fink (1445–1527) and Heinrich Isaac both created examples. So did Paul Hofhaimer (1459–1537). Outstanding examples of the form, however, are those of Ludwig Senfl (about 1490–1543). His ability to project a mood and his skill in handling the form are constantly in evidence.

The Spanish counterpart of the frottola was the *villancico.* Like the frottola, it was, in its early state, primarily harmonic in texture with a top melody supported by two lower voices. Juan del Encina (1468–1529) produced villancicos of this type. Later examples are polyphonic, with equal interest in the four or five voices that go to make them up. In this style are the villancicos of Juan Vasquez (flourished around 1550).

Several of the dark, intense villancicos of Vasquez match in quality the best writing of Josquin. His brighter, more playful songs suggest the influence of Spanish folk song.

English composers were slow to adopt the Flemish style. After John Dunstable, there was little English music of substance until the great triumvirate of John Taverner (about 1495–1545), Christopher Tye (about 1500–1572), and Thomas Tallis (about 1505–1585). Secular music flourished in England toward the end of the sixteenth century, and this period is one, of course, dear to players of the recorder. It was at that time that the madrigal, transplanted from Italy, took root in England and bore distinctively English fruit. Thomas Weelkes (about 1575–1623), John Wilbye (1574–1638), and Thomas Morley (1557–1602) published madrigals of excellent quality. There was instrumental music in England, too, particularly music for the consort of viols, that lends itself to performance on recorders.

The English music for viol consort was not the only music of the Renaissance designated as being for instruments. Such specifically instrumental music forms a relatively small but significant part of the total picture of the period. Before proceeding to the music of the late Renaissance, it seems appropriate to pause to examine the forms that instrumental music took. It must be remembered that music for the lute, vihuela, viol, and keyboard was usually designated as such. Lute and vihuela music, in its own distinctive notation, *tablature,* is quite inappropriate to the recorder. So, too, is the music written for keyboard instruments. One category of music for instruments, usually unspecified instruments, is music which is an adaptation of vocal models, as the canzona is an adaptation of the chanson. The *ricercar,* for example, is essentially a motet without words. But an area of music that belonged indisputably to instruments was that of the dance. The *basse danse* was the most important social dance of the early Renaissance. Its music seems to have been improvised over a series of given tenors, and only a few examples have been transmitted to us in notation. By the middle of the sixteenth century, however, dance music for instrumental ensemble was published in some quantity. Since most of it was intended for actual use in accompanying dancing, it is rhythmically regular and consists of distinct sections which are usually repeated. There is little polyphonic complexity. Often the dances were paired, as in the solemn pavane followed by the more vigorous galliard. Sometimes a brisk third dance rounded

Concert Champêtre, by Giorgione. Alinari/Editorial Photocolor Archives.

out the group. But there was little consistency in the contents of a group or the ordering of those contents. Toward the end of the century, dance music was often composed as chamber music, with no thought that it be used for actual dancing. These idealized dances are more polyphonic in texture and more intricate in rhythm.

The idea of using a given tune as a theme for a formal set of variations probably originated in Spain, but English composers quickly adopted the procedure and produced fine specimens, particularly for keyboard and lute. Another type of variation, that of creating constantly changing melodic ideas over a repeated bass line, must have originated as improvisation, but notated examples occur, often as instruction for the performer who would learn that improvisational process. Although fairly late, those contained in Jakob van Eyck's *De Fluyten Lusthof,* published about 1646 in Amsterdam, are typical examples of the first type—the formal set of variations on a given tune. Quite a few of van Eyck's tunes are English in origin, including the melodies of several of John Dowland's songs, and the variations on them demand virtuoso playing of a C recorder, the instrument for which they were written. Van Eyck was a blind organist, recorder player, and player of the carillon at Utrecht.

To turn once again to the general scene of music in the Renaissance, we find that the second half of the sixteenth century is dominated by three composers: Giovanni Pierluigi da Palestrina (about 1525–1594), Orlando di Lasso (1532–1594), and William Byrd (1543–1623). Palestrina's great art is almost completely closed to instrumental performers. Except for a small number of madrigals, his music is entirely sacred. But the music of di Lasso (originally Roland de Lassus) contains some delightful chansons constructed with his supreme skill. There are secular songs in parts by William Byrd, solo songs with the accompaniment of an instrumental ensemble, and fantasias for viols that may be played on recorders. All of them demonstrate Byrd's elegant melodic lines and his complete mastery of linear construction.

The Renaissance draws to a close with some experiments in intensity of expression that seem to call for the new forms that the Baroque era would supply. The madrigals of Don Carlo Gesualdo (1560–1613) are examples. Sudden cries of anguish, sighs of grief, and outbursts of rage are characteristic of them, as are the strongly dissonant and chromatic harmonies. The importance attached to the texts in the compositions of this composer make his music quite senseless in a performance without singers. Evidence of this "mannerism" is to be found in the music of John Dowland (1562–1626), too. But Dowland's grief-stricken *Lachrimae* pavans, "set forth for the Lute, Viols or Violons" are quite effective in a performance on recorders. Many of the part-songs of Dowland can be played instrumentally, as well. Several, as a matter of fact, seem to have been instrumental dances before being made into songs by the composer.

THE BAROQUE PERIOD

The serenity, restraint, and balance so typical of the Renaissance give way, as we move into the seventeenth century, to dramatic conflict, tension, deliberate distortion, and an emphasis on feeling and expression. Claudio Monteverdi (1567–1643), for instance, points with pride at how he has been able to increase the vocabulary of musical expression. It was not the highly personal expression of the nineteenth century that he sought, but rather the expression of the *affections,* a more stereotyped set of states of the soul as the seventeenth century recognized them.

The Baroque period, which we usually define as existing from the beginnings of Italian opera, around 1600, until the death of Johann Sebastian Bach in 1750, saw an enormous growth in the amount of music written for instruments. Early in the seventeenth century, composers began to write idiomatically for instruments, differentiating between instrumental and vocal styles. No longer was vocal music to be shared by instruments. Furthermore, the instruments to be used began to be specified by the composer. At times, the title page of an instrumental publication offered a choice of instruments, as was the case with Dowland's *Lachrimae.* Substitutions might, of course, be made. Providing the range of the music was appropriate, recorders might play music intended for viols, violins, or cornetti. The music for lute and that for keyboard instruments remained the distinct property of those instruments, however.

The use of the *basso continuo* in Baroque music is a feature so characteristic of the period that an understanding of it is essential to the performer. Basically, it was a shorthand system of indicating the chords of an accompaniment. It consisted of a bass line with figures, although in the earliest period those figures were few or even nonexistent. The line was to be played by two performers. A bass instrument was to play the line itself, and an instrument capable of playing chords was to play the line plus the indicated chords. In most modern editions of Baroque music the continuo part has been realized, that is, the editor has supplied the necessary chords. But some scholarly editions of Baroque music leave the bass unrealized, and it becomes the job of the accompanist to provide the harmonies, either through improvisation, or by writing out his part. Harpsichord and viola da gamba are the instruments most frequently used as continuo instruments in modern performances. But there are times when the bass instrument might be a trombone, or a cello, or a bassoon (in later music). And organ, lute, or guitar may be used as the chordal instrument. The necessity for two performers to play the single line of the figured bass leads to some odd inconsistencies: a solo sonata requires three performers, but a trio sonata requires four.

The titles given to instrumental compositions in the early Baroque are somewhat confusing. Canzona, ricercar, capriccio, fantasia, fancy, and sonata are some of them. And composers seem to have used them without consistency. The Baroque canzona consisted of a chain of musical events. Each of its links contained its own thematic material, mood, and tempo. The resulting series of strong contrasts produces the kind of dramatic conflict that is so characteristic of the period. The canzonas for ensembles of various sizes by Girolamo Frescobaldi (1583–1643) are of particular interest, as are those of Giovanni Gabrieli (about 1554–1612). Eventually the short, contrasting sections of the canzona were to become the longer, independent movements of the Baroque sonata. In similar manner, the more sedate ricercar, with its tendency toward polyphonic texture, eventually developed into the fugue. The titles "sinfonia" or "sonata" were often used in the early Baroque to designate canzonas.

Of particular interest to recorder players who enjoy performing in large groups are the canzonas for multiple choirs that are associated with the Venetian School of composition. In 1527 the Belgian composer Adrian Willaert (about 1490–1562) was made director of music at the Cathedral of St. Mark in Venice. This splendid eleventh-century structure, with its two organs, its distinctive architecture, and its resonant acoustics, lent itself particularly well to the idea of two choirs performing from the two sides of the building. Although Willaert himself composed polychoral music, he was not the first composer to do so. Nor was the Cathedral of St. Mark unique in being the setting for the performance of such music. But certainly Venice and St. Mark's became associated with the practice.

Motets composed for such circumstances stressed boldness in design, full chordal textures, and the bright colors of instruments uniting with the voices. The Venetian taste for magnificence reached its culmination in the polychoral works of Giovanni Gabrieli, who was a student of his uncle, Andrea Gabrieli (about 1510–1586), who had been, in turn, a student of Willaert. Polychoral instrumental canzonas, often called "sonatas," were an outgrowth of the tradition of sacred music for divided choirs. The division sometimes went as high as five separate groups. The brilliance of such music is best produced by viols, cornetti, and sackbuts. In a performance by recorders, however, some of that brilliance can be achieved by following a suggestion of Marin Mersenne in his *Harmonie Universelle* of 1636–37. He recommends the division of a recorder consort into two groups—one of high-pitched instruments and one of low, the high group doubling the low one at the octave. The result is similar to the 4-foot and 8-foot registrations of an organ.

A favored structural device of the Baroque composer was that of variation. The practice already observed in the Renaissance of varying a repeated bass line persisted into the Baroque. Several of these basses, or *grounds,* were used again and again, sometimes without being identified in the title of a composition. The *folia, passamezzo antico, romanesca,* and *ruggiero* are some of the ones most frequently used. And variations continued to be written as a series of transformations of a given melody.

More and more the dance music of the early Baroque was idealized —intended for the listener rather than the dancer. The pavane-galliard and passamezzo-saltarello pairing of dances were familiar in the Renaissance. To them were added new ones such as the allemande, courante, and sarabande. Each was characterized by a traditional rhythmic pattern. When presented in sets, the music of each dance was sometimes related to the others in the set. Early publications, however, are more apt to group all the dances of one type together, permitting the performer to arrange his own set, and confirming the fact that the Baroque suite was still to come. Keyboard and lute dances often contain written-out variations of repeated strains, and that this ornamenting of repeats was practiced by other instrumentalists, including recorder players, would seem highly likely.

To have proceeded this far into the Baroque period without some mention of Italian opera, perhaps its most characteristic form, may seem strange. Actually, however, the recorder is very little associated with opera in its early development. Called for briefly by Monteverdi in his *L'Orfeo,* the recorder was subsequently ignored by both him and his immediate followers in Italy. This was hardly the result of antipathy toward the instrument, but rather a tendency to use a string orchestra made up of the instruments of the new violin family, with their distinctive expressive capability. But the devices for expression, so necessary to opera, quickly found their place in instrumental chamber music. These included jagged melodic lines, chromatic and dissonant harmonies, and strongly contrasting rhythms. Both Frescobaldi and Monteverdi mention an elasticity in the pulse as an aid to representing the affections, something that few modern performers seem to be willing to tackle. The most revolutionary device of early opera was *monody,* a harmonically conceived vocal line with the rhythms closely allied to those of the text, and with the support of a chordal accompaniment. This new harmonic texture, too, exerted an influence on chamber music.

The early chamber sonatas extended the principles already in evidence in the canzona. Several sections of music were presented in strong contrast. One of the sections, at least, was fugal, and the others, whether slow or fast in tempo, were indebted to the dance. The violin was the preferred instrument in both the solo and trio sonata. It was only after the middle of the seventeenth century that the recorder was used with any degree of frequency in chamber music. It was then that the Hotteterres, that extraordinary French family of instrument makers, effected the changes in recorder design which resulted in the Baroque form of the instrument. From their workshops, in the same period, came the Baroque oboe and the one-keyed Baroque flute. The Baroque recorder was less full and bright in tone than its predecessor, replacing that brightness with a thinner, reedier quality, but the extension of its upper register made it more suitable for virtuoso use. In addition, its construction in three sections instead of only one made it more portable than its predecessor and permitted adjustments in tuning.

With the development of the Baroque recorder, the relative neglect that the instrument had suffered in the early years of the seventeenth century was at an end. It was the alto recorder, referred to as "flute," "flauto," or "flauto dolce," that became the vehicle for solo and chamber performance. In addition, one or two alto recorders were frequently used in the opera or theater orchestra. Henry Purcell (1659–1695) made particularly effective use of the recorder in incidental music composed for various plays, in his occasional odes and welcome songs, and in his chamber cantatas. The chaconne from *Dioclesian*, "Two in One upon a Ground," is an especially moving expression of grief. It uses two alto recorders winding about one another in canon over the inexorable descents of a ground bass.

At a later date, about a dozen of the sacred cantatas of Johann Sebastian Bach (1685–1750) feature the recorder in some of the most expressive writing for the instrument in the entire Baroque period. Bach carefully indicated in his scores whether he required a recorder (flauto) or a flute (traverso), and he assigned them very different roles, the recorder being considered the more intimate of the two. Purity, innocence, tenderness, and sorrow are moods he saw as appropriate to the recorder. Less frequent are the instances where he expects the instrument to be festively brilliant. Two recorders contribute, for example, to the tender mood of the soprano aria "Father, all I bring thee," from the cantata *Brich dem Hungrigen dein Brot* (BWV 39). They intensify the mood of sorrow in the cantata *Meine Seufzer, meine Thränen* (BWV 13). And in the funeral cantata *Gottes Zeit ist die allerbeste Zeit* (BWV 106), they summon up, not so much the feeling of grief over death, as the serene acceptance of it. The opening sonatina of this cantata, scored for two alto recorders and two viole da gamba with continuo, uses the darkly veiled sonorities of the instruments in a poignant depiction of loss and final farewell. The most familiar appearance of recorders in a Bach cantata is in the aria "Sheep may safely graze," from the secular cantata *Was mir behagt* (BWV 208). Here they assume the pastoral role so frequently assigned to the recorder by Baroque composers.

There are other roles that are regularly delegated to the recorder in the Baroque period. One of these is the imitation of birdsong. In *Acis and Galatea* by George Frederick Handel (1685–1759) the sopranino is called upon to do just such an imitation in the song "Hush, ye pretty warbling Quire." In "Heart, the seat of soft delight," from the same work, two altos are asked to assist, with gentle undulations, in suggesting the emotion of romantic love—another typical assignment.

Of the musical forms from this later period in which the recorder is involved, the sonata is perhaps most important. There were two basic types, the *sonata da chiesa,* or church sonata, and the *sonata da camera,* or chamber sonata. The sonata da chiesa consisted of four movements with tempos of slow, fast, slow, fast. The sonata da camera grouped together dance movements in a sequence determined by the composer. The familiar sonatas for recorder of the Opus 1 of Handel are mostly typical of the first type, although occasionally Handel slips in a dance movement to mix the types.

The *concerto grosso* pitted a small group of agile soloists, the *concertino,* against a larger and more formidable group, usually made up of strings, called the *ripieno.* There were three movements: fast, slow, fast. The alto recorder is a member of the solo group in both the second and fourth of Bach's *Brandenburg Concertos.*

The three so-called "piccolo concertos" of Antonio Vivaldi (1687–1741) are examples of the *solo concerto.* Scored for *flautino* and strings, they pose a performance problem. What instrument did Vivaldi mean by *flautino?* Sopranino recorder seems most likely, although flageolet and small transverse flute have both been suggested as possibilities. The concertos are brilliant pieces, demanding a high degree of technical proficiency. Chamber works which include recorder also exist by Vivaldi. *Il Pastor Fido,* a set of six sonatas for "musette, vielle, flûte [recorder], hautbois, violon, avec la basse continue," have been ascribed to Vivaldi, but seemingly incorrectly. They are, at any rate, rather uninteresting works.

The recorder was occasionally included in the orchestral *overture* or *suite*. The suite opened with a French overture which consisted of a majestic slow section with many dotted rhythms followed by a fugal allegro. Often the slow opening, or a variant of it, then returned. The overture was followed by a series of dance movements. The Suite in A Minor of Georg Philipp Telemann (1681–1767) is an example.

Telemann, as a matter of fact, might very well assume the position of patron saint of the recorder movement. In his incredibly large output there is a substantial amount of music for recorder in all sorts of combinations, in a variety of forms, and at all levels of difficulty. Much of it is of high quality, and this fact was apparent to recorder players long before the musical world in general had divested itself of the myth that Telemann was a third-rate composer. The present revival of interest in Telemann's music may indeed be traced back to recorder players seeking to increase their repertory of Baroque music.

A convention of the late Baroque permitted the substitution of instruments in chamber music when it seemed appropriate, particularly in the trio sonata. This is true in the music of Telemann as it is in the music of other composers. The recorder might substitute for the flute or oboe, for instance. Solo music for the flute was sometimes transposed to fit the recorder range. The usual transposition was up a minor third. An unusual substitution, sanctioned by the composer, occurs in Telemann's Quartet in D Minor for recorder, two flutes, and basso continuo. The recorder part may be played two octaves lower by bassoon or cello!

Among the examples chosen to illustrate the principal Baroque forms appropriate to the recorder, music by French composers has been notably absent. Indeed there is recorder music of elegance and charm from France, but early in the period French composers showed a marked preference for the more expressive transverse flute. The more substantial French works are, then, for that instrument.

The Baroque period represents the golden age of the recorder. The instrument itself reached the end of its technical development, and the music written for it represented a rich variety of forms, styles, and composers. By the end of the eighteenth century, however, it had been almost completely replaced by its longtime rival, the transverse flute.

THE TWENTIETH CENTURY

With the advent of the Viennese classical period, the recorder finally became silent, remaining so during the whole of the nineteenth century. Its modern revival was due mainly to the efforts of Arnold Dolmetsch, who in 1926, at Haslemere, introduced a consort of recorders playing instruments from his own workshop. In the ensuing period, although used as an educational tool or folk instrument in Germany, most of the interest in the recorder was in using it to play its traditional repertory. Gradually, however, composers of the twentieth century began to show an interest in writing for it. At first it was difficult for them to use the instrument without being in awe of its history, and early efforts by both English and German composers leaned heavily on a pseudoantique style modified by postimpressionist harmonies. Later efforts utilized the tonal chromaticism of Paul Hindemith, who was himself a major figure in the revival of early music. The compositions of Hans Ulrich Staeps, a name familiar to most recorder players, show an indebtedness to Hindemith. Neoclassicism, as practiced in the United States, produced some attractive works such as those by Gail Kubik and William Bergsma. Benjamin Britten, who was himself a player, also wrote effectively for the instrument.

Although not used in jazz, there have been jazz-inspired works for recorders, and the instrument has occasionally found its way into rock groups. Even the serial procedures of Arnold Schönberg have been used in writing for the recorder, although none of the three giants of the first half of our century, Schönberg, Stravinsky, or Bartok, showed an interest in writing recorder music. Some fascinating recent compositions, mainly inspired by the virtuoso playing of Frans Brüggen, have demanded a whole new vocabulary of sounds. These include harmonics, multiphonics (playing two or more pitches at once), microtones, fluttertonguing, and singing into the instrument. Luciano Berio's *Gesti* falls into this category, as does this writer's *Meadow, Hedge, Cuckoo.*

Certainly if the recorder is to continue to flourish, it must take its place in the music of our own time. As the world body of players continues to grow, perhaps so will its modern repertory. The time is ripe for the recorder to attract the efforts of the best of our composers.

Chapter 9

REPERTORY
OF THE RECORDER:
A SELECTIVE LIST

WITH MARTHA BIXLER AND JOAN MUNKACSI

In this chapter we present a selected repertory for the recorder player, carefully chosen from the vast and possibly bewildering amount of music that has been composed or arranged for our instrument, but the reader should realize that there is an even vaster quantity of music that one can find and arrange for oneself if one wishes.

For the scholarly-minded, the historical editions of early music found mostly in music schools and libraries are good sources of material. *Jacobean Consort Music,* Volume IX in the Musica Britannica series (Stainer & Bell), to name one example, contains much excellent music that is suitable, even though it is not specifically written or arranged for recorders. The *Historical Anthology of Music,* first published by Harvard University Press in 1947, is still a very good source. There are dozens of volumes of *opera omnia*—the complete works of a composer—ranging from the Middle Ages to the Baroque.

Perhaps more accessible to the average recorder player is the vocal music we encounter everywhere in daily life. Some of this, of course, has already been arranged for recorder, but the amateur can easily make his or her own arrangements. Folk and art songs, popular songs, show tunes, even operatic arias, are grist for the recorder player's mill, although they may need to be simplified and/or transposed from possibly outlandish keys. The *Antiqua Chorbuch* series, published by Schott, is full of German

part-songs that are particularly lovely performed on a consort of recorders. There are English, French, Italian, Spanish, and Russian part-songs
as well that will suit with a minimum of rearrangement. Rounds, madrigals, hymns, and Christmas carols may be played on the recorder.

In the field of instrumental music there is an almost infinite amount
that a recorder player may find and arrange for himself or a group of
friends. Just because the recorder is considered an instrument primarily
for early music, there is no need to shy away from the music of the
eighteenth and nineteenth centuries. Much of the chamber music and
even orchestral music of the Classical and Romantic periods can be and
has been arranged for recorders. Jazz, either written out or improvised,
is marvelous on the recorder and has been used to good effect in recordings and television commercials. Pop and bop duos for clarinets or saxo-
phones are ready-made for the recorder. There is almost no area of music
that cannot be explored. We are not purists in this regard and would urge
you not to be. It is no more inappropriate to play a Schubert song on the
recorder than it is to play a Machaut virelai. In each instance the composer never intended his vocal piece to be played on a recorder, but we
feel sure that he would have enjoyed hearing it performed that way. If
the music fits, play it!

Some general statements should be made concerning the bibliography set forth in this chapter. We have used the following criteria in
selecting the editions: suitability for recorders, quality of the music, price
(much of the published literature has, alas, been priced outrageously
high, particularly the foreign editions), availability (although some of the
music listed will inevitably be out of print by the time you read this),
and quality of the editing. This last has sometimes been sacrificed for
other considerations. A good edition will give the player both guidance
and choice as to style, phrasing, articulation, and instrumentation. The
player will be able to see what is editorial and what is original and will
be able to reconstruct the original music and the composer's intentions.
A good edition will be edited by someone who understands the recorder,
its capabilities, and its idiosyncrasies.

One of the oldest and certainly the most extensive of the recorder
catalogs is that of Schott (B. Schott's Söhne, Mainz; and Schott & Co.,
Ltd., London). Both the German and the London offices were pioneers
in the publication of music for recorders. Many of the older items in the
catalog were edited at a time when publications for the recorder were few
and sorely needed. Because of its age, the editing is somewhat old-

fashioned. Slurs and staccato markings appear, with no indication that they are editorial additions and, in fact, often anachronistic (slurring became an acceptable articulation only in the Baroque era). Musicological niceties such as background information, original instrumentation and phrasing, and so on are not always provided. However, these editions are included in this listing because the music is so fine and is not otherwise easily available.

The same criticisms may be made of the early American Recorder Society editions. They are full of changes from the original music, with parts rearranged and parts added, editorial meter changes and accidentals, and nary a caveat to the player. They were enormously useful when they were first published, but they are beginning to be supplanted now by more modern publications. Only the later A.R.S. editions (published by Galaxy Music) are listed here, with one exception—an anthology of the best of the early editions.

Certain editions should be used with great care because of the unreliability of the editing. Many Hargail editions, for example, although containing much excellent music, have been edited by non-recorder players and contain distortions and mistakes, particularly in phrasing and articulation. The newer London Pro Musica editions, by contrast, are exemplary. They are legible and have comfortable page turns or parts. Incipits (indications of original clefs and notation, showing original ranges), texts, translations, even pronunciation guides, as well as musical and historical background, are provided. The editor gives suggestions for instruments other than recorders and occasionally provides an alternate top part, appropriately ornamented. The modern recorder player wants to know more about the music he or she is playing, and the modern editor takes note of this.

The listing that follows includes four categories—first, recorder methods, then music on three levels: easy, intermediate, and difficult. Within each level the music is arranged in this order: exercises; music for recorder, according to the number of parts; music for recorder and keyboard; music for recorder and other instruments.

There is of necessity some overlap in the categories. All editions requiring bass recorder are listed as being intermediate or difficult, as most novices do not play bass, but some may actually be very easy to play. There is overlap of instrumentation as well; anything listed for two sopranos can of course be played on two tenors instead, and so forth.

Low soprano parts may be played on altos; high bass parts may be played on tenors. Much of this music can be sung as well as played; indeed we encourage singing wherever a text is provided, as singing is an aid to phrasing and general musicianship.

We have commented on the music or on the edition where it seems appropriate. We consider all the listed music by Handel, Bach, and Telemann to be first class, so no comments concerning its quality have been made. Instruments listed in parentheses are substitutes for the one immediately preceding. Recorders often play up an octave from the written pitch, particularly in arrangements (the solo alto recorder music of the eighteenth century is an exception), but this is not always indicated in the edition, so we have mentioned it each time it is a possibility. Editions of medieval, Renaissance, and contemporary music provide a score only, unless otherwise indicated; Baroque editions will come with parts.

METHODS

BURAKOFF, SONYA AND GERALD. *The Beginners Method for Soprano and Alto Recorder,* 2 vols. Hargail, H-51 and H-52.
  Soprano and alto.
  This method teaches C and F fingerings simultaneously (both volumes include fingering charts). Musical terms and symbols are systematically introduced, but the music tends toward the simpleminded. We recommend it for self-teaching.
DUSCHENES, MARIO. *Method for the Recorder,* 2 vols. Berandol/Associated Music.
  Soprano (tenor) or alto (sopranino, bass).
  The first volume, called Part I, presents music notation terms and symbols, as well as the complete gamut of fingerings; the literature is sometimes not terribly well suited to the recorder. Part II stresses playing in all keys; it includes ornaments, a trill-fingering chart, and some material from the original recorder repertoire with suggestions on how to practice it. This is probably the best method for someone working entirely on his or her own, but is not ideal in all respects. (Two volumes for C fingering, two for F.)
GIESBERT, FRANZ J. *Method for the Treble Recorder.* Schott, RMS 427, Ed. 4469.
  Alto.
  This method really requires a teacher to accompany it: The musical material, all of it in duet form, is excellent, but both the text and the fingering chart are unreliable and should be ignored. An appendix contains useful technical material and fifteen solo pieces by masters of the eighteenth century.

KATZ, ERICH. *Recorder Playing: A New and Comprehensive Method.* Carl Van Roy.
Soprano and alto.
This is an extremely systematic and comprehensive method for C and F
recorders combined. Music of rhythmic complexity is introduced somewhat too soon for a beginner.
ORR, HUGH. *Basic Recorder Technique,* 2 vols. Berandol/Associated Music.
Soprano or alto.
This is particularly good for self-teaching and for the musically sophisticated. There is much text and many photographs, though not all this
material is ideal. Volume I covers the range of only a ninth. Volume II
completes the range and gives a great deal of technical information by means
of text and exercises. In both volumes the music is of very high quality, but
little help is given with articulation and none with phrasing. Both volumes
include fingering charts. (Two volumes for C fingering, two for F.)

EASY
Exercises

LINDE, HANS-MARTIN. *The Little Exercise.* Schott, RMS 1051, Ed. 4882.
Soprano.
The translation of the text is at times imprecise, but the notes are clear.
ROHR, HEINRICH, AND FRANZ LEHN. *Treble Recorder Pieces.* Schott, RMS 267, Ed.
4248A.
Alto.
Starts at the very beginning and gives some instruction. Good material,
systematically presented; includes reading up an octave.

Recorder Alone

ONE RECORDER

O Mistress Mine. Harold Newman, ed. Hargail, H-131.
Soprano.
Shakespearean and Elizabethan tunes and dances. Guitar chords included.

TWO RECORDERS

CORELLI, A. *Short Duets for Descant and Treble Recorders.* Kaestner, ed. Schott, RMS 17,
Ed. 2729a.
Soprano and alto.
First Duets and *Second Duets.* Walter Bergmann, arr. Schott, RMS 225 and 401, Eds.
10112 and 10496.
Two sopranos.
Some folk, some Baroque.
HANDEL, GEORGE FRIDERIC. *Pieces and Dances,* 2 vols. Schott, RMS 79A and 79B, Eds.
2704 and 2742.
Soprano and alto.
Old Dances. Ruth Kaestner, ed. Hofmeister, B102.
Soprano and alto.

PURCELL, HENRY. *Fifteen Short Duets.* H. Kaestner, ed. Schott, RMS 141, Ed. 2726.
Soprano and alto.
Spielt auf zur Weihnacht. Fritz Koschinsky, ed. Noetzel, 3054.
Two altos.
Christmas and other pastoral music.
Three Thirteenth-Century Dances. Transcribed by Peter Hedrick, ed. Consort, CM 1034.
Soprano and alto.
Includes an optional percussion accompaniment.
Treble and Tenor Duets by Purcell, Handel, Bach and Other Masters. Dom Gregory Murray, arr. Schott, RMS 419, Ed. 10539.
Alto and tenor.
Zes Suites. Gerrit Vellekoop, arr. XYZ, 729.
Two altos.
Typical French Baroque pieces, written for the amateur.

THREE RECORDERS

Elizabethan Trios. Erich Katz, ed. Anfor, RCE 3.
Soprano, alto, and tenor.
Five 13th Century Pieces. Bruno Turner, ed. Schott, RMS 1114, Rec. Bibliothek 22.
Various.
House Music. Reba Paeff Mirsky, ed. Hargail, H-50.
Soprano, soprano (alto reading up an octave), and alto (tenor).
Easy homophonic Baroque music. The instrumentation specified at the beginning of the edition is incorrect.
MONTEVERDI, CLAUDIO. *Eight Pieces and Balletto.* Colin Sterne, arr. Hargail, Classical Anthology 11.
Soprano, alto reading up an octave, and tenor.
Short, light pieces.
Recorder Consort (Book I). Erich Katz, ed. E. C. Schirmer, Earls Court Repertory for Rec. 2053.
Soprano, soprano (alto reading up an octave), and alto (tenor).
Various Elizabethan composers.

FOUR RECORDERS

BACH, JOHANN SEBASTIAN. *Twelve Chorales.* Theo Wyatt, arr. Schott, RMS 277, Ed. 10405.
Soprano, soprano (alto), alto, and tenor (parts and piano score).
HAUSSMANN, VALENTIN. *New Pleasant and Delightful Dances.* R.-F. Callenberg, ed. Moeck, Zeitschrift für Spielmusik 56.
Soprano, soprano (alto reading up an octave), alto (tenor), and tenor (bass reading up an octave).
Very simple four-part Renaissance dance music, with an optional fifth part for alto or tenor.

Nine Sixteenth-Century Dances, 2 vols. Freda Dinn, arr. Schott, RMS 426 and 428,
    Archive 1 and 2.
    Soprano, two altos, and tenor.
    Separate optional percussion part included.
Three Canzoni. Erich Katz, ed. Anfor, RCE 1.
    Soprano, alto, tenor, and bass (tenor).
    Late-sixteenth-century Italian instrumental pieces. Includes a separate
    tenor part as an alternative to the bass.

VARIOUS NUMBERS OF RECORDERS

Elizabethan & Shakespearean Musicke for the Recorder and *Jacobean & Restoration Musicke
    for the Recorder.* Claude Simpson, arr. E. C. Schirmer, 2009 and 2010.
    Various; two, three, four, five, and six parts.
    Some pieces are presented in more than one arrangement, using different
    recorders and/or numbers of parts.
The Recorder Book. Collected by Steve Rosenberg. Schott, RMS 1408, Ed. 11380.
    Various; one, two, three, four, and five parts.
    An anthology of music from the Middle Ages to the present, including one
    avant-garde piece, notated somewhat cryptically, that is considerably more
    difficult than the rest of the collection. Very accessible to the novice,
    although there are a few misprints. Contains a fingering chart.

Recorder with Keyboard

ONE RECORDER

HANDEL, GEORGE FRIDERIC. *Pieces for Treble Recorder and Basso Continuo.* Willi Hil-
    lemann, ed. Schott, RMS 85, Ed. 2563.
    Alto and basso continuo.
HOOK, JAMES. *Sonata in G.* Walter Bergmann, ed. Schott, RMS 106, Ed. 10108.
    Soprano and piano.
    Early classical.
Kleine Vortragsstücke. Heinz Kaestner, ed. Schott, RMS 1007, Ed. 4857.
    Alto and piano (harpsichord).
    Baroque arrangements.
19 Small Pieces from a Book of 1740. Kalmus, Rec. Series.
    Soprano (tenor) and piano.
Old Dances and Airs. H. Kaestner and H. Spittler, eds. Schott, RMS 131, Ed. 2567A.
    Soprano (tenor) and piano.
    Twenty-four pieces by composers of the seventeenth and eighteenth cen-
    turies.
Pieces from the Fitzwilliam Virginal Book. Kalmus, Rec. Series 9012.
    Soprano and piano.
    Charming arrangements of Elizabethan harpsichord pieces.

INTERMEDIATE

Exercises

DONINGTON, MARGARET AND ROBERT. *Scales, Arpeggios, and Exercises for the Recorder.* O.U.P.
All sizes.
Exercises at various levels of difficulty for all sizes of recorder.

DUSCHENES, MARIO. *Studies in Recorder Playing.* Berandol.
Soprano (tenor) or alto.
Scales and arpeggios methodically presented; exercises in transposition. (One volume for C fingering, one for F.)

HÖFFER-VON WINTERFELD, LINDE. *40 Studies for Alto-Recorder Adapted from the Solfeggios of Frederick the Great.* Sikorski, Ed. 318.
Alto.
Frederick's flute teacher, the great Johann Joachim Quantz, probably devised these studies for his royal pupil. Here they have been adapted for recorder.

ROODA, G. *95 Dexterity Exercises and Dances for Recorders in C* and *95 Dexterity Exercises and Dances for Recorders in F.* Hargail, HRW-3 and HRW-4.
Soprano (tenor) or alto (sopranino and bass).
Excellent exercise material, interspersed with pleasing tunes. (One volume for C fingering, one for F.)

STAEPS, HANS ULRICH. *Das tägliche Pensum.* Universal, UE 12614.
Alto.
Modern exercises; unusual scales, meters, and rhythms.

Recorder Alone

ONE RECORDER

The Bird Fancyer's Delight. Stanley Godman, ed. Schott, RMS 281, Ed. 10442.
Sopranino (alto).
Eighteenth-century tunes for teaching birds to sing.

Fifteen Solos for Treble Recorder by Masters of the 18th Century. F. J. Giesbert, ed. Schott, RMS 39, Ed. 2562A.
Alto.

Fifty Old English Folk Dance Airs. Edgar H. Hunt, arr. Schott, RMS 43, Ed. 10007.
Soprano.

For the Sopranino (also Soprano, Alto, Tenor, Bass) Recorder Player. Walter Bergmann, ed. Magnamusic, M-21 (M-22, M-23, M-24, and M-25).
Sopranino (soprano, alto, tenor, or bass).
Five volumes of selections from the literature (and some adaptations).

Preludes and Voluntaries (1708). Rene Colwell, ed. Schott, RMS 251, Ed. 10013.
Alto.
Charming eighteenth-century études.

TWO RECORDERS

Bicinia: 16th Century Pieces for Soprano and Alto Recorders. Gerald Burakoff and Edward
    G. Evans, eds. Hargail, H-57.
    Soprano and alto.
CHÉDEVILLE, ESPRIT PHILIPPE. *6 Galant Duos for 2 Recorders.* Kalmus.
    Two sopranos.
    French Baroque.
Easy Duets by Old Masters of the 16th Century. Kalmus.
    Various.
    Those pieces that were originally vocal have texts printed.
FESCH, WILLEM DE. *Fourteen Duets.* Audrey Abbott and Theo Wyatt, arrs. Schott,
    RMS 211, Ed. 10406.
    Alto and tenor.
    Baroque.
FONGHETTI, PAOLO. *Four Duets.* William E. Hettrick, ed. Sweet Pipes, Musica Selecta
    III, SP2311.
    Various (parts in original notation).
    Bicinia from a collection of 1598. The editor provides a guide for reading
    the notation of the facsimile parts.
French Chansons. Joel Newman, ed. Galaxy, ARS 81.
    Various.
    Includes texts and translations.
KATZ, ERICH. *A Miniature Suite.* Anfor, RCE 9.
    Two altos.
    Contemporary.
LASSO, ORLANDO DI. *Bicinien.* Gerhard Pinthus, ed. Bärenreiter, Hortus Musicus 2.
    Various.
    One of the best collections of Renaissance bicinia.
LE ROY, ADRIAN, AND ROBERT BALLARD. *Premier Livre de Chansons à Deux Parties (1578),*
    2 vols. Bernard Thomas, ed. London Pro Musica, LPM RM1 and RM2.
    Various.
LOEILLET DE GANT, JEAN BAPTISTE. *Sechs Duette,* 2 vols. Hugo Ruf, ed. Schott, RMS
    1062 and 362, Ed. 4737 and 5591.
    Two altos.
    Loeillet's own arrangements of his sonatas for recorder and basso continuo.
————. *Sonata in D Minor.* Elloyd Hanson, ed. Galaxy, ARS 55.
    Two altos.
    The editor provides an ornamented version of the sarabande.
MATTHESON, JOHANN. *Four Sonatas.* M. Kolinski, ed. Hargail, Ed. Newman 505.
    Two altos.
    Somewhat pedestrian, but fun.
MORLEY, THOMAS. *Two-Part Canzonets for Voices and Instruments.* D. H. Boalch, ed.
    Peters, Ed. H-1998.
    Various.
    Charming Elizabethan pieces originally for voices and viols.

Music of the Baroque. Erich Katz, arr. Anfor, RCE 6.
  Soprano and alto.
Music of the Renaissance. Erich Katz, arr. Anfor, RCE 5.
  Soprano and alto.
RHAW, GEORG. *Bicinia Germanica (1545).* Bernard Thomas, ed. London Pro Musica,
  Thesaurus Musicus LPM TM2.
  Various.
Seven Canons of the Sixteenth Century. Bernard Thomas, ed. London Pro Musica,
  Thesaurus Musicus LPM TM1.
  Two sopranos.
Seven Renaissance Bicinia. Transcribed by Edward G. Evans and Kenneth Wollitz,
  eds. Consort, CM 1012.
  Soprano and alto.
SUSATO, TYLMAN. *Le Premier Livre des chansons à 2 ou à 3 parties,* 2 vols. Aimé Agnel,
  ed. Heugel, Cahiers de Plein Jeu CPJ 5 and CPJ 6.
  Various.
  Each of these sixteenth-century chansons can be performed as a duet or
  with the addition of an optional third part.

THREE RECORDERS

BARAB, SEYMOUR. *Six Pieces for Three Recorders.* Boosey & Hawkes, B. H. Bk. 405.
  Soprano, alto, and tenor.
  Pleasantly modern.
BOISMORTIER, JOSEPH BODIN DE. *Sonata for Three Flutes or Alto Recorders, Oeuvre 7, No. 1,
  1725.* Conrad Rawski, Ed. Boosey & Hawkes.
  Three altos.
BYRD, WILLIAM, AND ORLANDO GIBBONS. *Fantasias a Tre (Trios of the 16th & 17th
  Centuries).* Erich Katz, ed. Hargail, H37-B.
  Soprano, alto, and tenor.
CRECQUILLON, THOMAS. *Twelve Chansons.* Bernard Thomas, ed. London Pro Musica,
  LPM PC8.
  Various.
  Sixteenth century.
DAVENPORT, LaNOUE. *Variations on Three Ravens.* Anfor, RCE 8.
  Soprano, alto, and tenor.
  Modern variations on an old English ballad.
EAST, MICHAEL. *20 Light Fantasias (The Fift Set of Bookes, 1618).* David Goldstein, ed.
  Provincetown Bookshop Eds.
  Two sopranos and tenor.
  Handwritten music and *Mensurstriche* make this a bit difficult to read.
Eight Chansons of the Late Fifteenth Century. Bernard Thomas, ed. London Pro Musica,
  Thesaurus Musicus LPM TM3.
  Various.
HENRY VIII. *Quam pulchra es.* C. F. Simkins, Ed. Schott, RMS 116, Rec. Library 15.
  Two altos and tenor.

ISAAC, HEINRICH. *Two Carmina (a 3)*. William E. Hettrick, ed. Sweet Pipes, Musica Selecta IV, SP2312.

> Soprano (alto reading up an octave), tenor, and bass (parts in original notation).
>
> Instrumental pieces. The editor provides a guide for reading the Renaissance notation of the facsimile parts.

KATZ, ERICH. *Three Movements*. Galaxy, ARS 50.

> Soprano, alto, and tenor.
>
> Modern. Rhythmically tricky; unusual time signatures.

LOCKE, MATTHEW. *Consort*. Elli McMullen, ed. Schott, RMS 480, Ed. 5692, Archive 9.

> Soprano, alto, and tenor.
>
> Late English Renaissance.

MATTHESON, JOHANN. *Acht Sonaten für drei Altblockflöten*. Nagel, Ed. 506.

> Three altos.
>
> Staple Baroque music.

MOORE, TIMOTHY. *Suite in G.* Schott, RMS 824, Ed. 10554.

> Soprano, alto, and tenor (parts).
>
> Contemporary English composer.

Motets and Hymns of the 16th Century. Erich Katz, arr. Carl Van Roy.

> Soprano, soprano (alto reading up an octave), and alto (tenor).

Music of the Fifteenth Century. Walter Gerboth, ed. Hargail, HCA-18.

> Soprano, alto, and tenor.

Musik aus dem Frühbarock. Helmut Mönkemeyer, ed. Schott, RMS 1022, Ed. 4676.

> Two sopranos and alto reading up an octave (alternate at-pitch alto part).
>
> Early Baroque music from different countries.

REGNART, JAKOB. *Ten Lieder in Villanella Style.* Bernard Thomas, ed. London Pro Musica, Thesaurus Musicus LPM TM4.

> Various.
>
> German pieces in a sixteenth-century Italian form.

Seven Chansons. Bernard Thomas, ed. London Pro Musica, LPM PC9.

> Various.
>
> Sixteenth century.

Tudor Trios. Joel Newman, ed. Galaxy, ARS 45.

> Various.
>
> Includes two pieces by King Henry VIII.

FOUR RECORDERS

AICHINGER, GREGOR. *Three Ricercars.* William E. Hettrick, ed. Galaxy, ARS 84.

> Various.
>
> Early Baroque. The first ricercar has an amusing part consisting of just two notes in alternation.

ATTAINGNANT, PIERRE. *Fourteen Chansons (1533).* Bernard Thomas, ed. London Pro Musica, LPM PC1.
    Alto reading up an octave, two tenors, and bass.
————. *Second Livre de Danceries (1547).* Bernard Thomas, ed. London Pro Musica, LPM DP2.
    Soprano (alto reading up an octave), alto (tenor), tenor, and bass.
BACH, JOHANN SEBASTIAN. *Canzona for Recorder Quartet.* Dom Gregory Murray, ed. Schott, RMS 718, Archive 38.
    Soprano, two altos, and tenor.
————. *Chorales for Christmas.* Jonathan Grove, arr. Carl Van Roy.
    Soprano, alto, tenor, and bass.
BYRD, WILLIAM. *Fantazia a 4.* Marylin Wailes, ed. Schott, RMS 796, Archive 64.
    Soprano, alto, tenor, and bass (parts).
    Measures with large note values—tricky to read from parts.
————. *Two In Nomines.* Terrill Schukraft, ed. Galaxy, ARS 71.
    Soprano, alto, tenor, and bass.
    One slow-moving part in each piece carries the *In nomine* theme.
Five Quodlibets of the Fifteenth Century. Bernard Thomas, ed. London Pro Musica, Thesaurus Musicus LPM TM6.
    Various.
    Based on French popular songs of the time.
GERVAISE, CLAUDE. *Troisième Livre de Danceries (1557)* (also *Quart Livre [1550], Cinquièsme Livre [1550],* and *Sixième Livre [1555]).* Bernard Thomas, ed. London Pro Musica, LPM DP3 (DP4, DP5, and DP6).
    Soprano (alto reading up an octave), alto (tenor), tenor, and bass.
HOFHAIMER, PAUL. *Seven Tenor Songs.* Bernard Thomas, ed. London Pro Musica, Thesaurus Musicus LPM TM8.
    Various.
    German Renaissance. Melody in the tenor part.
ISAAC, HEINRICH. *A la Bataglia.* Bernard Thomas, ed. London Pro Musica, LPM AN1.
    Alto reading up an octave, two tenors, and bass (parts).
    A lively example of the sixteenth-century genre of battle pieces.
Italian Masters Around 1600. Helmut Mönkemeyer, ed. Pelikan, Ed. 745, Musica Instrumentalis Book 6.
    Soprano, alto, tenor, and bass.
JOSQUIN DES PRÈS. *Seven Secular Pieces.* London Pro Musica, LPM AN6.
    Alto reading up an octave, two tenors, and bass.
LASSUS, ROLAND DE. *Ten Chansons.* Bernard Thomas, ed. London Pro Musica, LPM AR1.
    Soprano, alto, tenor, and bass.
PHALÈSE, PIERRE. *Antwerpener Tanzbuch,* 2 vols. Helmut Mönkemeyer, ed. Heinrichshofen, Consortium 1066 and 1067.
    Soprano, alto reading up an octave, tenor, and bass (parts).
    Renaissance dances.

————. *Löwener Tanzbuch,* 2 vols. Helmut Mönkemeyer, ed. Heinrichshofen, Consortium 1064 and 1065.
Soprano, alto reading up an octave, tenor, and bass (parts).
Renaissance dances.

POSER, HANS. *Rendsburger Tänze.* Sikorski, Ed. 410.
Soprano, alto, tenor, and bass (parts).
Modern dances.

PURCELL, HENRY. *Suite "The Fairy Queen."* Universal, UE 12604.
Soprano, alto, tenor, and bass (parts).
An arrangement of music from Purcell's opera.

SENFL, LUDWIG. *Liedsätze für Blockflötenquartett.* Hartmut Strebel, ed. Hänssler, Series XI, No. 3.
Various.
Lovely pieces by the sixteenth-century Swiss composer.

Seven Comical Chansons, c. 1530. Bernard Thomas, ed. London Pro Musica, Thesaurus Musicus LPM TM7.
Various.

Seven Double Canons of the Early Sixteenth Century. Bernard Thomas, ed. London Pro Musica, LPM RB2.
Alto reading up an octave, two tenors, and bass.
Mainly based on popular tunes of the time.

SUSATO, TIELMAN. *Danserye,* 2 vols. F. J. Giesbert, ed. Schott, RMS 169a and 169b, Eds. 2435 and 2436.
Various.
The best of the Renaissance dance collections. Most of the triple-time pieces (basse danses and galliards) are misbarred and presented as being in duple time—a serious example of bad editing. The funny-looking clef used is a peculiar invention of Giesbert's and is equivalent to treble clef down an octave.

TERTRE, ETIENNE DU. *Septième Livre de Danceries (1557).* Bernard Thomas, ed. London Pro Musica, LPM DP7.
Soprano (alto reading up an octave), alto (tenor), tenor, and bass.

VECCHI, ORAZIO. *Seven Canzonette (1585).* Bernard Thomas, ed. London Pro Musica, Thesaurus Musicus LPM TM5.
Various.

FIVE RECORDERS

AGOSTINI, LUDOVICO. *Canzoni alla Napolitana (1574).* Bernard Thomas, ed. London Pro Musica, Thesaurus Musicus LPM TM9.
Various.

GABRIELI, GIOVANNI. *Canzon Prima (1615).* Bernard Thomas, ed. London Pro Musica, LPM VM1.
Soprano, alto, two tenors (two altos), and bass (parts).
This edition is a bit confusing: The score is in A minor, but the parts have been transposed down a tone to fit recorders.

PRAETORIUS, MICHAEL. *Two Christmas Hymn-Settings on "A Solis Ortus Cardine."* Erich Katz, ed. Galaxy, ARS 61.
Soprano, alto, two tenors, and bass.

SCHEIDT, SAMUEL. *Dances in Five Parts.* Linde Höffer-von Winterfeld, ed. Moeck, Zeitschrift für Spielmusik 184.
Two sopranos, alto, tenor, and bass.
Early-seventeenth-century German dances.

SCHEIN, JOHANN HERMANN. *Two Suites in Five Parts.* Rudolf Gutman, ed. Moeck, Zeitschrift für Spielmusik 43.
Soprano, soprano (alto reading up an octave), alto (tenor), tenor, and bass.
Dances from Schein's 1617 *Banchetto Musicale.*

WILDER, PHILIP VAN. *Four Chansons.* Bernard Thomas, ed. London Pro Musica, Thesaurus Musicus LPM TM10.
Various.
French songs by a Flemish composer in the employ of King Henry VIII.

WOODCOCK, CLEMENT. *"Browning" Fantasy.* London Pro Musica, LPM EM1.
Two sopranos, alto, tenor, and bass (parts).
An instrumental setting of the late-sixteenth-century English popular tune also known as "The Leaves Be Green."

SIX RECORDERS

PURCELL, HENRY. *In Nomine 1.* Walter Bergmann, arr. Faber, FO 258.
Soprano, two altos, alto (tenor), tenor, and bass (parts).
A very late and very beautiful example of the enormous number of English seventeenth-century fantasias incorporating the plainsong antiphon *Gloria tibi trinitas* as a cantus firmus.

SEVEN RECORDERS

PURCELL, HENRY. *In Nomine 2.* Walter Bergmann, arr. Faber, FO 268.
Two sopranos, alto, tenor, tenor (bass reading up an octave), and two basses (parts).

EIGHT RECORDERS

ALTENBURG, MICHAEL. *Puer Natus in Bethlehem.* Helmut Mönkemeyer, ed. Moeck, Zeitschrift für Spielmusik 379.
Double choir: Two sopranos, alto reading up an octave, and tenor (bass); alto reading up an octave, two tenors, and bass.
A seventeenth-century Lutheran setting of a medieval Latin hymn. Difficult page turns.

BARTOLINI, GABRIELI, AND GUSSAGO. *Drei doppelchörige Canzonen.* Helmut Mönkemeyer, ed. Heinrichshofen, Consortium 996.
Double choir: various (parts).
Typical Venetian instrumental pieces for double choir.

FRESCOBALDI, GIROLAMO, AND GIOSEPPE GUAMI. *Zwei doppelchörige Kanzonen.* Helmut
Mönkemeyer, ed. Heinrichshofen, Consortium 1012.
Double choir: various (parts).
More Venetian instrumental pieces.

GRILLO, GIOVANNI BATTISTA. *II. Canzone.* Paul Winter, ed. Peters, Canticum 5902.
Double choir: Two sopranos, alto reading up an octave, and tenor (bass);
tenor, tenor (bass), bass, and great bass.
Four of the parts in this 1618 composition are in bass clef.

JOSQUIN DES PRÈS. *Tulerunt Dominum Meum.* LaNoue Davenport, arr. Row, 3007-8.
Two sopranos, two altos, tenor (alto), two tenors (two altos), and two
basses (two tenors) (parts).
An instrumental arrangement of a motet of surpassing beauty.

MASSAINO, TIBURTIO. *Canzona XXXIV.* Reginald Johnson, ed. and arr. Universal, UE
12641.
Double choir: Soprano, soprano (alto reading up an octave), alto, and bass;
two altos, tenor, and bass (parts).
An easy and effective early-seventeenth-century piece.

ROGNONI TAEGGIO, G. D. *La Porta.* Paul Winter, ed. Peters, Canticum 4822.
Double choir: Soprano, soprano (alto reading up an octave), alto reading up
an octave, and bass (tenor); alto reading up an octave, tenor, bass (tenor),
and bass (parts).
An early-seventeenth-century canzona.

VIADANA, LUDOVICO GROSSI DA. *Canzona "La Padovana."* Reginald Johnson, ed. Universal, UE 14037.
Double choir: Soprano, alto, tenor, and bass; soprano, alto, tenor, and bass
(parts).

TEN RECORDERS

GABRIELI, GIOVANNI. *X. Canzone.* Paul Winter, ed. Peters, Canticum 5901.
Double choir: Two sopranos, two altos reading up an octave, and bass; alto
reading up an octave, tenor, tenor (bass reading up an octave), bass (tenor),
and great bass (parts).
From the *Sacrae symphoniae* (1597).

TWELVE RECORDERS

GABRIELI, GIOVANNI. *Canzona XIII.* Reginald Johnson, ed. Universal, UE 14000 L.
Triple choir: Soprano, soprano (alto reading up an octave), alto (tenor), and
bass; soprano, alto, alto (tenor), and bass; soprano, alto, tenor (alto), and
bass (parts).

VARIOUS NUMBERS OF RECORDERS

Ein altes Spielbuch, 2 vols. F. J. Giesbert, ed. Schott, RMS 67a and 67b, Eds. 2439
and 2440.
Various; three, four, and five parts.
A marvelous compendium of secular pieces by Josquin, Isaac, Obrecht, and

many other composers of the late fifteenth century. The strange-looking F clef used, Giesbert's invention, is equivalent to treble clef down an octave.

Nine Medieval Songs. Martha Bixler and Judit Kadar, arrs. Anfor, RCE 34.
   Various; one, two, and three parts.
   Medieval music arranged to fit alto recorders.

PRAETORIUS, MICHAEL. *Terpsichore.* Horst Weber, ed. Fidula, 5407 Boppard.
   Various; four and five parts.
   First-class late-Renaissance dances.

Renaissance Songs and Dances. Erich Katz, ed. Associated Music, ARS Eds.
   Various; three, four, five, and six parts.

Recorder with Keyboard

ONE RECORDER

CORELLI, ARCANGELO. *Sonata in A Minor* (Op. 5, No. 8). Fritz Koschinsky, ed. Noetzel, Pegasus 3127.
   Soprano and basso continuo.
   Originally for violin; very effective on recorder.

The Division Flute (1706). Hans-Martin Linde, ed. Schott, RMS 2026, Ed. 5737.
   Alto and basso continuo.
   Original divisions for recorder over a ground bass; improvisatory in character.

FRESCOBALDI, GIROLAMO. *Five Canzonas.* Bernard Thomas, ed. London Pro Musica, LPM GF1.
   Soprano and basso continuo.
   Early Baroque patchwork canzonas with frequent meter changes.

Greensleeves to a Ground. Arnold and Carl F. Dolmetsch, arrs. Schott, RMS 58, Ed. 10366; Schott, RMS 856, Ed. 10596.
   Soprano and harpsichord (Ed. 10366) or alto and harpsichord (Ed. 10596).
   A set of variations on the familiar tune.

HAND, COLIN. *Plaint.* Schott, RMS 1372, Ed. 11147.
   Tenor and harpsichord (piano).
   Elegiac modern piece in a blues vein.

HANDEL, GEORGE FRIDERIC. *Sonata in B Flat.* Thurston Dart and Walter Bergmann, arrs. Schott, RMS 92, Rec. Series 20.
   Soprano and piano.
   A good arrangement of an oboe sonata.

LINDE, HANS-MARTIN. *Sonatine française.* Gerhard Braun, ed. Hänssler, Series XI, No. 14.
   Soprano and harpsichord.
   Modern. Idiomatic for both recorder and keyboard; well-constructed.

L'OEILLET, JEAN BAPTISTE. *Sonatas,* 3 vols. Johann Philipp Hinnenthal, ed. Bärenreiter, Hortus Musicus 43, 162, and 165.
   Alto and basso continuo.
   The editor provides written-out ornaments in the French style for the slow movements.

MARCELLO, BENEDETTO. *Sonaten,* 3 vols. Jörgen Glode, ed. Bärenreiter, Hortus
    Musicus 142, 151, and 152.
    Alto and basso continuo.
PEPUSCH, J. C. *Sonata in G.* F. J. Giesbert, arr. Schott, RMS 158, Rec. Series 10.
    Soprano (tenor) and piano.
    By the English arranger and composer of *The Beggar's Opera.*
REID, JOHN. *Sonata.* Alexander Silbiger, ed. Galaxy, ARS 66.
    Alto and basso continuo.
    Authentic Scottish flavor. Originally for flute.

TWO RECORDERS

CORELLI, ARCANGELO. *Drei Sonaten.* Dietz Degen, ed. Peters, Ed. 4567.
    Two altos and basso continuo.
    Originally for two violins.
FRESCOBALDI, GIROLAMO. *Five Canzonas.* Bernard Thomas, ed. London Pro Musica,
    LPM GF4.
    Two sopranos and basso continuo.
    Early Baroque patchwork canzonas with frequent meter changes.
HANDEL, GEORGE FRIDERIC. *Twelve Original Trio Pieces.* Willi Hillemann, ed. Nagel,
    Ed. 514.
    Two altos and piano (optional cello part).
    Excerpts from trio sonatas.
PURCELL, HENRY. *Chaconne: "Two in One upon a Ground."* Walter G. Bergmann, arr.
    Schott, RMS 170, Rec. Series 23.
    Two altos and piano.
    A gem.
SCHICKHARDT, JOHANN CHRISTIAN. *Triosonate, e-moll.* Hugo Ruf, ed. Schott, RMS 380,
    Ed. 5594.
    Two altos and basso continuo.
TELEMANN, GEORG PHILIPP. *Trio-Sonate in F dur.* Adolf Hoffmann, ed. Breitkopf &
    Härtel, Collegium Musicum 1967.
    Two altos and basso continuo.

THREE RECORDERS

Anonymous Master of Breslau. *Sonada.* E. H. Meyer, ed. Schott, RMS 4, Ed.
    10107.
    Soprano, two sopranos (two altos) and basso continuo.
SCARLATTI, ALESSANDRO. *Quartettino.* Waldemar Woehl, ed. Peters, Ed. 4559.
    Three altos and basso continuo.

FOUR RECORDERS

FRESCOBALDI, GIROLAMO. *Canzona on "Romanesca."* Colin Sterne, ed. Associated
    Music.
    Soprano, alto, tenor, and bass and keyboard.

FIVE RECORDERS

BERTALI, ANTONIO. *Sonatella.* E. H. Meyer, ed. Schott, RMS 38, Ed. 10106.
Soprano (sopranino), soprano, alto, tenor (alto), bass (tenor), and basso
continuo (ad lib).
One short, light movement.

SIX RECORDERS

BONONCINI, GIOVANNI MARIA. *Two Suites a 6.* Layton Ring, ed. Universal, Dolmetsch
Rec. Series, UE 14018 L.
Sopranino (soprano), soprano, alto (soprano), alto, tenor, and bass and
basso continuo.
Originally for strings.

SEVEN RECORDERS

SCHMELZER, J. H. *Sonata.* E. H. Meyer, ed. and arr. Schott, RMS 182, Ed. 10105.
Soprano (sopranino), soprano, two altos, tenor (alto), tenor, and bass and
basso continuo (ad lib).
A war-horse from the mid-Baroque.

Recorder with Other Instruments

TELEMANN, GEORG PHILIPP. *Trio-Sonate in C dur.* Adolf Hoffmann, ed. Breitkopf &
Härtel, Collegium Musicum 1968.
Alto; violin (alto recorder); and basso continuo.
Canonic.

DIFFICULT

Exercises

COLLETTE, JOANNES. *Melodische Studies.* XYZ.
Alto.
Very difficult; modern idiom.
———. *12 Melodious Exercises.* Universal, UE 12643.
Soprano.
Very difficult; modern idiom.
LINDE, HANS-MARTIN. *Modern Exercises for Treble Recorder.* Schott, RMS 1014, Ed.
4797.
Alto.
Modern exercises of very high musical quality, stressing articulation.
———. *Quartet Exercise for Recorders.* Schott, RMS 1058, Ed. 5262.
Soprano, alto, tenor, and bass.
Exercises for the recorder consort.
MÖNKEMEYER, HELMUT. *Handleitung für das Spiel der Alt-Blockflöte,* Vol. II. Moeck, Ed.
2001.
Alto.

Challenging exercises with related excerpts from eighteenth- and twentieth-century recorder literature.

ROWLAND-JONES, A. *A Practice Book for the Treble Recorder.* O.U.P.
Alto.
Very difficult exercises based on excerpts from Baroque, Classical, and modern literature.

STAEPS, HANS ULRICH. *Tonfiguren.* Universal, UE 14933.
Alto.
A continuation of Staeps's *Das tägliche Pensum.*

Recorder Alone

ONE RECORDER

BASSANO, GIOVANNI. *Vier Ricercate (1598).* Hans-Martin Linde, ed. Hänssler, HE 11.217.
Alto.
Virtuoso display pieces.

COOKE, ARNOLD. *Serial Theme and Variations.* Schott, RMS 1286, Rec. Library 52.
Alto.
Well-crafted.

FREILLON-PONCEIN, JEAN-PIERRE, AND JACQUES HOTTETERRE LE ROMAIN. *Preludes.* Betty Bang and David Lasocki, eds. Faber.
Alto.
Good preface dealing with French Baroque performance practice.

LINDE, HANS-MARTIN. *Four Caprices.* Galaxy, ARS 59.
Alto.
An accessible modern piece.

MILLER, EDWARD. *Song for Recorder or Flute.* McGinnis & Marx.
Tenor (soprano) or alto.
Rhapsodic; contemporary idiom. (The second page of music is the alto version.)

The Recorder in J. S. Bach's Cantatas, Vol. I. Linde Höffer-von Winterfeld, ed. Sikorski, Ed. 502a.
Alto.

STERNE, COLIN. *Meadow, Hedge, Cuckoo.* Galaxy, ARS 87.
Alto.
Employs avant-garde techniques.

TELEMANN, GEORG PHILIPP. *Six Fantasias.* Frans Brüggen, ed. Hargail, BRS-1.
Alto.
Challenging and interesting music, originally for flute.

VAN EYCK, JACOB. *De Fluyten Lusthof*, 3 vols. Gerrit Vellekoop, ed. XYZ.
Soprano.
A very important collection of seventeenth-century tunes and variations written for recorder.

TWO RECORDERS

DAVENPORT, LaNOUE. *Three Duets for 2 Equal Instruments.* Omega.
    Two sopranos.
    Pleasing; in a mildly modern idiom.
From J. S. Bach's Cantatas with Two Recorders, Vol. 2. Linde Höffer-von Winterfeld,
    ed. Sikorski, Ed. 502b.
    Two altos.
    Treasures of the original recorder repertoire.
GIBBONS, ORLANDO. *Three Fantasias.* Douglas Ritchie, ed. Faber.
    Two altos.
    Viol music that is miraculously effective on recorders; the first fantasia is
    particularly delightful. No bar lines. Marred by awkward page turns.
HOTTETERRE, JACQUES. *Première Suitte de Pièces* and *Deuxième Suitte de Pièces.* Gerrit
    Vellekoop, ed. XYZ, 641 and 718.
    Two altos.
    The essence of the early French Baroque; requires knowledge of the style
    for effective performance.
LASSO, ORLANDO DI. *Six Fantasias,* 2 vols. Walther Pudelko, ed. Bärenreiter, Hortus
    Musicus 18 and 19.
    Soprano and alto reading up an octave (HM 18); various (HM 19).
    HM 19 includes a piece using alto clef.
LOCKE, MATTHEW. *Six Suites in Two Parts.* Helmut Mönkemeyer, ed. Pelikan,
    865.
    Soprano and alto.
    Originally written for viols; arranged for recorders.
QUANTZ, J. J. *Duette für 2 Altblockflöten.* Gerhard Braun, ed. Hänssler, Series XI, No.
    2.
    Two altos.
    Challenging; rococo style (originally for flutes; arranged for recorders).
STAEPS, HANS ULRICH. *Collection of Little Duets.* Schott, RMS 294, Ed. 4082.
    Two altos.
    Well-written, idiomatic contemporary music.
TELEMANN, GEORG PHILIPP. *6 Duette (Sonaten),* 2 vols. Hans-Ulrich Niggeman, ed.
    Hofmeister, FH 2998 and 2999. *Six Duets,* 2 vols. Mieczyslaw Kolinski, ed.
    Hargail, EN 106 and 106a.
    Two altos.
    Standards of the repertoire, of higher quality than most other Baroque
    duets. The Hofmeister edition is free of editorial corruption, but has some
    incorrect and missing notes; the Hargail edition has the correct notes but
    is a victim of outmoded editing (changed meters, editorial articulations not
    so identified and often ill judged).
————. *Six Canonic Sonatas.* Greta Richert, ed. Schott, RMS 334, Ed. 4088.
    Two altos.
    Ingenious; great fun to play.

THREE RECORDERS

Carols for Recorders and *More Carols for Recorders.* LaNoue Davenport, ed. Galaxy.
Various.
Fifteenth-century English carols. Dubious editorial accidentals, but lovely music.

DOROUGH, ROBERT. *Homophonic Suite.* Anfor, RCE 35.
Soprano, alto, and tenor.
Forties-style jazz and blues for recorder, by a composer who really knows the idiom and the instrument.

HINDEMITH, PAUL. *Trio for Recorders.* Schott, RMS 474, Ed. 10094.
Soprano and two altos (parts).
Classic modern trio from the *Plöner Musiktag.* It works much better on soprano, alto, and tenor than with the specified instrumentation.

LINDE, HANS-MARTIN. *Trio für Blockflöten.* Hänssler, Series XI, No. 19.
Alto, tenor, and bass (parts).
Difficult contemporary piece. The alto player switches to sopranino during two of the movements.

Music from Shakespeare's Day. Joel Newman, ed. Galaxy, ARS 51.
Various.

PURCELL, HENRY. *Fantasia (No. 1).* George Hunter, adap. E. C. Schirmer, Earls Court Repertory for Rec. 2048.
Soprano, alto, and tenor.
Difficult, gorgeous music.

WOOLLEN, RUSSELL. *Sonatina.* Berandol.
Two altos and tenor.
Charming, well-written modern piece with impossible page turns.

FOUR RECORDERS

ALEMANN, EDUARDO ARMANDO. *Spectra.* Galaxy, ARS 79.
Soprano, alto, tenor, and bass.
Extremely difficult; avant-garde techniques. Includes a recording of the piece.

CHARLTON, ANDREW. *Three Movements for Four Recorders.* Galaxy, ARS 76.
Soprano, alto, tenor, and bass (parts).
Contemporary.

COOK, DOUGLAS. *Octave Variations.* Schott, RMS 1342, Ed. 10845.
Soprano, alto, tenor, and bass (parts).
Modern. Complicated rhythms.

Four Pieces of the Late Fifteenth Century. Bernard Thomas, ed. London Pro Musica, LPM AN2.
Alto reading up an octave, two tenors, and bass (parts).
Three of the pieces have one very slow-moving part.

HANDEL, GEORGE FRIDERIC. *Rodrigo-Overture.* Harold Newman, arr. Hargail, EN 508.

Soprano, alto, tenor, and bass.

Only the first movement presents difficulties (rhythmic).

KATZ, ERICH. *Suite.* Carl Van Roy, Rec. Library 3.

Soprano, alto, tenor, and bass (parts).

Contemporary; well written. Has an optional percussion accompaniment.

————. *Toccata.* Associated Music.

Soprano, alto, tenor, and bass (parts).

Acerbic modern piece.

MORTARO, ANTONIO. *Four Canzoni.* George Houle, ed. Galaxy, ARS 67.

Soprano, alto, tenor, and bass.

Shifting time signatures. Includes an ornamented version of the top part of one of the canzoni by an early-seventeenth-century contemporary of Mortaro.

RAKSIN, DAVID. *Serenade from "The Unicorn in the Garden."* Schott, RMS 850, Rec. Ensemble 10.

Two altos, tenor, and bass.

Composed for an animated film version of the Thurber short story. A sweet piece.

FIVE RECORDERS

BRADE, WILHELM. *Newe ausserlesene Paduanen/Galliarden/Cantzonen (1609).* Helmut Mönkemeyer, ed. Heinrichshofen, Consortium 1010.

Various (parts).

Fine examples of English late-Renaissance dances.

————. *Newe lustige Volten, Couranten, Balletten, Paduanen (1621).* Helmut Mönkemeyer, ed. Heinrichshofen, Consortium 1011.

Various (parts).

More fine Brade.

BYRD, WILLIAM. *The Leaves Be Green.* Timothy Moore, arr. Schott, RMS 792, Archive 58.

Soprano, two altos, tenor, and bass (parts).

The best of the five extant instrumental settings of the late-sixteenth-century English popular tune also known as "Browning."

DOWLAND, JOHN. *Lachrimae Pavans, Galiards and Almands,* 7 vols. Edgar Hunt, ed. Schott, RMS 518, 520, 522, 524, 526, 528, and 530; Archive 19, 20, 21, 22, 23, 24, and 25.

Soprano, alto, alto (tenor), tenor, and bass.

Dances by the greatest Elizabethan master of the lute song. The first piece in each volume is based on Dowland's own "Lachrimae," or "Flow, My Tears."

EAST, MICHAEL. *Desperavi.* Nathalie Dolmetsch, ed. Schott, RMS 798, Archive 65.

Two sopranos, alto, tenor, and bass (parts).

An emotionally charged, expressive fantasia by the English madrigalist.

HOLBORNE, ANTHONY. *Dances, Grave and Light.* Dorothy Dana and Jennifer Lehmann, eds. Galaxy, ARS 58.

Soprano, alto, alto (tenor), tenor, and bass.
Elizabethan.
———. *Pavan & Galliard.* Edgar Hunt, ed. Schott, RMS 532, Archive 26.
Soprano, alto, alto (tenor), tenor, and bass.
———. *Quintets (First, Second,* and *Third Sets).* Royston Barrington, ed. Schott, RMS
750, 752, and 754; Archive 50, 51, and 52.
Two sopranos, alto, tenor, and bass.
More dances.
———. *Suite for Five Recorders.* John Parkinson, ed. Schott, RMS 496, Archive 17.
Soprano, two altos, tenor, and bass.
Still more delightful dances.
JOSQUIN DES PRÈS. *La Spagna.* Bernard Thomas, ed. London Pro Musica, LPM RB3.
Alto reading up an octave, two tenors, and two basses (parts).
Magnificent polyphonic setting of the basse-danse tenor, with two delight-
fully active bass parts.
Lachrimae. Joel Newman, ed. Heinrichshofen, 1182.
Soprano, alto, two tenors, and bass (parts).
Pavans and galliards by Holborne and others, inspired by John Dowland's
famous lute song "Flow, My Tears."
MARENZIO, LUCA. *Solo e Pensoso.* Marylin Wailes, ed. Schott, RMS 598, Archive 35.
Soprano, two altos, tenor, and bass.
A late, highly chromatic Italian madrigal.
SIMPSON, THOMAS. *Dances.* William E. Hettrick, ed. Galaxy, ARS 77.
Two sopranos, alto, tenor, and bass.
Very pretty, elegant dances by a contemporary of William Brade.
T'Andernaken. Bernard Thomas, ed. London Pro Musica, LPM RB1.
Alto reading up an octave, two tenors, and two basses (parts).
One of the numerous Renaissance settings of the Flemish popular tune.
The elaborate rhythms of the piece are similar to those of late-fifteenth-
century basse-danse settings. Spurious vagant.

SIX RECORDERS

BRADE, WILHELM. *Newe ausserlesene Paduanen und Galliarden (1614).* Helmut Mön-
kemeyer, ed. Heinrichshofen, Consortium 1133.
Two sopranos, alto reading up an octave, alto (tenor), tenor, and bass
(parts).
Superb.
BYRD, WILLIAM. *Fantazia No. 2.* Robert Salkeld, arr. Faber, FO 363.
Two sopranos, alto, alto (tenor), tenor, and bass (parts).
Byrd weaves popular Renaissance material into a highly aristocratic form.
HAND, COLIN. *Fanfare for a Festival, Op. 64.* Schott, RMS 1280, Rec. Ensemble
39.
Two sopranos, alto, two tenors, and bass (parts).
Contemporary; harder to read than to play. Works well with many instru-
ments on a part.

JOSQUIN DES PRÈS. *Three Chansons.* LaNoue Davenport, ed. Galaxy, ARS 73.
Various (parts).

PHILLIPS, PETER. *Passamezzo Pavan.* Thurston Dart and William Coates, eds. Stainer
& Bell, Jacobean Consort Music 12.
Two sopranos, alto reading up an octave, tenor (alto), and bass.
Six Jacobean variations on the *passamezzo* ground bass.

TEN RECORDERS

SCARLATTI, DOMENICO. *Capriccio Fugato.* Francis Baines, arr. Schott, RMS 1308, Rec.
Bibliothek 37.
Four sopranos, alto (tenor), alto, two tenors, and two basses (parts).
A surprising piece.

VARIOUS NUMBERS OF RECORDERS

Comment peult avoir joye/Wohlauf gut Gesell von hinnen. Richard Taruskin, ed. Ogni
Sorte Editions, RS 1.
Various; three, four, and five parts (parts in original notation).
Settings by Franco-Flemish composers of a very popular Renaissance tune.
Includes a guide to reading Renaissance notation. The parts in original
notation are not facsimiles but rather modern renderings. A few of the
settings will not fit on recorders.
Een vrolic wesen. Richard Taruskin, ed. Ogni Sorte Editions, RS 2.
Various; two, three, and four parts (parts in original notation).
See *Comment peult,* above.
Instrumental Music from the Baldwine-Manuscript (1581–1606), Vol. I. Kees Boeke, ed.
Zen-On.
Various; two and three parts.
Some of these are extremely complex rhythmically. Pages (up to six!) fold
out to avoid turns.
L'Homme armé. Richard Taruskin, ed. Ogni Sorte Editions, RS 4.
Various; two, three, four, five, and seven parts (parts in original notation).
See *Comment peult,* above.
O venus bant. Richard Taruskin, ed. Ogni Sorte Editions, RS 3.
Various; three and four parts (parts in original notation).
See *Comment peult,* above. (All these settings will fit on recorders.)

Recorder with Keyboard

ONE RECORDER

BACH, JOHANN SEBASTIAN. *Drei Sonaten.* Greta Richert, arr. Hofmeister, V. 1061.
Alto and basso continuo.
Arranged from the original flute sonatas.
BARSANTI, FRANCESCO. *Sonata in C Major; Sonata in B-Flat Major.* Hugo Ruf, ed.
Bärenreiter, Hortus Musicus 183 and 185.
Alto and basso continuo.
In the Italian style, floridly ornamented.

CORELLI, ARCANGELO. *La Follia* (Op. 5, No. 12). Bernard Krainis, ed. McGinnis & Marx.
Alto and piano.
An eighteenth-century recorder arrangement of Corelli's variations for violin of the *La Follia* ground bass and tune.
————. *Sonata in C Major* (Op. 5, No. 3). David Lasocki, ed. Musica Rara. *Sonata in F Major* (Op. 5, No. 4). David Lasocki, ed. Hargail, H-101.
Alto and basso continuo.
Both sonatas are eighteenth-century recorder arrangements with ornaments of the violin originals.
COUPERIN, FRANÇOIS. *Le Rossignol en Amour.* Fleury, ed. Schott, RMS 52, Rec. Series 6.
Sopranino (alto) and basso continuo.
Originally for harpsichord.
DANICAN-PHILIDOR, ANNE. *Sonata d-moll.* Bärenreiter, Hortus Musicus 139.
Alto and basso continuo.
Interesting example of the French style.
HANDEL, GEORGE FRIDERIC. *Fitzwilliam Sonatas.* Thurston Dart, ed. Schott, RMS 82, Ed. 10062.
Alto and basso continuo.
————. *Four Sonatas.* Edgar H. Hunt, ed. Schott, RMS 86, Ed. 5056. *Vier Sonaten.* Waldemar Woehl, ed. Peters, Ed. 4552.
Alto and basso continuo.
The cornerstone of the Baroque recorder literature. Peters' *Urtext* edition is more accurate; the Schott edition has a better keyboard realization.
————. *3 New Sonatas.* Kalmus, Rec. Series 9027.
Alto and basso continuo.
HOTTETERRE, JACQUES. *Suite in E Minor.* Hugo Ruf, ed. Bärenreiter, Hortus Musicus 198.
Alto and basso continuo.
The French style at its best.
STERNE, COLIN. *Sonata.* Galaxy, ARS 74.
Alto and harpsichord (piano).
Modern.
TELEMANN, GEORG PHILIPP. *Partita No. 4 in G Minor.* Walter Bergmann, ed. Schott, RMS 1302, Ed. 11015.
Soprano and piano (harpsichord).
An arrangement of the fourth partita from Telemann's *Petite Musique de chambre.* Originally for oboe, violin, or flute.
————. *Vier Sonaten.* Dietz Degen, ed. Bärenreiter, Hortus Musicus 6. *Sonatas 1–4.* Walter Bergmann, ed. Schott, RMS 1382, Ed. 11238.
Alto and basso continuo.
Two very good editions of the same four sonatas. The third sonata is in different keys in the two editions.

————. *Zwei Sonaten.* Waldemar Woehl, ed. Peters, Ed. 4551.
Alto and basso continuo.

————. *Zwölf Methodische Sonaten.* Max Seiffert, ed. Bärenreiter, 2951.
Soprano (tenor) and basso continuo.
Each sonata has a slow movement with Telemann's embellishments in the *stile galant.* Originally for flute or violin.

VIVALDI, ANTONIO. *Il Pastor Fido.* Walter Upmeyer, ed. Bärenreiter, Hortus Musicus 135.
Alto and basso continuo.
Six sonatas.

TWO RECORDERS

TELEMANN, GEORG PHILIPP. *Trio Sonata in C Major.* Dietz Degen, ed. Bärenreiter, Hortus Musicus 10.
Two altos and basso continuo.
Short, charming movements, many bearing names of antique heroines.

THREE RECORDERS

PURCELL, HENRY. *Chaconne: "Three Parts upon a Ground."* Layton Ring, ed. Schott, RMS 510, Ed. 10340.
Three altos and basso continuo.
Elaborate variations on a ground bass.

FOUR RECORDERS

SCHICKHARDT, JOHANN CHRISTIAN. *Concertos,* 2 vols. R. V. Knab, ed. Bärenreiter, 1285 and 1286.
Four altos and basso continuo.
Musically uneven, but great fun to play.

Recorder with Other Instruments

ONE RECORDER

FASCH, JOHANN FRIEDRICH. *Sonata in B Flat Major.* Waldemar Woehl, ed. Bärenreiter, Hortus Musicus 26.
Alto; oboe (violin) and violin; and basso continuo.

HANDEL, GEORGE FRIDERIC. *Sonate II, F dur.* Helmut Mönkemeyer, ed. Schott, RMS 310, Ed. 3657.
Alto; violin; and basso continuo.

————. *Trio Sonata in C Minor.* Helmut Mönkemeyer, ed. Schott, RMS 88, Ed. 3656a.
Alto; violin; and basso continuo.

LINDE, HANS-MARTIN. *Serenata a tre.* Schott, RMS 2002, Ed. 5536.
Soprano, alto, and bass; guitar and cello (viola da gamba).
Contemporary. (The recorder player uses three instruments.)

PEPUSCH, JOHANN CHRISTIAN. *Triosonate g moll.* Walter Birke, ed. Peters, Ed. 4556.
Alto; oboe; and basso continuo.
QUANTZ, JOHANN JOACHIM. *Trio Sonata in C Major.* Walter Birke, ed. Bärenreiter,
Hortus Musicus 60.
Alto; flute (violin); and basso continuo.
SAMMARTINI, GIUSEPPE. *Concerto in F.* Johannes Brinckmann and Wilhelm Mohr,
eds. Schott, RMS 894, Rec. and Strings 25.
Soprano; two violins and viola; and basso continuo.
SCARLATTI, ALESSANDRO. *Quartett F dur.* Waldemar Woehl, ed. Peters, Ed. 4558.
Alto; two violins; and basso continuo.
TELEMANN, GEORG PHILIPP. *Concerto a tre, F Major.* Felix Schroeder, ed. Noetzel,
Pegasus 3286.
Alto; horn (viola); and basso continuo.
———. *Concerto in E minor.* Herbert Kölbel, ed. Bärenreiter, Hortus Musicus 124.
Alto; flute, two violins, and viola; and basso continuo.
———. *Quartett G dur.* Waldemar Woehl, ed. Peters, Ed. 4562.
Alto; oboe and violin; and harpsichord (piano).
———. *Quartett in d moll.* Max Seiffert, ed. Breitkopf & Härtel, Collegium Musi-
cum 59.
Alto; two flutes; and basso continuo.
Brilliant recorder part.
———. *Sonata a tre.* Helmut Mönkemeyer, ed. Moeck, Ed. 1001.
Alto; violin; and basso continuo.
———. *Sonate a-moll.* Gerhard Braun, ed. Hänssler, Series XI, No. 1.
Alto; oboe; and basso continuo.
———. *Suite, A minor.* Horst Büttner, ed. Eulenberg, Ed. 882 (score) and 5713
(parts).
Alto; two violins and viola; and basso continuo.
A recorder-player's dream; perhaps the most exciting piece in the literature.
———. *Trio, D Minor.* Manfred Ruëtz, ed. Schott, RMS 210, Ed. 3654.
Alto; violin (tenor recorder, oboe); and basso continuo.
The violin part was written for pardessus de viole.
———. *Trio in F Major.* Walter Upmeyer, ed. Nagel, Musik-Archiv 131.
Alto; viola da gamba; and basso continuo.
———. *Trio Sonata in B Flat.* Manfred Ruëtz, ed. Bärenreiter, Hortus Musicus 36.
Alto; harpsichord and basso continuo.
———. *Triosonata in E Minor.* Manfred Ruëtz, ed. Bärenreiter, Hortus Musicus 25.
Alto; oboe (flute, violin); and basso continuo.
———. *Trio Sonata in G Minor.* Manfred Ruëtz, ed. Schott, RMS 212, Ed. 3655A.
Alto; violin; and basso continuo.
The violin part was written for pardessus de viole.
———. *Triosonate a moll.* Waldemar Woehl, ed. Peters, Ed. 4560.
Alto; violin; and basso continuo.
———. *Triosonate c moll.* Waldemar Woehl. ed. Peters, Ed. 4561.
Alto; oboe (violin, viola da gamba); and basso continuo.

TWO RECORDERS

BACH, JOHANN SEBASTIAN. *Konzert.* Adolf Hoffman, ed. Möseler, Corona 32.
  Two altos; string orchestra; and harpsichord (piano).
  Bach's own F-major version of the G-major Brandenburg Concerto No. 4.

L'OEILLET, JEAN BAPTISTE. *Quintett h-moll.* Rolf Ermeler, ed. Bärenreiter, Hortus
  Musicus 133.
  Two flutes; two tenors; and basso continuo.
  The recorder parts were originally written for two voice flutes. All four
  melody parts can be played on tenor recorders.

APPENDIX

THE BEGINNER'S FIRST LESSON

For those of you who have never played the recorder before, the first chapter of this book, "Technique," doesn't really do the trick. You probably don't even know how to get started. You want to learn how to assemble the recorder, how to hold it, where to put your fingers to cover all of the holes, how to blow and how to use your tongue. So this is the section for you. We begin with the concrete and take simple, easy steps.

The notes in this lesson are presented in terms of the alto recorder, because that is the best size for the adult beginner. If you have inherited or been given another size, say a soprano or a tenor, it would be better to set it aside for the time being, and go out and buy yourself a good inexpensive plastic alto. Advice on buying recorders, both plastic and wood, will be found at the beginning of the chapter "Selecting and Caring for Your Recorder," p. 159.

The first three or four notes introduced in this lesson (E, D, C, and A) will be enough—maybe too much—for the absolute beginner to absorb at one sitting. The first note, E, may be sufficient for your first session, if music, let alone the instrument for making it, is totally new to you. However, the lesson does encompass further notes, so first read the chapter through for an overview, and then go back and learn one note at a time. Remember, novices need practice material, much more than the few musical examples contained in this lesson. I recommend Hugh Orr's book if you are absolutely new (or returning after a long hiatus) to music. He spells out everything. For people with some musical experience, I suggest Franz Giesbert's *Method for Recorder in F* (i.e., the alto). The text is totally unreliable, but the musical material is excellent; so if you can ignore the printed word and devote your attention exclusively to the

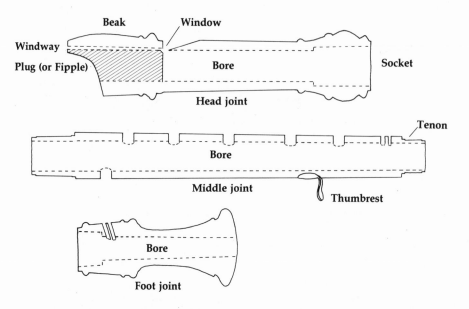

Beak   Window

Windway

Plug (or Fipple)   Bore   Socket

Head joint

Tenon

Bore

Middle joint   Thumbrest

Bore

Foot joint

printed notes, you will love this book. Both of these books are listed in Chapter 9 under "Methods," page 201.

Take the recorder out of its case or box. There are three pieces, or "joints," as they are usually called. The head joint is narrowed at the top into a curved beak with a slot through which one blows air into the windway, a flat, narrow passage which exits about an inch and a half further down at the window, a rectangular hole on the front of the head joint. The lower edge of the window is a thin blade. Air issuing from the windway is directed against this blade to produce the recorder's sound, the whistle system of tone production. Do not touch the blade. It is delicate.

The center is a slightly tapering tube with tenons on either end. The wider, upper tenon slides into the head joint, and the narrower, lower tenon slides into the foot joint. The center joint has six holes on top, for the fingers. (The sixth, lowest hole is usually a double hole.) On the back, near the upper end, is a thumbhole. The foot joint has a seventh finger hole, also usually doubled.

Assembling the Recorder

If your instrument is plastic, you will probably find the tenons of the center joint covered with plastic caps. The tenons are lightly greased so the parts of the instrument will slide together easily, and the caps keep the grease from spreading around when the instrument is disassembled and in its case. A little tube of the lubricant is usually supplied with the instrument. Slip the caps off, and if you don't want them to get lost, put them back in the case, particularly if you have cats. Otherwise you will find them under the refrigerator someday. Slide the center joint into the head joint so that the finger holes on top are aligned with the window. The foot joint, however, should be turned slightly so that its double hole, looking down the instrument, is a bit to the right of the finger holes on the center joint, making it easier for the right little finger to cover that hole.

Be sure all parts are pushed snugly together. If you have a wooden recorder, the tenons will probably be lapped with cork and there will be a little container of cork grease to keep them lubricated. The cork on new recorders is usually dry and will need an application of cork grease before the instrument is assembled.

Basic Fingerings

Here are the basic fingerings. Once you have mastered them, consult pages 21–29 for more explicit details about the fine points of playing each note perfectly.

THE FIRST NOTE, E:

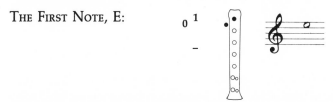

The left hand is held uppermost on the recorder, index, middle, and ring fingers governing holes 1, 2, and 3, and the thumb covering the hole in back. The left little finger is not employed. We begin by placing the thumb on the thumbhole and the index finger on hole 1. Hold the recorder out in front of you between thumb and forefinger rather as though you were holding a single, long-stemmed rose, and with your right hand gently swing the bottom of the recorder from side to side. As you do so, be aware of the sensation under the finger and thumb which are holding the recorder. They should feel the circles of the edges of the holes beneath them. This is to be sure the digits are properly centered and sealing the holes beneath them. Now place the lower edge of the beak about midway onto your lower lip at the center of your mouth, and let your upper lip rest on the upper edge of the beak, drawing the edges of the mouth slightly together to ensure that no air will escape from the sides. The recorder should not be placed too far into the mouth, certainly not far enough to get wet! Since the right hand is not involved in fingering this note (or the next two notes we will meet, D and C,) you can use it to steady the recorder by holding the foot joint below its double holes. Air is released into the slot by a stroke of the tip of tongue, rather like saying "du." Do not start the tone by placing the tongue on the recorder! You'll get it wet. When the tongue moves away, a steady supply of air should follow. Remember that you are blowing *through* the recorder, not at it. There should not be too much buildup of air pressure behind the tongue; this will result in a harsh, explosive attack. On the other hand, do not start the air flow *after* you have taken the tongue away, for that will make the start of the tone weak and unclear. Let your ear be your guide, and after a few tries you should get the right balance which starts the note cleanly but without any explosive quality.

Try playing a series of four short E's and one long, to get a feel of how to use the tongue in starting notes, and how to sustain the air for longer notes: "du, du, du, du, du—."

To get a sense of the tongue's action in stopping the notes, play the same series with spaces in between: "dut, dut, dut, dut, du—."

Note that you stop the notes by returning your tongue to the hard palate. In a smooth series of notes, the moment of stopping one is the same stroke that begins the next. For a spaced series, the tongue stops on the palate *between* each note. The longer it stops, the shorter the notes become. Playing the series at the same speed, experiment with various degrees of articulation—from the smoothest possible, a mere flick of the tongue between each note, to very short notes with silences between that are much longer than the notes themselves. Note that, whether the notes are played smoothly or very short, the tongue's action is always the same at the beginning of the note. You do not attack harder as the notes get shorter; you simply bring the tongue back to the palate sooner.

THE SECOND NOTE, D

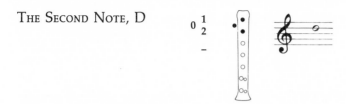

Add the left middle finger to cover hole 2 and you produce the note D. Make the same experiments in articulation with D that you did with E. If the D is not coming out distinctly, one of the holes is probably not being securely covered. Check for finger placement, and the sensation of circles under your fingertips. When your D's are coming out correctly, try moving back and forth between E's and D's. Note that finger action must move exactly with the tongue stroke. The more smoothly the notes are played, the more instantaneous the coordination must be. Try playing the notes with separation first, so that you have time to think about both finger and tongue action; then, as the actions become more automatic, move toward the smoothest possible articulation between the two notes.

You will find that the tongue is the better-disciplined muscle and the fingers must strive to move exactly with it. In general, fingers tend to get ahead of themselves. The tongue should hold the reins.

THE THIRD NOTE, C:

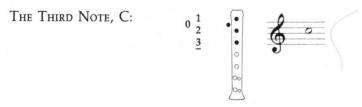

Add the left ring finger to cover hole 3 and you have C. Again, for this note to sound clearly, all three fingers and thumb must be securely sealing their holes. Some beginners experience difficulty with C, and the trouble usually is in not getting hole 3 properly covered. Be sure the ring finger is sufficiently on the recorder to make a good seal. When you have solved C, proceed to patterns of E, D, and C, moving from separate articulation to smooth as the fingers get their coordination with the tongue.

You are now in a position to play a couple of tunes: the well-known "Hot Cross Buns" and a simplified version of "Mary Had a Little Lamb."

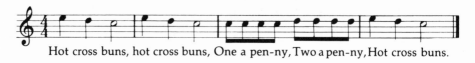

Hot cross buns, hot cross buns, One a pen-ny, Two a pen-ny, Hot cross buns.

Ma - ry had a lit - tle lamb, lit - tle lamb, lit - tle lamb,

Ma - ry had a lit - tle lamb, its fleece was white as snow.

THE FOURTH NOTE, A:

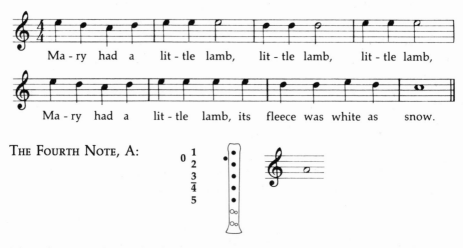

Most beginner's methods at this point proceed to give the next two higher lefthand notes, F' and G'. I prefer instead to introduce the low A which gets the right hand into the action and gives it more than a mere supporting role. The low A is nothing more than a C with two more holes covered, right index and middle fingers on holes 4 and 5. You will notice that the tongue's action in starting low A's must be somewhat gentler than for E, D, and C. The right thumb does indeed have nothing but a supporting role. It takes its humble but useful position on the back of the recorder, more or less midway between holes 4 and 5 (see "The Thumbrest," p. 15). Low A is an easy note, and many pleasing patterns can be made with it and the notes you've already got. Start with the usual series of repeated notes, then proceed to various combinations, including the obscure Chinese "Temple Bells."

Hear   the   tem - ple   bells   as   they   soft - ly   chime,

call - ing   the   peo - ple   to   come   for   wor - ship   time.

THE FIFTH NOTE, LOW G:

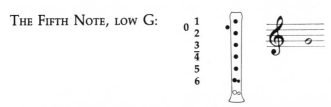

Low G is obtained by covering hole 6 with the right ring finger. As with the corresponding lefthand note, C, care must be taken that the finger is far enough on the recorder, particularly since on most recorders there are two little holes to be covered instead of the usual single hole. Tongue action must be quite gentle on the low G; otherwise the note will overblow and sound an octave higher than it is supposed to. Also, since there are now six fingers plus thumb down, particular attention is needed to be sure all the holes are sealed. Low G can be a frustrating note for beginners, but if you get it you can play the first phrase of "Far Above Cayuga's Waters."

Far   a - bove   Ca - yu - ga's   wa - ters,

Cross-fingered Notes

The logic of fingering on the recorder is not the simple and apparent one of the piano keyboard where one key follows the next as you step up and down the scale. There are simple whistle flutes, such as the six-holed pipe and the Irish penny whistle, that do have the straightforward fingering system of lifting or dropping successive fingers to go up and down the gamut of notes, but these are designed to play one scale only, without accidental sharps and flats. On such instruments you can play tunes only in the single key to which they are built. The recorder has more sophisticated aspirations. It is designed to play *all* the notes, so although the alto recorder (and sopranino and bass) has a basic scale of F major, and the soprano (and also tenor and great bass) has a basic scale of C major, recorders can play in any key, major or minor, although some keys, obviously, are easier than others. The price we pay for this flexibility is cross-fingering. A cross-fingering can be defined as one which requires one or more holes covered below an open hole. It can also be defined as a fingering which makes the player cross. We now begin our acquaintance with cross-fingerings. Make your peace with them, for they are more numerous than the simple one-finger-up-or-down variety.

F′ AND G′:

The fingering for F′ is not really so formidable. You can just think of it as a D with hole 1 uncovered. Likewise, G′ is nothing more than an F′ with the thumbhole uncovered. With the acquisition of these two notes we can restore the true rendering of "Mary Had a Little Lamb."

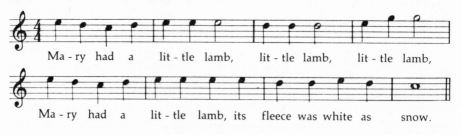

Ma - ry   had   a   lit - tle   lamb,   lit - tle   lamb,   lit - tle   lamb,

Ma - ry   had   a   lit - tle   lamb, its   fleece was white as   snow.

LOW F AND B-FLAT:

Since the basic scale of the alto recorder is F Major, the two remaining notes we need to play it are B-flat and low F.

B-flat is an easy enough note to produce, but its fingering is by far the most complicated we have met so far. Low F is not an easy note to produce. There are eight holes to be securely covered, and even when we have got them all, the note must be started very gently lest it overblow, which, by its nature, it easily tends to do. On the other hand, its fingering is easy to remember; just cover everything. Therefore it helps to think of B-flat as a low F with hole 5 uncovered. Whether thinking of low F as a B-flat with hole 5 covered is helpful or not, I'm not quite sure; but in any case, the relation between the two fingerings is obvious. Practically speaking, neither note, or the low G, for that matter, belongs in a beginner's first lesson. Only someone whose fingers have already been trained by playing some other woodwind, such as the oboe or clarinet, should be able to assimilate so many fingerings and caveats all at once. Fingers for which these tasks are new are likely to get confused and frustrated, and start gripping.

More Notes

Besides the notes of the B-flat major scale, plus an extra G' on top, that have been presented so far, there are of course several other notes: F'-sharp, E-flat, C-sharp, B, A-flat, and low F-sharp. Most of these are cross-fingered notes, with the exception of low A-flat and F-sharp, which are obtained by covering only one of the double holes on 6 or 7. Fingerings for all of these notes appear in the fingering chart on p. 238, and they are discussed in greater detail under "Fingers," p. 12. These are the notes of the lower register. By means of slightly opening the thumbhole and overblowing we extend the range higher, into the upper registers. The exact technique for this thumb action is described under "Cracking the Thumbhole" on p. 16.

All the fingerings for the upper registers are modified versions of the fingerings in the lower register. In the simplest instances, the only modification is to slightly open the thumbhole. For example, to get an A' above the G' at the top of the staff, we finger as for the low A, crack the thumbhole, give a little more air, and produce A' an octave higher.

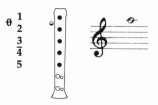

High C' is fingered in this simple fashion.

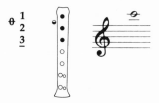

And so is high D'.

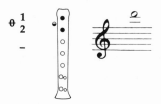

Cross-fingered notes in the second register are not the same as their counterparts in the lower register, the difference being that only one hole is covered below the open hole rather than two.

For the Absolute Beginner

If the recorder is your first musical instrument (or your first one in a long time), I have already carried you into deep water, and we must back up. I hope, as I suggested at the beginning of this lesson, that you are using a beginner's method book that will provide you with lots of practice material. If you are taking up the recorder as an introduction to the field of music overall (and the recorder is excellent for this purpose), you will find it helpful to obtain a beginner's book on musical notation and theory, to introduce you to the basic grammar of music. Among the many texts available, I prefer *Learn to Read Music* by Howard Shanet. The book is divided into two sections; the first deals with the notation of rhythm, and the second with the notation of pitch plus sundry other items of basic music theory. Learning pitch notation comes automatically with learning the recorder, so it is the section dealing with rhythm that will be most useful to the novice.

Mr. Shanet starts at the very beginning. His language is simple and clear, but in no way condescending. He progresses in the smallest possible steps, and there is an exercise to illustrate every point. You learn and internalize the information by doing the exercises. The steps are so simple and logical that you will know when you have succeeded in doing each exercise correctly. The only way his method can fail is if someone with a little bit of knowledge chooses to skip over the material he already knows to begin with what is new to him. There will always be some bit of information that is missed, and the lack will cause trouble further along the line. Knowing, for example, that a dotted quarter note in 4/4 time is counted "one-and-two" is not the same as actually tapping, and counting out the rhythm with your voice. You must know "one-and-two" with the muscles of your body as well as with your mind in order to have a full, useful understanding of how long to count a dotted quarter in 4/4.

By the same token, you must have had the recorder under your fingers, and in front of your tongue and breath stream before you can understand what is discussed under "Technique." Now that you have played "Hot Cross Buns," and "Temple Bells," and "Mary Had a Little Lamb," and many other simple tunes and exercises from the beginner's method of your choice, "Technique" will make sense to you; and I think you will find it fun to read. I think you will also enjoy reading "How to Practice," even though at a certain point it will go beyond your beginner's capabilities. The chapter will show you what's to come, and will give you the steps for getting there. Likewise, the chapter on ensemble playing will provide you with intimations of that happy day when you begin to make music with others. The beauty of the recorder is that the ensemble experience comes soon. My purpose in this book is to help you to it sooner, and to do it better. Read and enjoy!

FINGERING CHART

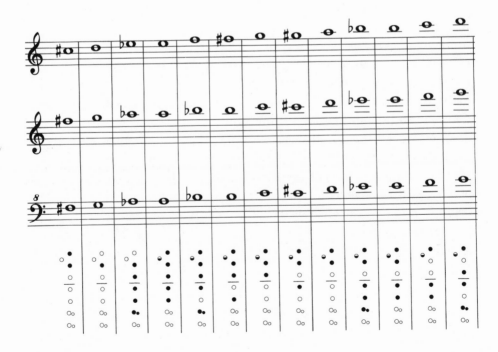

MAJOR AND MINOR SCALES

Scales in the twelve major keys are presented with their relative minor scales immediately below them. The minor scales are given in the natural minor form, i.e., without the chromatic alterations of the melodic or harmonic forms. The scales are given in the order of the circle of fifths, each successive scale beginning on the note five steps higher than the tonic of the previous scale. Thus the scale following C Major is G Major, G being five steps up from C. Five steps up from G is D, so D Major follows G Major, and so on it goes. When we get to the thickest part of the woods the scales can be written either in terms of sharps or flats; thus B Major (five sharps) could also be written as C-flat Major (seven flats), F-sharp Major (six sharps) could be written as G-flat Major (six flats), and C-sharp Major (seven sharps) can also be written as D-flat Major (five flats). The term *enharmonic* is used when a note, a scale, or even a piece can be notated in two ways. Thus C-sharp is the enharmonic equivalent of D-flat, and vice versa. I have not presented the enharmonic equivalents of those scales which have them, feeling that to do so would make the page too confusing to read, but if you prefer to think in five flats (D-flat Major) rather than in seven sharps (C-sharp Major) by all means do so. Or you can think sharp one time and flat the next.

The three forms of the minor scale—natural, melodic, and harmonic—are spelled out for you in the following pages, as well as the two ways minor scales connect with major scales, i.e., relative minor and tonic minor. No getting away from it, you can see there is plenty to think about. Since the historical recorder literature rarely calls for so many as four sharps or flats, and almost never more, playing scales and arpeggios in the twelve major and minor keys serves mostly as a matrix for practicing long tones and vibrato. However, I do have a couple of students who regularly begin each lesson by playing a tune in all twelve keys, starting in C and proceeding through the circle of fifths. It's always fun to see which of the hairy keys will be most daunting for a particular tune.

I have not written out the arpeggios for the scales since these always consist of the same notes of a given scale, namely, one, three, five, and eight. Thus in C Major, C is one, E is three, G is five, and C an octave higher is eight. Similarly, in A Minor, A is one, C is three, E is five, and A an octave higher is eight, and so on.

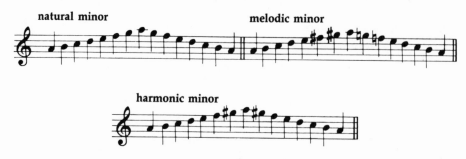

Note that in the melodic minor, steps 6 and 7 are sharped going up but are natural going down. The natural and harmonic forms of the minor scale are the same both ascending and descending.

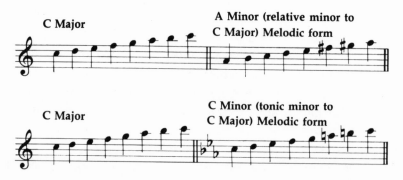

Note that the relative minor has the same key signature as its relative major but starts two steps lower (a minor third). The tonic minor begins on the same note as its corresponding tonic major but must have a different key signature in order to preserve the proper sequence of whole steps and half-steps.

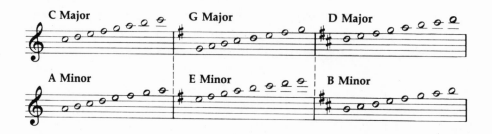

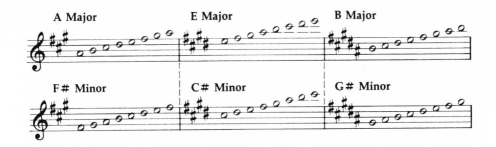

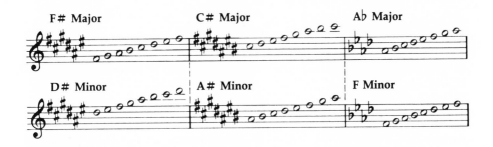

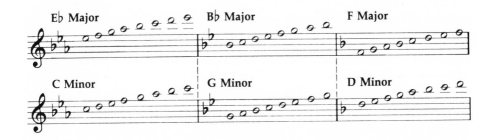

NOTES AND SUGGESTIONS

Music Stands

The most important quality to be desired in any music stand, be it a folding metal one or a beautifully turned wooden one, is that it be adjustable. You should be able to adjust it to any height you wish, and the music rack should be movable to various angles. Usually the most flexible can be found among the folding metal types. Often wooden stands, though very handsome in appearance, cannot be adjusted sufficiently for optimum playing comfort, so give them a test before you invest. Inexpensive metal stands will not have an adjustable music rack and they usually cannot be set low enough to suit some players, especially those who are reading through the lower half of their bifocals. In the long run, then, the more expensive varieties are worth the extra cost, since you can set them any way you want. When performing, for example, one usually wants to set the stand quite low so that the music will not be between the player and the audience. If you find a model, with all the necessary virtues, that also folds up into a small package, so much the better. Be sure to tape your name on it.

Where to Put All of Your Music

As anyone who has played for a while knows, the quantity of music one acquires mounts steadily, and soon the problems of storage and retrieval arise. Legal-size file cabinets are the answer. How the music is organized in the drawers depends on how much you've got. A small collection fits easily into categories like *Methods, One recorder, Two recorders,* etc., up to *Recorder with Keyboard, Trio Sonatas, Larger Ensembles.* All of these categories can be contained in manila folders or between drawer separators, appropriately labeled. As your collection grows, so must your categories. *Methods* becomes *Methods, Beginner's* and *Methods, Advanced. One recorder* becomes *Solo, soprano* and *Solo, alto. Two recorders* becomes *Duos, soprano; Duos, s & a; two altos; two altos, Baroque,* etc. *Trios* becomes *Trios, small format; Trios, large format; and Trios w. pts."* Do you begin to perceive the oncoming madness? *Quartets with parts* becomes *Quartets with parts, Ger. Ren.* or *Ital. Ren.* or *Ger. Bar.* (Bach fugues transcribed for recorders would go in the last category, of course, but does Handel's *Rodrigo Suite* go here, or in *Eng. Bar. 4ttes w. pts.?*).

It's best to get organized early in the game. Learn to be flexible, and change your strategy as new forces appear. Always try to keep half a drawer ahead of the horde, and have lots of manila folders to segregate the unruly. Keep a name stamp at hand to brand every item as it enters into your keeping. If you choose to maintain a dossier, a card file, do so from the beginning. Otherwise there will be many escapees, and where one went another will follow.

All this says nothing of that motley crew of separate sheets, the scarcely legible copy of someone's transcription of some marvelous piece, or the twenty copies of the ten rounds which you selected and wrote out for last year's Christmas party, of which the first two got sung although the other eight are just as good. Where do we put them so we'll see them again? Everyone must find his or her own answer to the grim realities; just don't be complacent before an innocent-looking pile of music on the dining-room table or a minor mess in the piano bench.

How to Carry Your Music

How to carry music is a simpler matter: Carry it in a folder. If the folder is nice, carry it in a plastic bag. If you don't have a folder, carry the music in a plastic bag. That's what I do. The point is to keep it from getting wet, or bent, or dispersed. The most important moment, in carrying music, occurs just before you pick it up, when you check to be sure it is all there. Like Santa Claus, on important occasions I make a list and check it twice. I always try to assemble things well in advance of departure because in the final moments my memory is undependable. This is my best advice about carrying music.

Sundry Items

You can assemble a little recorder first aid kit with a few simple items that come in handy for emergencies, perhaps keeping them all in a little bag that can be easily tucked into one of your recorder cases or carryall. This could include: an extra container of cork grease, since those little boxes get lost so easily; a roll of tape for repairing torn music or securing loose thumbrests; an extra thumbrest in case one has fallen off and gotten lost; rubber bands for the temporary repair of keys which have lost their springs; a tiny screwdriver for tightening key screws that have worked loose; some fine thread for wrapping the tenons of joints that have become loose; a couple of small, delicate feathers for clearing clogged windways. Such feathers should have very thin, flexible spines so there is no danger of scratching or marring the surfaces of the windway. Anything as large as a chicken feather is too big. Finally, any other little items that you have found to be useful.

Page Turns

All too many editions of music contain awkward, or downright impossible, page turns. You find yourself at the bottom of the page playing notes that require both hands, and what are you to do? There are several solutions, but they all must be arranged in advance. If there are just a few notes before there is time for a turn, those few notes can be copied at the bottom of the previous page. If this isn't feasible, you can make a photocopy of the following page. Sometimes it is possible to make a horizontal cut from the edge of the page to the spine so that after you have played the upper part you can turn it and go on playing from the lower part and on to the upper part of the following page until you have a chance to turn the lower half. It is wise to make a note in the music to remind you of just when to make these turns. You must, of course, hold the music up to the light before making such a cut to be sure that it is in between the staves on both sides of the page.

When we are playing from photocopied sheets of some multi-page composition taken from one of the large scholarly editions which are too cumbersome and expensive for everyone to own a copy, the page-turn strategy is as follows: Place the first page on the lefthand side of the music rack, and the second page on the right, and beneath it the third page, and beneath that, the fourth, and so on, for however many pages there are. As you begin to read from the second page, take the first opportunity when you have a hand free to slide it across on top of the first page, and do the same with the following pages. With a little training you will get used to remembering to slide the pages across, and things will go quite smoothly. This system is much preferable to precariously balancing all the pages side by side across a couple of stands. Invariably

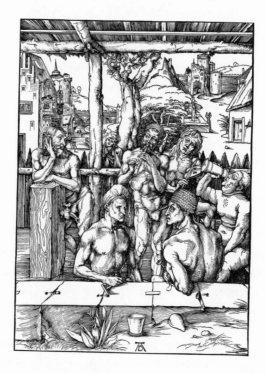

sheets tumble, and it is uncomfortable craning from side to side to read the nether ends of such a display.

Records

There are by now so many recordings featuring the recorder that to list them all would create a sizable discography. Even a selective list of recommended discs is beyond my ken, since I don't listen to records much, and when I do it is usually vintage Billie Holiday, or Rossini operas, or something equally far afield. However, there is a group of recordings which I think will interest many readers of this book, the Music Minus One series, a number of which are for recorder players. These include duets, trios, and larger ensembles, from both the Baroque and Renaissance literature. You are provided with the music and a recording with one part left out which *you* supply, so you can play ensemble music even when nobody else is around. There are two potential drawbacks to the Music Minus One records. One is that some players will find the tempos too fast to keep up, for some of the performances do move at a very lively clip. However, the recording will obligingly start over again as often as you want it to. The other possible drawback is that unless your turntable is going at exactly the right speed you may have trouble getting in tune with the record. A turntable with a fine-speed adjuster solves this problem.

You can write to Music Minus One, and they will be happy to send you a catalogue of what is available. The address is:

Music Minus One
243 West 55th Street
New York, N.Y. 10019

The American Recorder Society: A Source of Up-to-date Information

I have not included lists of instrument makers and music shops in this book. Such lists, in order to be fair to all concerned, would have to be very long, and the longer they are the sooner they would begin to go out of date. There is a much better way for you to obtain this kind of information, which is to join the American Recorder Society. Membership dues are a modest $15.00 per year. There are many good reasons for being a member, but the most immediate benefit is that you will receive the Society's quarterly journal, *The American Recorder,* which contains articles on topics of interest to recorder players, reviews of recorder music and of relevant books and recordings, and, what is perhaps most useful, advertisements from instrument makers, music shops, publishers, forthcoming workshops, etc. From these ads you learn what is currently available. As a specialty publication, *The American Recorder* contains only ads geared to its special readership, so you will find them interesting and informative. The Society sells its mailing list, so members receive announcements of early-music concerts, workshops, and other events. You will also find in your mailbox brochures offering antique books and music prints, hand-crafted walnut music stands, gothic harps, special carrying cases, and a host of other things; and though you may not want all of them you will be glad to know about them.

Besides being a source of up-to-date information, the American Recorder Society offers other benefits. There is an annual Directory which lists all members' names and addresses, and often phone numbers. Thus, if you find yourself in Wichita, Kansas, with an urge to play recorder music, you will know whom to call. The Society has local chapters, seventy-two as of this writing, throughout the United States (including Wichita, Kansas) which have monthly playing meetings, and sponsor other events. The Society itself sponsors several week-long workshops each summer, taught by the most outstanding performers and teachers in early music. You can learn to play anything from recorder to rommelpot. These workshops provide a wonderful vacation at a modest fee, if you regard playing all day and half the night as a vacation, as most aficionados do.

The American Recorder Society offers an educational program with guidelines for the aspiring player: what fingerings, scales, and rhythms a novice should first master, what an intermediate player should be able to do for his ongoing musical enjoyment, and so on. The Society has much to offer its members, and lovers of the recorder should join it so it can offer even more.

> The American Recorder Society
> 13 East 16th Street
> New York, N.Y. 10003 (phone: 212 675–9042)

In England, The Society of Recorder Players provides similar services. For specific information, write *Recorder & Music* magazine, 48 Great Marlborough Street, London W1V 2BN, England.

GLOSSARY

ADAGIO: a moderately slow tempo, literally "at one's ease."

AGRÉMENT: short, specific ornamental figures of the French Baroque.

ALLEGRO: a fast tempo, literally "happy."

ALLEMANDE: a dance in moderate duple time.

ALTO CLEF: a clef sign designating the third line of the staff as middle C.

ANTIPHONAL: descriptive of music in which the musical phrases are performed in sequence first by one group, then by another (or by a solo voice and then a choir).

ARPEGGIO: the notes of a chord played one after the other rather than together. From Italian *arpa,* harp.

BALLATA: Medieval Italian song form.

BASSE DANSE: a slow and gliding French dance.

BASSO CONTINUO: an accompaniment improvised from a written bass part, played by a harpsichord, lute, organ, or other chordal instrument. The bass line is usually doubled by a bass instrument.

BEL CANTO: in Italian, "beautiful singing"; eighteenth-century vocal style emphasizing beauty of tone and brilliant performance.

BELL KEY: a key devised to stop the bottom of the recorder's bore to obtain special effects and to extend the upper range. A modern device.

BRANLE: a fast circle dance of the sixteenth century.

BUTTRESS FINGER: the sixth finger used to steady the recorder; an eighteenth-century expedient obviated by the use of a thumbrest.

CADENCE: a pause at the end of a section of music, generally signaled by a succession of chords leading back to one of the piece's principal chords.

CANTATA: a Baroque musical form for voice(s) and instruments, usually in several movements.

CANTIGA: Spanish monophonic song of the thirteenth century.

CANTILLATION: chanting in plainsong style.

CANTUS FIRMUS: an underlying given melody, often traditional, around which other polyphonic voices are woven.

CANZONA: an instrumental form derived from the sixteenth-century French chanson.

CHACONNE: a series of variations over a reiterated bass line.

CHANSON: French, song, a sixteenth-century musical form, for voices, either polyphonic or homophonic.

CHORALE: a hymn, especially as developed for sixteenth-century Lutheran worship.

CHROMATIC: tones extraneous to the diatonic scale.

CITTERN: a fig-shaped instrument of the guitar family with four double courses of wire strings.

CLAVICHORD: a very soft keyboard instrument whose strings are sounded by metal tangents fixed to the back of the keys.

CONCORDANT: pleasing or harmonious to the ear; often used to describe combinations of notes such as triads.

CONSORT: a group of instruments, either all of the same family (whole consort) or of different kinds (broken consort).

CONTINUO: see basso continuo.

CORNAMUSE: a soft double-reed instrument of the sixteenth century. The reed is enclosed by a windcap.

CORNETT: a wooden instrument with finger holes, sounded by buzzing of the player's lips, as with brass instruments. The chief virtuoso wind instrument of the sixteenth century.

COUNTERTENOR: a very high tenor voice, usually sung in falsetto.

COURANTE: a dance form of moderate speed alternating between 6/4 and 3/2.

CRESCENDO: to grow gradually louder.

DECRESCENDO: to grow gradually softer.

DESCANT: English term for the soprano recorder.

DIATONIC: the natural scale, a succession of whole steps and half-steps, as produced by playing the white keys of the piano from C to C.

DOUBLE: to have more than one voice or instrument on the same part.

DRONE: a single note (or notes) held continuously through a piece, as with the bagpipe.

DULCIAN: a one-piece instrument with a doubled back bore, ancestor of the bassoon.

ESTAMPIE: a medieval dance form consisting of many repeated sections.

FANTASIA: a polyphonic composition for instruments.

FIPPLE: the plug which is inserted into the head joint of the recorder and similar whistle-type instruments.

FLATTEMENT: a vibrato produced by trilling a finger over a partially covered finger hole, employed by French Baroque wind players.

FONTANELLE: a perforated barrel covering and protecting keywork of the larger Renaissance wind instruments.

FROTTOLA: Italian secular song, homophonic and often folklike

GALLIARD: a lively dance alternating 6/4 and 3/2 meters.

GIGUE: a lively dance in triple meter.

GLOCKENSPIEL: a percussion instrument consisting of a series of gradated metal bars, set over a sound box, which are struck with hard mallets.

GROUND BASS: a bass line which repeats a short figure throughout a piece.

HARMONY: a combination of two or more notes sounding simultaneously.

HARPSICHORD: a keyboard instrument whose mechanism plucks the strings rather than striking them as with the piano or clavichord.

HOMOPHONY: a style of composition in which the melody is dominant and the other lines provide chordal accompaniment.

KRUMMHORN: a capped double-reed instrument with a cane-like curve at the end of its slender body.

LARGO: Italian, broad, a slow, stately tempo.

LEAKING: a technique of partially covering a finger hole to facilitate production of certain notes on the recorder.

LIED: a form of German secular song, polyphonic in structure.

LUTE: a plucked string instrument with a very light body, fretted fingerboard, and a peg box bent back almost at right angles with the fingerboard.

MADRIGAL: a complex polyphonic song form that evolved from the *frottola.*

MASS: a musical setting of the five fixed parts of the Mass, known as the Ordinary (Kyrie, Gloria, Credo, Sanctus, and Benedictus).

MESSA DI VOCE: a swelling and then diminishing of volume on a single note.

MINNESINGER: aristocratic German poet-musicians of the twelfth through the fourteenth century, influenced by the French troubadours.

MODULATION: a change of key within a composition.

MONOPHONIC: music consisting of a single melodic line.

MOTET: a sacred composition for unaccompanied voices, set to a short religious text.

MUSETTE: a small, elegant bagpipe, favored at the court of Louis XIV.

NEO-BAROQUE: a term used to describe the fingering system of modern recorders, which differs slightly from that of their Baroque prototypes.

PASSAMEZZO: a dance of the second half of the sixteenth century in duple meter with a moderately quick tempo.

PAVANE: (or pavan): a slow and stately dance.

PLAINCHANT, PLAIN SONG: the unmeasured melodies sung in unison as part of devotional services.

POLYPHONY: a style of composition in which two or more independent melodies are combined, none subordinate but all in harmony with each other.

PSALTERY: a plucked string instrument consisting of a number of strings stretched across a sound box.

RACKETT: a Renaissance double-reed instrument whose narrow, cylindrical bore doubles back a number of times within the body of the instrument. It has a deep, soft, buzzing sound.

RECERCADA: see RICERCAR.

RESOLUTION: the change of a dissonant note within a chord into a note that is consonant within the chord.

RICERCAR: a fantasia-like composition with much imitation among the voices.

ROMMELPOT: a Dutch Renaissance folk instrument consisting of a stick fixed into the center of a skin stretched over the mouth of a clay pot. A sound of indefinite pitch but great presence is produced by rubbing the stick with a damp rag.

SACKBUT: the Renaissance ancestor of the modern trombone, from which it differs in having more slender tubing and a less flaring bell, thus producing a softer, more covered sound.

SALTARELLO: a quick, leaping, Italian dance of the sixteenth century in triple meter.

SARABAND: a slow, stately dance of the seventeenth and eighteenth centuries in triple meter.

SEGUE: to proceed from one piece to the next without pause.

SEQUENCE: a musical pattern repeated on successive degrees of the scale.

SHAWM: a loud double-reed instrument, predecessor of the modern oboe.

SLUR: a curved line over two or more notes indicating that they are to be played with a single breath, with no interruption by articulation.

SONATA: a form of instrumental music usually consisting of four movements in the order slow, fast, slow, fast.

STACCATO, STACCATISSIMO: an articulation instruction, usually indicated by dots or dashes over the notes, which are to be played short, or very short.

STILE GALANT: a mid-eighteenth-century style of composition and performance, which combines the earlier French and Italian Baroque styles, characterized by an almost excessive preoccupation with nuances of dynamics and ornamentation.

SUITE: an instrumental form consisting of a series of dances.

TABOR, TABOR PIPE: a deep drum, suspended from the player's waist and beaten with one hand while the other hand manipulates a three-holed pipe; used to accompany dancing.

TACET: Latin, "it is silent," i.e., a given part does not play for a section or a movement.

TACTUS: a sixteenth-century term for beat or pulse, implying a tempo of MM 50–60.

TAMBOURINE: a flat drum with jingles set into the hoop, usually played with the hand.

THEORBO: a bass lute.

TREBLE: the English designation for the alto recorder.

TREMOLO: in recorder playing, a quick, shallow, uncontrolled vibrato.

TROUBADOUR: aristocratic poet-musicians of medieval Southern France who had great influence on the literary forms and themes of the Late Middle Ages and Early Renaissance.

TROUVÈRE: the Northern French counterpart of the troubadours, whom they imitated.

VARIATION: the repetition of a melody with ornamental changes of figuration, tempo, and rhythm.

VENETIAN SCHOOL: the sixteenth-century school of composition initiated by Adrian Willaert and continued by his pupils, inspired by the cruciform plan of St. Mark's Cathedral, which suggested placing antiphonal choirs of voices and instruments in each bay of the church.

VIBRATO: the steady, even pulsing of pitch and intensity in the tone of a voice or instrument, used to increase expression.

VIELLE: a bowed string instrument of the twelfth and thirteenth centuries, usually held vertically on the lap.

VIHUELA: in medieval Spain, the vielle (vihuela de arco); in sixteenth-century Spain, an early form of the guitar (vihuela da mano).

VILLANCICO: a form of Spanish secular song which was first written in homophonic style but in the later Renaissance became more polyphonic.

VIOL, VIOLA DA GAMBA: a six-stringed, bowed instrument with frets on the fingerboard, held between the legs (thus the Italian viola da gamba, or leg viol, as opposed to the viola da braccio, or arm viol). In England the instrument was termed "viol," so why many leading players refer to their instrument as a "gamba" I cannot understand.

VOICE: one line of a piece written for two or more instruments or voices.

FOR FURTHER READING

This bibliography is selective. I have included books you should know about, books I would like you to know about, and books that lead you to what you want to know about.

ARBEAU, THOINOT: *Orchesograply,* translated by Mary Stewart Evans, with an introduction and notes by Julia Sutton. Dover, New York, 1967.
We thank Julia Sutton and Dover for reprinting this delightful treatise on sixteenth-century dance.

BAINES, ANTHONY, editor: *Musical Instruments Through the Ages.* Penguin Books, London, 1961.
Readable articles by various authorities. Informative plates.

BAINES, ANTHONY: *Woodwind Instruments and Their History.* Norton, New York, 1963.
Anthony Baines's erudition and love of the instruments illuminate this indispensable book.

BAKER'S BIOGRAPHICAL DICTIONARY OF MUSICIANS: 6th Edition, revised by Nicolas Slonimsky. Schirmer Books, New York, 1978.

BENADE, ARTHUR H.: *Horns, Strings and Harmony.* Anchor, Garden City, New York, 1960.
A layman's guide to acoustics.

BERGELYK, WILLIAM, PIERCE, JOHN, AND DAVID, EDWARD: *Waves and the Ear.* Anchor, Garden City, New York,. 1960.
A basic exposition of hearing and sound. Difficult but revealing.

BRIFFAULT, ROBERT: *The Troubadours.* Indiana University Press, Bloomington, 1965.
A fascinating study of how the troubadours got their music, poetry, and themes from the Spanish Moors.

BROWN, HOWARD MAYER: *Embellishing Sixteenth Century Music.* Oxford University Press, London, 1976.
The best analysis of the topic.

BUKOFZER, MANFRED: *Music in the Baroque Era.* Norton, New York, 1947.
The standard survey.

CLEMENICIC, RENÉ: *Old Musical Instruments.* Octopus Books, London, 1973.
Many pictures of fabulously beautiful instruments.

CLOUGH, JOHN: *Scales, Intervals, Keys, and Triads.* Norton, New York, 1964.
An excellent programmed book of elementary music theory.

DART, THURSTON: *The Interpretation of Music.* Harper Colophon Books, New York
and Evanston, 1963.
A short, authortative survey of musical style from the Middle Ages
through the Baroque period. Indispensable.

DOLMETSCH, ARNOLD: *The Interpretation of the Music of the Seventeenth and Eighteenth
Centuries.* Washington Paperbacks, Seattle and London, 1969.
This seminal study is filled with quotes and musical examples from the
period.

DOLMETSCH, MABEL: *Personal Recollections of Arnold Dolmetsch.* Macmillan, New York,
1958.
Familial glimpses of the great pioneer.

DONINGTON, ROBERT: A *Performer's Guide to Baroque Music.* Charles Scribner's Sons,
New York, 1973.
Clear advice, but most of it is in his *Interpretation* volume.

————: *The Interpretation of Early Music.* St. Martin's Press, New York, 1974.
Evidence from the original sources. The best modern study.

DORIAN, FREDERICK: *The History of Music in Performance.* Norton, New York, 1966.
An insightful survey from the Renaissance to the present.

DUCKLES, VINCENT: *Music Reference and Research Materials.* The Free Press, New York,
1974.
This is the *Ultima Thule* of guidance to what you want to know about music.
Of bibliographies, the state of the art. Read with care.

GANASSI, SYLVESTRO: *Opera Intitulata Fontegara,* Venice, 1535. Edited by Dr. Hildemarie Peter. English translation (1959) by Dorothy Swainson from the
German edition (1956) of Robert Lienau (Berlin: Lichterfeld).

GROUT, DONALD: *A History of Western Music,* Norton, New York, 1973.
A standard one-volume survey.

THE NEW GROVE DICTIONARY OF MUSIC AND MUSICIANS: Edited by Stanley Sadie.
Macmillan, London, 1980.
This, the sixth edition, has much new material, but omits Robert Doning-
ton's excellent article, "Ornamentation," which ornamented the fifth.

HARMAN, ALEC: *Man and His Music.* Schocken, New York, 1969.
A multi-volume paperback reissue. Parts I and II, "Medieval and Early
Renaissance Music," and "Late Renaissance and Baroque Music," give us
insights into our repertoire.

HARVARD DICTIONARY OF MUSIC: 2nd Edition, edited by Willi Apel. Belnap Press, Cambridge, Mass., 1969.
The standard, one-volume American reference dictionary.

HINDEMITH, PAUL: *Elementary Training for Musicians,* 2nd Edition. Associated Music Publishers, New York, 1949.
Correct, rigorous practice material for the professional. Amateurs do well to digest chapters I through III, or maybe IV.

HOTTETERRE, JACQUES: *Principles of the Flute, Recorder, and Oboe,* translated and edited by David Lasocki. Praeger, New York and Washington, 1968.
This is the best modern edition.

HUNT, EDGAR: *The Recorder and Its Music.* Eulenburg Books, London, 1977.
An excellent historical survey of the recorder.

KRASSEN, MILES: *O'Neill's Music of Ireland.* Oak Publications, New York, 1976.
Over 1000 fiddle tunes. Most go nicely on a recorder played with C fingering. As refreshing as a field of shamrocks.

LINDE, HANS-MARTIN: *The Recorder Player's Handbook.* Schott, London; Maintz, New York, 1974.
Brevity and poor translation obscure this contemporary virtuoso's insights.

HARMAN, ALEC: *Man and His Music,* Part One, "Medieval and Early Renaissance Music," Part Two (with Anthony Milner), "Late Renaissance and Baroque Music." Schocken, New York, 1969.
Good popular paperback surveys.

MANN, THOMAS: *Doctor Faustus.* Alfred A. Knopf, New York, 1948.
A difficult novel, but very astute about music.

MATHER, BETTY BANG: *Interpretation of French Music from 1675 to 1775.* McGinnis and Marx, New York, 1973.
What the composers said about how to play and ornament their music. Highly recommended. Many musical examples.

MATHER, BETTY BANG, AND LASOCKI, DAVID: *Free Ornamentation in Woodwind Music, 1700–1775.* McGinnis and Marx, New York, 1976.
An anthology of written-out examples from the period. Invaluable.

NEWMAN, WILLIAM S.: *The Sonata in the Baroque Era.* Norton, New York, 1972.
Not much about recorders, but a lot about the form.

ORTIZ, DIEGO: *Tratado de Glosas.* Rome, 1553. Edited by Max Schneider, Bärenreiter, Kassel, 1967.
Introduction in German; Ortiz's remarks, facsimile, in Spanish. Some music in unfamiliar clefs. The best source for Renaissance embellishment.

PEPYS, SAMUEL: *Diary,* edited by Richard Lord Braybroke. Dent, London, 1924.

PETER, HILDEMARIE: *The Recorder, Its Traditions and Its Tasks.* Robert Lienau, Berlin, 1953.
Outdated pioneer study, chiefly useful for historical fingering charts and ornamentation.

PETZOLDT, RICHARD: *Georg Philipp Telemann.* Oxford University Press, New York, 1974.
A welcome study of the life and work of one of our favorite composers.

QUANTZ, JOHANN JOACHIM: *On Playing the Flute,* translated and edited by Edward Reilly. The Free Press, New York, 1966.
A lode of information on style, ornamentation, and performance in the mid-eighteenth century. Thank Quantz that he wrote it all down. Not easy reading, but very exact.

REESE, GUSTAVE: *Music in the Middle Ages.* Norton, New York, 1963.
The standard work, awaiting a compendious revision based on new research. Not easy reading.

————: *Music in the Renaissance.* Norton, New York, 1959.
The standard reference. A superb bibliography and index lead you to anything you want to find.

ROWLAND-JONES, A.: *Recorder Technique.* Oxford University Press, London, 1959.
Much useful material, but false advice on tonguing and blowing.

SEAY, ALBERT: *Music in the Medieval World.* Prentice-Hall, Englewood Cliffs, New Jersey, 1965.
An excellent short survey.

SHANET, HOWARD: *Learn to Read Music.* Simon and Schuster, New York, 1956.

STARER, ROBERT: *Rhythmic Training.* MCA Music, Melville, New York, 1969.
Good practice for those who are unsure about rhythm.

STEVENS, DENIS, AND ROBERTSON, ALEC: *The Pelican History of Music.* Penguin Books, Baltimore. Volume One, *Ancient Forms to Polyphony,* 1960. Volume Two, *Renaissance and Baroque,* 1963.
Excellent surveys in paperback.

TERRY, C. S.: *Bach's Orchestra.* Oxford University Press, London, 1961.
What Bach thought the instruments meant, including the recorder.

VETTER, MICHAEL: *Il Flauto Dolce ed Acerbo.* Moeck, Celle, 1969.
A treatise on avant-garde techniques.

WAITZMAN, DANIEL: *The Art of Playing the Recorder,* AMS Press, New York, 1978.
A difficult book, directed to the aspiring virtuoso, reflecting the author's preoccupation with the bell-keyed recorder.

WHITE, B. F., AND KING, E. J.: *The Sacred Harp,* facsimile of the third edition, 1859. Broadman Press, Nashville, Tenn., 1968.
The most famous of numerous early-nineteenth-century American Protestant hymnals. This beautiful music sounds wonderful played by recorders.

INDEX

A NOTE ABOUT THE AUTHOR

Born in Spokane, Washington, Kenneth Wollitz started playing the recorder when in college at Berkeley. He has taught at the University of California and has given private lessons for more than twenty years, including instructing children in the recorder at the Brearley School in New York City. In 1963–64 he studied early music on a Fulbright scholarship in Amsterdam. He has performed with the New York Pro Musica and has taught at recorder workshops from Montreal to Mexico, from the East to West coasts, and in Sienna, Amsterdam, and England.

A NOTE ON THE TYPE

The text of this book was set, via computer-driven cathode-ray tube, in a film version of Palatino, a type face designed by the noted German typographer Hermann Zapf. Named after Giovanbittista Palatino, a writing master of Renaissance Italy, Palatino was the first of Zapf's type faces to be introduced in America. The first designs for the face were made in 1948, and the fonts for the complete face were issued between 1950 and 1952. Like all Zapf-designed type faces, Palatino is beautifully balanced and exceedingly readable.

Composed by The Haddon Craftsmen, Inc., Allentown, Pennsylvania

Printed and bound by
The Maple-Vail Book Manufacturing Group, York, Pa.

Line drawings by Marcia Goldenberg

Typography by Joe Marc Freedman